Bulletin 65
1954

RESEARCH ON LABOR MOBILITY

An Appraisal of Research Findings
in the United States

By

HERBERT S. PARNES

SOCIAL SCIENCE RESEARCH COUNCIL
230 PARK AVENUE   NEW YORK 17

The Social Science Research Council was organized in 1923 and formally incorporated in 1924 for the purpose of advancing research in the social sciences. Its members are chosen from seven associated professional organizations in the social sciences and from related fields.

ASSOCIATED ORGANIZATIONS

American Anthropological Association

American Economic Association

American Historical Association

American Political Science Association

American Psychological Association

American Sociological Society

American Statistical Association

COMMITTEE ON LABOR MARKET RESEARCH

FOREWORD

Over a period of several years the Committee on Labor Market Research of the Social Science Research Council has sought to stimulate and improve basic research on the behavior of labor markets. Much of this effort has been focused specifically on studies of the factors affecting the occupational, industrial, and geographic mobility of labor. The program planned by the committee included as one of its integral parts an intensive appraisal of the research done within this field during the past two decades. Inasmuch as several members of the committee have themselves been actively engaged in research on labor mobility, it was concluded that the appraisal project should be undertaken by an independent scholar whose observations and judgments would not be heavily influenced by his own prior decisions concerning the scope and methodology of mobility studies.

The committee was most fortunate in persuading Herbert S. Parnes, of the Department of Economics of The Ohio State University, to undertake this task. The results, which are presented in this bulletin, reflect close cooperation between the committee and Mr. Parnes, but a cooperative relation in which the committee served as a panel of discussants rather than as an employer or as a directing body. Members of the committee from time to time gave Mr. Parnes their comments on successive portions of his manuscript, and the manuscript as a whole was reviewed with him in committee meetings as well as at a research conference in the spring of 1953. While the committee is certainly in general agreement with the judgments and conclusions of the final document, these are to be attributed to the author rather than to the committee.

The present bulletin concludes—for the time being—the series of steps planned by the committee on behalf of research on labor mobility. The first of these was a *Research Planning Memorandum on Labor Mobility* by Gladys L. Palmer, published by the Council in 1947 but now out of print. In subsequent years the committee organized several research conferences; stimulated the preparation of sundry research papers by individuals; planned and directed the major study of mobility patterns and factors summarized in the monograph, *Labor Mobility in Six Cities,* which was prepared by Gladys L. Palmer and published by the Council in June 1954; and sponsored a volume of essays by members of the committee, *Labor Mobility and Economic Opportunity,* which was recently published jointly by The Technology Press and John Wiley & Sons. It is the committee's hope that these publications, and the many preceding discussions with scholars in the field of labor mobility and related areas will have contributed to continuing efforts to extend our still all too limited knowledge of mobility phenomena. Suggestions concerning further research which may be especially profitable are set forth in the concluding chapter of Mr. Parnes' report.

PAUL WEBBINK

ACKNOWLEDGMENTS

It was the rare good fortune of the author to have many expert advisers in the preparation of this bulletin. The members of the Committee on Labor Market Research of the Social Science Research Council were his faithful allies from the planning of the study to its completion. Several conferences with the committee were helpful, but even more so were the thoughtful comments which most of the individual members wrote on each chapter. The author is particularly indebted to Paul Webbink, Vice-President of the Council, for the encouragement and assistance given at every stage of the study.

Of material aid also was the opportunity to be present at the Conferences on Industrial Relations Research held in 1952 and 1953 at the University of Minnesota Center for Continuation Study. These conferences, sponsored jointly by the Committee on Labor Market Research and the University of Minnesota Industrial Relations Center, were devoted to discussions of important theoretical and methodological problems in research on labor mobility, and made substantial contributions to the author's thinking. A preliminary draft of the present report was distributed to the participants in the 1953 conference, many of whom were kind enough to provide critical comments.

In addition to the members of the Committee on Labor Market Research, the following persons read the manuscript and made many helpful suggestions: Robert L. Aronson of Cornell University, Herbert G. Heneman, Jr. of the University of Minnesota, Margaret S. Gordon of the University of California, A. J. Jaffe of Columbia University, Wilbert E. Moore of Princeton University, Lloyd G. Reynolds of Yale University, George P. Shultz of the Massachusetts Institute of Technology, Joseph Shister of the University of Buffalo, and Joseph J. Spengler of Duke University. Grateful acknowledgment is made also to Melvin Seeman of The Ohio State University for valuable suggestions during the initial planning of the study. Finally, especial appreciation is expressed to Atha R. Parnes, for her cheerful and expert assistance in the preparation of the several drafts of the manuscript.

To acknowledge the generous assistance received is not to suggest that any of the persons mentioned are responsible for the shortcomings of the finished product. For whatever errors there may be in either fact or judgment the author alone is responsible.

HERBERT S. PARNES

The Ohio State University

CONTENTS

TABLES

1 A FRAMEWORK FOR RESEARCH ON LABOR MOBILITY

IN A dynamic, free enterprise economy, labor mobility lends flexibility to productive activity. Variations in the total labor requirements of the economy and in their distribution among firms, industries, occupations, and geographic areas necessitate shifts in the amount, location, and function of the human resources used in production. The significance of labor mobility in this context has long been recognized by economists, and a considerable amount of relevant empirical research has been done. Such research has received increasing emphasis during the past two decades, as first the problem of unemployment in the 1930's and then labor shortages in the 1940's and early 1950's directed the attention of investigators to the effect of mobility on the adjustment of labor supply to the demand for labor.

The research done in this field, however, has been extremely diverse with respect to specific hypotheses, research design, and methodology. The findings of studies in different local labor markets have frequently appeared to be conflicting, but whether the ostensible differences in findings are "real" or whether they result principally from conceptual and methodological differences is not clear.

OBJECTIVES AND LIMITATIONS OF THE PRESENT APPRAISAL

This report represents a stocktaking of past research on labor mobility—an attempt to fit the findings of many individual studies into a single framework. The aim is to ascertain and summarize what is known about the mobility of workers and what remains to be discovered in order to permit answers to important theoretical and practical questions concerning labor market processes. Thus a critical analysis of the problems that have been studied and the methods that have been employed is required, as well as a review of the findings of the various relevant investigations. The former is particularly important, for the results of research can be interpreted only with reference to the methods that produced them.

1

The scope of the present appraisal is limited in at least three important respects. First, it deals with labor mobility only in relation to flexibility of the labor supply. There are several other frames of reference in which labor mobility can be studied. Although these are largely neglected in this report, some of the more important will be described at this point so that the nature of the omissions can be fully appreciated.

Mobility can be studied with reference to the goals of workers and their opportunities to attain them. That is, the series of job changes made by workers during their lives can be examined with a view to determining the extent to which such changes constitute a ladder of self-improvement. Whether mobility performs this function has important implications with respect to the psychological satisfactions or the frustrations present in an industrial system. Incidentally, it may be that the movement of workers among various jobs contributes to psychological well-being even when movement is not "upward" in any real sense: mere variety of work experience at only one occupational level may constitute a safety valve for the pressures created by the minutely specialized and repetitive tasks involved in so many jobs in an industrialized economy.

Another context in which labor mobility can be studied concerns the class structure of society. Although occupation is not the only determinant of social class, it is an important one.[1] Consequently, the ease or difficulty of "climbing the occupational ladder," whether from the standpoint of an individual or of a family over several generations, is indicative of how "open" the class structure is. American ideology postulates an open class system, with equality of opportunity, mobility among occupational levels, and a resultant fluidity in the class structure. The degree of truth in this assumption is important in interpreting current sociopolitical developments and in predicting the nature and the direction of future social change.[2]

[1] See Wilbert E. Moore, *Industrial Relations and the Social Order* (rev. ed.; New York: Macmillan Company, 1951), Chapter 23.

[2] See Seymour M. Lipset and Reinhard Bendix, "Social Status and Social Structure: A Re-examination of Data and Interpretations," *British Journal of Sociology*, 2:150–168, 230–254 (1951), or University of California Institute of Industrial Relations Reprint No. 35 (Berkeley, 1952). The authors, in objecting to the design and the interpretation of some of the recent research on social stratification, argue that the proper purpose of the study of social class is to contribute to an understanding of social change: "We are interested to learn how new political movements . . . arose, or how the values and behaviour patterns of, say, the American 'middle class'

Finally, labor mobility is of significance not only as a functional process, but as a phenomenon that has important effects quite independent of whatever "functions" it may be conceived to have. These effects are both personal and social and are of interest to both psychologists and sociologists. The movement of workers is in many ways a disruptive influence. It often involves the breaking of established patterns of behavior and interpersonal relations, and the formation of new ones. Geographic movement over any great distance, for example, not only compels the worker to substitute a new circle of friends for the one he has known, but requires him and his family to adjust to an entirely new environment. These disorganizing influences are not confined to individuals and families, but may affect entire communities. The shortages of housing and schools, the overburdening of transportation and sanitation facilities, and the strains placed upon service industries of all types in many metropolitan areas during World War II are illustrative of the ways in which the large-scale movement of workers can affect the entire social fabric.

The foregoing discussion is not a complete outline of the several facets of labor mobility, but merely a reminder that mobility can be studied from various points of view. Although all are interrelated, the specific orientation of the investigator—the framework within which he chooses to work—will largely determine the problems that he considers important and influence the methods of analysis that he uses and perhaps even the interpretations that he draws from his data.

The delimitation of the present inquiry to the relationship between mobility and flexibility of the labor supply implies no judgment as to the relative importance of various approaches to the subject of labor mobility. Nor does the fact that the study is confined to what might be regarded as the economic, as opposed to the sociological, implications of mobility suggest that each of these is a distinct domain, not to be trespassed upon by specialists in the other. Since the boundaries that divide the social sciences reflect no comparable compartments in real life, research will probably be most fruitful if investigators roam wherever the specific nature of their problems leads them, so long as their competence assures a firm footing.

Second, within the framework of flexibility of the labor supply, the present appraisal is restricted to what might be called short-run, as

have changed over time. . . . the analysis of social class is concerned with an assessment of the chances that common economic conditions and the common experiences of a group will lead to organized action" (pp. 247–248).

opposed to long-run, mobility. Job shifts and changes in labor force status by persons of working age are clearly not the only means whereby labor supply adjusts to changing requirements. Variations in the rates of entry into different occupations and industries by those newly entering the labor force perform the same function. Thus, over time, the industrial or occupational structure of the economy could change without any job shifting at all. This aspect of flexibility of the labor supply is not considered in this bulletin.

It should be noted that even in the short run there are factors other than labor mobility that contribute to economic flexibility. Although the emphasis throughout this report is on the adjustment of labor supply to changes in labor requirements, adjustment of demand to supply must also be taken into account in any complete analysis of economic flexibility. Expanding industries and firms may meet their labor requirements not only by attracting workers from other areas, but also by moving into areas where the labor supply is more adequate. Adjustment of supply and demand can be accomplished by adapting jobs to the existing occupational skills of workers as well as by fitting workers into the molds of existing job requirements.[3]

Third, the research reviewed here is restricted as to place and time. Only investigations relating to labor mobility in the United States are examined. Nevertheless, there is abundant evidence that the amount (and perhaps the character) of labor mobility in the United States differs substantially from that in most European countries.[4] To what extent the lesser mobility of European, as compared with American, workers is associated with differences in the structure and organization of industry and with other cultural differences merits intensive study.

The fact that most of the studies of labor mobility in the United States relate to the 1930's and 1940's dictates caution in generalizing from their results. Without implying that there are norms in labor market processes, it should be noted that rather extreme conditions prevailed during both decades. In the 1930's the economy suffered the severest industrial depression on record. During much of the 1940's acute manpower shortages prevailed, and labor market processes were influenced by manpower controls, by conversion to war production in

[3] See A. J. Jaffe and Charles D. Stewart, *Manpower Resources and Utilization* (New York: John Wiley & Sons, 1951), pp. 332–336.

[4] Gladys L. Palmer, "Social Values in Labor Mobility," in E. Wight Bakke and others, *Labor Mobility and Economic Opportunity* (Cambridge, Mass.: Technology Press, and New York: John Wiley & Sons, 1954).

the early part of the decade, by reconversion at the end of the war, and by the movement of millions of workers and potential workers into and out of the armed services.

The great variation in economic conditions during the two decades for which labor mobility has been most intensively studied has increased the value of the findings, since analysis of the effect of changing economic conditions on mobility is made possible. It must be kept in mind, however, that the labor market processes during this period may not be typical of those in less "disturbed" periods.

PLAN OF THE REPORT

A review and appraisal of research in any area logically begins with an examination of the questions and hypotheses that have been investigated. It is useful to inquire whether the studies of labor mobility, considered collectively, can be fitted into an integrated framework. The remainder of this chapter describes the questions with which mobility research has been concerned and indicates their relationship to the framework for research in this field outlined in the preceding section.

Chapter 2 examines some of the conceptual and methodological problems in mobility research. Special attention is paid to the appropriateness of various concepts to the problems that have been investigated, and to the possible effects of alternative concepts, definitions, and classification systems on the findings of past studies. Also, some of the research designs and methods of analysis are described and evaluated, and suggestions are made concerning methods which appear to be most appropriate for certain purposes.

In Chapters 3, 4, and 5, the evidence produced by mobility research is summarized for the principal problems that have been studied. For each problem considered, the findings of various investigators are compared with reference to the methodology used. Judgments are made as to the degree of confidence with which certain conclusions can be accepted, and as to the questions on which additional research is needed. Some suggestions for further research are presented in Chapter 6.

MAJOR QUESTIONS IN MOBILITY RESEARCH

Research on labor mobility does not deal with a neat group of hypotheses that can be clearly distinguished from those examined in research on labor market dynamics in general. The movement of workers is only one of the factors affecting labor supply and is almost inextricably related to a host of other factors affecting the supply, to say nothing of the many factors affecting the demand for labor. For this reason, research on labor mobility necessarily blends into and is frequently inseparable from other labor market research.

There is a degree of artificiality, therefore, in attempting to describe mobility research by pulling out of studies of labor markets those portions that deal with mobility. Nevertheless, progress in empirical research depends on the formulation and testing of specific hypotheses. This in turn requires the breaking down of major problems into specific components for separate analysis. Considering only one aspect of a problem does not imply that it is independent of the whole, or even that it can be fully understood without consideration of the whole. Indeed, distinguishing labor mobility research from research on other aspects of labor markets is not a division in subject matter so much as it is a differentiation in the viewpoint of the observer. In investigating labor mobility one is really studying the total operation of labor markets, but with specific reference to the interaction between the movement of workers and the other factors and processes involved.

With this perspective it is possible to indicate the major problems with which mobility research has been concerned. Although investigators have raised innumerable specific questions, a review of the literature suggests three major headings under which they may be classified: (1) the extent and character of labor mobility, (2) the determinants of mobility, and (3) mobility and the process of labor allocation. Each of these topics is illustrated in the following paragraphs by reference to specific questions that have been investigated. At the same time, an effort is made to appraise the relevance of the questions to flexibility of the labor supply.

Extent and Character of Labor Mobility. Attempts have been made to measure the amount of mobility in the entire economy or in specific labor markets, the proportion of the work force that is responsible for the shifting that takes place, and the relative frequency of various kinds of job shifts. Examples of specific questions investigated are: How prevalent are simple interfirm job shifts relative to the more complex shifts that involve changes in occupational or industrial assignments? What proportion of job shifts is geographic, and does geographic movement involve occupational or industrial patterns differing from those within a local labor market? Do workers show a greater tendency to change occupations, or to change industries? Are there "families" of occupations and industries among which movement is more likely to occur than among others, or are the industrial and occupational changes made by workers essentially random?

Conclusive answers to questions of this kind would permit generalizations not only about the degree of flexibility in the labor supply, but also about the precise character of that flexibility. For example, is the labor force more adaptable to industrial or to occupational changes in labor requirements? What types of changes in the industrial structure can most readily be met by the voluntary movement of workers? Given an increase in the labor requirements of a particular industry, from what industries and in what relative numbers are workers likely to be recruited? With such information, it would be possible to develop labor supply models on both a local and a national basis for estimating the degree to which assumed levels and patterns of manpower requirements could be met by the existing labor force.

Determinants of Labor Mobility. A second group of questions with which mobility research has been concerned relates to the factors that affect the extent, character, and incidence of labor mobility. These questions have been approached in two ways: (1) by analyzing the employment histories of workers to determine whether mobility varies according to readily ascertainable characteristics of individuals, and (2) by studying the impact of environmental factors on labor mobility. Illustrative of the first are attempts to determine differences in the degree and patterns of mobility according to age, sex, race, or marital status of workers, and according to various socioeconomic characteristics, such as home ownership, union membership, and education. Among the environmental, or institutional, factors whose influence on mobility has been analyzed are the policies of unions, employers, and government; the level of business activity; and the industrial structure of the labor market. For example, what are the net effects on labor mobility of the hiring preferences of employers, of their recruitment and promotion policies, and of their attitudes toward using the public employment service? Does the union's attempt to control job opportunities, to protect job rights, and to ameliorate unsatisfactory working conditions inhibit the voluntary movement of workers? Do certain aspects of such government programs as social security influence the volume or the character of mobility? Are mobility rates and patterns in local labor market areas affected by the industrial characteristics of those areas?

Information on questions of this kind is clearly pertinent in any analysis of the flexibility of labor supply. Knowledge of the characteristics of mobile workers is at least a first step toward a qualitative analysis. A given volume and pattern of job shifts means one thing if the workers involved are predominantly young and inexperienced, but quite another if they are primarily experienced workers with records of long service. Similarly, the implications of a given volume of movement vary, depending on whether the moving workers are predominantly men or women. Of even clearer significance are occupational and industrial differentials in mobility.

An understanding of the environmental, or institutional, forces that affect labor mobility is important both in developing theories of labor market behavior and in formulating policies for the effective allocation and utilization of labor resources. Models of labor supply can be constructed only in the light of the impact of institutional arrangements on the distribution of the labor force and on the propensity and ability of workers to make job shifts. Moreover, if the relationship between these institutional arrangements and the mobility of workers is known, controls can be devised to produce the kinds of results appropriate to particular manpower requirements. To illustrate, if government wage controls should again become desirable, they could be formulated with a view not only to their effect on the prevention of inflation, but also to their incidental effects on the composition of the labor supply. Decisions relating to the location of new productive facilities and to the letting of contracts among existing facilities could be based on analyses of the extent to which the structures of various local labor markets would permit a ready adaptation of the labor supply to a new pattern of manpower requirements.

Mobility and the Process of Labor Allocation. In research on labor mobility considerable attention has been given to the relation between the labor market behavior of workers and the process of labor allocation in a free enterprise economy. What criteria do workers use in assessing the relative desirability of job opportunities? What considerations prompt them to make voluntary job changes? Do workers in fact make careful decisions about the relative advantages and disadvantages of alternative job opportunities and gravitate toward those jobs that offer the greatest "net advantage"? What light is thrown on this question by the ways in which workers find out about jobs? How much do workers actually know about labor market conditions and about the nature of available job opportunities? Is there any evidence that the movement of workers among jobs in a local labor market operates to reduce or eliminate wage differentials among similar jobs?

These questions are fundamental in labor mobility research. In an economic system in which job choices are made freely by individuals, an understanding of how and why their choices are made is prerequisite to the development of labor market theory. If labor mobility is "functional" in the sense of adapting the labor supply to changing labor requirements, individual workers must tend to choose employment where the need for them is greatest. Traditional economic theory suggests that this will be the case because of the responsiveness of workers to wage differentials. According to this theory, differentials in wages among comparable jobs reflect differences in the relative "need" for workers. The movement of workers toward higher paying jobs thus assures the most effective allocation of the labor supply. Also, the movement or threat of movement of workers from the less to the more attractive jobs tends to equalize the net attractiveness of all jobs in the economy. More succinctly, economic differentials produce necessary movement, and this movement continues until the economic differentials are eliminated. In empirical research on the actual labor market behavior of workers, the basic assumptions of this theory may be tested.

But questions on the process of labor allocation have practical as well as theoretical significance. In a mobilization program, for example, it is crucially important to know what factors have the greatest influence on workers' job choices and decisions. Manpower policy based on the assumption that wage differentials are the major factor inducing workers to change jobs will be quite different from policy based on the assumption that wages are of relatively minor importance. The question is also important for the personnel policies of individual employers. Although it is doubtful whether employers spend much time speculating about the shape of the labor supply curve for the individual firm, they frequently face the practical problem of attracting and retaining an adequate work force. Whether workers evaluate jobs chiefly in terms of wages, or whether other elements in personnel policy are of equal or greater importance, has great relevance to these problems.

All the major questions with which mobility research has been concerned are highly interrelated, as indicated in the preceding discussion. The institutional factors that affect mobility and the considerations that motivate the labor market behavior of workers are clearly interacting; their labor market behavior is largely a product of institutional influences. Also, many institutional factors affect mobility only because of the prevalence of certain motivational patterns. Specifically, if seniority arrangements restrict mobility, this is largely because workers value job security highly. For these reasons the classification of research questions presented above is not to be regarded as a hard and fast delineation of areas of research on labor mobility, but as a convenient, if somewhat arbitrary, procedure for analyzing the work that has been done and for summarizing its results.

To say that the questions discussed in this section have been raised in research on labor mobility is not to imply that they have been fully answered. Data gathered on some of the questions do point rather conclusively to definitive answers. On others the evidence is conflicting, and further research is needed before confident judgments are warranted. Still other questions which have been suggested have not yet been empirically investigated at all.

2 SOME CONCEPTUAL AND METHODOLOGICAL PROBLEMS

In research on labor mobility there have been not only variations in the classes of workers studied, the sources of data on job histories, and the methods of measurement and analysis, but also differences even with respect to the meaning of the concept of mobility itself. The present chapter describes and evaluates some of the concepts and methods that have been used. Its purpose is twofold. First, in appraising the research it is necessary to inquire whether the concepts and methods employed are appropriate to the problems investigated, and whether certain techniques and concepts are superior to others for specific purposes. Second, the research findings reviewed in subsequent chapters can be interpreted only with reference to the techniques that produced them. To illustrate, the "fact" that skilled workers are less mobile than unskilled workers has one set of implications if mobility is taken to mean the actual movement of workers among jobs, but quite another if the relative propensity of workers to make voluntary job shifts is meant. As another example, a study that considers all the job shifts made by workers during a period of a year and a study that compares the job status of workers at the beginning and end of the year are bound to yield different measures of mobility. The second study not only disregards the actual frequency of job changes but probably also understates the proportion of mobile workers, for it ignores those who moved from one job to another and then back to the original one.

An analysis of the definitions and the procedures used, and of the probable influence of alternative procedures upon the findings, is particularly important if the conclusions of different research projects are to be compared. Ostensibly different findings with respect to a given question may be attributable to differences in methodology; and a similarity between the findings of two studies may be more apparent than real if different definitions or analytical methods have been used.

In empirical research the usefulness of a concept depends upon its

11

appropriateness or relevance to the basic problems on which the research is focused, and upon the extent to which it can be operationally defined. In the field of labor force description and measurement, for example, the concept of "unemployment" refers to a situation in which persons able and willing to work are unable to find jobs. Insofar as it is the purpose of labor force statistics to measure the extent to which the economy is not affording opportunities for remunerative employment to those who want to work, this concept is reasonably appropriate. Moreover, it lends itself fairly well to operational definition, in that willingness to work may be determined in specific cases by whether the individual declares himself to be looking for a job. On the other hand, if manpower statistics had the sole purpose of indicating the extent of unutilized human resources, unemployment might more appropriately be conceived as a situation in which persons *able* to work do not have jobs. Between these extremes it would be possible to define unemployment in terms of various degrees of willingness to work, short of actually seeking a job.[1]

[1] Cf. A. J. Jaffe and Charles D. Stewart, *Manpower Resources and Utilization.* The authors maintain that *"working force analysis,* including the very definition of the term, emerges from the entire social, economic, political, and cultural milieu . . . The nature of any specific definition of or method of analysis of *working force* is conditioned by the particular problem for the solution of which the nation wishes to formulate social policy" (p. 1).

See also Samuel C. Kelley, *A Case Study in the Measurement of Manpower Resources* (Columbus: Ohio State University Research Foundation, 1951, mimeo.). Kelley points out that the present concept of unemployment is in part a carry-over from concern with the problems of the 1930's, when workers were plentiful and jobs scarce. Although admitting the usefulness of the present concepts of the labor force and unemployment for certain purposes, he suggests that a concept of labor resources that would include all those *not unwilling* to take jobs would be useful in making estimates of labor supply in a mobilized or semimobilized economy. To test the feasibility of preparing such estimates, a questionnaire survey of a random sample of the population of Columbus, Ohio was conducted in 1951. A number of persons equal to 8 percent of the current labor force who were neither working nor seeking work at the time said they would take jobs if they were trained for them.

That the current definition of unemployment excludes some persons who would undoubtedly take jobs if employment opportunities were abundant has been rather commonly recognized. See, for example, W. S. Woytinsky, *Three Aspects of Labor Dynamics* (Washington: Social Science Research Council Committee on Social Security, 1942), p. 106. Jaffe and Stewart make the same point (*op. cit.,* pp. 457–461). They conclude that "unemployment is a state of mind as well as an economic fact. To that extent then, there is no uniquely correct way of measuring it. Unemployment and 'seeking work' must be defined in that manner which supplies the data of most use in the given social and economic situation" (p. 461).

THE CONCEPT OF LABOR MOBILITY

Labor mobility may be conceived in three quite different ways: (1) as the capacity or ability of workers to move from one job to another, or into and out of employment, or into and out of the labor force; (2) as their willingness or propensity to make such moves, given the opportunity; or (3) as their actual movement. Each of these concepts of mobility will be examined to determine its relevance to the problems raised in the preceding chapter, and its susceptibility to operational definition.

Mobility as Ability To Move. The *ability* of workers to make job changes of various kinds has meaning only in the context of the aptitudes and skills required for particular jobs. Research on the ability of workers to shift from one type of employment to another, in other words, is equivalent to investigating the transferability of specific skills. To what extent can unskilled workers serve satisfactorily in semiskilled jobs? For example, is a hand trucker ordinarily qualified to take a job as an automatic punch press operator?

The implications of this concept of mobility for describing and measuring the flexibility of the labor supply are important. Use of this concept of mobility would seem to be essential in any attempt to determine the *maximum potential* flexibility in the distribution of human resources in production. For example, if one assumes a fully mobilized economy in which freedom of job choice is suspended and in which workers can be "drafted" for civilian employment, knowledge of the extent to which workers are able to perform alternative jobs would permit estimates of the levels and patterns of production that could be achieved by shifting workers among jobs and by "inducting" new workers into the labor force. But such knowledge is useful in other connections. By indicating the maximum potential transferability of the work force, it furnishes a basis for estimating actual flexibility under assumed conditions, provided that the effects of institutional and motivational factors on the voluntary movement of workers are known. Indeed, it is difficult to imagine how models of labor supply such as those suggested in the preceding chapter could be developed without detailed knowledge of the alternative kinds of jobs that can be performed by workers in each occupational category.

There are serious difficulties, however, in giving operational meaning to this concept of mobility. Both the training of workers and the hiring specifications of employers have to be taken into account. The ability of an automobile mechanic to become a machinist, or of a housewife without previous experience in the labor force to take a semiskilled job, is related to available training programs. It is therefore necessary to define the transferability of workers from one occupation to another in terms of some minimum training time. Moreover, employers' specifications of the requirements of particular jobs are rather flexible, in that they are affected considerably by the tightness or the looseness of the labor market. Under ordinary circumstances, female school teachers or department store clerks do not have the "ability," even with training, to become aircraft riveters, but during World War II literally thousands of women made such shifts.

These considerations suggest that even detailed knowledge of the skill and aptitude requirements of various jobs would not permit precise description of patterns of transferability. However, if it becomes possible to define families of jobs with common skill and aptitude requirements, it should be possible to construct models based on a number of different assumptions relative to the tightness of labor supply and to the consequent patterns of employers' hiring specifications.

Relatively little attention has been given to this concept of mobility despite its relevance to some of the fundamental problems in labor market research. Although some investigators have defined mobility as the willingness *and ability* of workers to make job shifts, in elaborating the definition and analyzing their data they have generally been concerned with propensity rather than ability.[2] There has been some investigation of the transferability of skills. The Occupational Analysis Branch of the U. S. Employment Service has approached this problem with the specific objective of facilitating the placement and the vocational counseling services of the public employment offices, and is currently experimenting with the possibility of developing a functional classification of occupations based on the aptitudes, personality traits, and other factors which they require.[3] In the literature of

---

[2] See, for example, Clark Kerr, "Migration to the Seattle Labor Market Area, 1940–1942," *University of Washington Publications in the Social Sciences*, 11:151, note 1 (August 1942). See also Sumner H. Slichter, "The Impact of Social Security Legislation upon Mobility and Enterprise," *American Economic Review*, 30(suppl.): 44 (March 1940).

[3] The ultimate aim of this project is to "develop an occupational structure that will more adequately group like jobs together, enable the conversion of experience and training into a more workable occupational framework, suggest transfer possibilities both within groups and among groups of the same vertical level, offer a better foundation for promotion and upgrading, and present a more comprehensive

mobility research, however, there is little evidence of concern with the problem.[4]

Mobility as Propensity To Move. Some investigators have held that labor mobility properly refers to the propensity of workers to make job changes and should be distinguished from the actual movement of workers. Thus, Kerr differentiates between "actual movement" and "latent mobility." The former, he says, "can be observed and serves as an indication of latent mobility—the willingness and ability to move with given incentives—but it is not a precise measurement of it. Relatively immobile groups may move in large volume, and potentially mobile groups may remain stationary depending upon the circumstances they face." [5] Reynolds, also, prefers to regard mobility as the propensity or willingness to move. He observes that the actual movement of workers is a function not only of their willingness, but also

means of . . . analyzing the labor market in terms of groups of jobs." (U. S. Department of Labor, Bureau of Employment Security, Occupational Analysis Branch, *Classification Factor Reports,* August 1950, mimeo., p. 1.) The project is still in an experimental stage, involving a trial run of some 4,000 jobs selected from the Bureau's *Dictionary of Occupational Titles* (1949). The components in terms of which these jobs are being classified are the following: work performed, industry, aptitudes, physical demands and working conditions, interests, temperament traits, and training time.

[4] It is not implied that this is an oversight on the part of those concerned with labor mobility. The failure to integrate the problem of transferability of workers into the framework of mobility research doubtless stems from the fact that most investigators have been concerned with the flexibility of labor supply in a free enterprise economy, in which the relevant consideration is not so much what workers *can* do as what they appear to be willing to do. As one authority on the subject has put it, "one cannot assume that workers in a given category will necessarily be either potentially or actually interchangeable just because the job requirements indicate that this interchange is possible. The Army *can* allocate men on the basis of job requirements alone, but civilian manpower cannot necessarily be allocated on this basis only." (Letter to the author from Gladys L. Palmer, November 18, 1952.)

This point of view is unquestionably valid on the assumption that there is little likelihood that manpower controls more stringent than those employed during World War II will ever be imposed. The theoretical objectives of mobility research, however, should not be circumscribed by any assumption of this kind. It is instructive to note that even during the last war there were some officials who saw compulsory mobilization of civilian manpower as the only real solution to the nation's pressing manpower problems, and that according to at least one public opinion poll, such a program would probably have received popular support. See John J. Corson, *Manpower for Victory* (New York: Farrar & Rinehart, 1943), pp. 273–275.

[5] Kerr, *op. cit.,* p. 151n.

of their opportunities for movement.[6] Reynolds goes further, arguing that the propensity to move is actually a heterogeneous concept "embracing a variety of motives and activities." He therefore suggests differentiation among three kinds of propensity:

"a. Propensity to move to an apparently more attractive job whose terms and whose permanence are not known with certainty. . . .

"b. Propensity to quit a job which has proved unsatisfactory without having a new job in sight. . . .

"c. Propensity of an unemployed worker to change his usual occupation, industry, or place of residence in order to secure employment." [7]

Slichter also distinguishes propensity from movement, but on somewhat different grounds. Mobility, he holds, implies willingness and ability to move, while actual movement may be initiated by employers.[8]

For purposes of describing the flexibility of the labor supply in a free enterprise economy, the willingness or propensity of workers to make job shifts of various kinds is indeed a fundamental consideration. The mere capacity of workers to shift from one type of job to another is bound to overstate the actual degree of flexibility, for a worker's ability to make a given job change is no assurance that he will choose to make it. At the same time, the actual volume of voluntary job shifting almost certainly understates flexibility because the movement that would have occurred had the opportunities and the incentives for it been present and known is not included. Thus the willingness of workers to make job changes of specific types provides the best single indication of the extent and the nature of the flexibility in labor supply in an economy characterized by free job choice.[9]

Another advantage in regarding mobility as the propensity to change jobs is that this is the concept embodied in the traditional theory of labor allocation and wage determination; and the use of the same

[6] Lloyd G. Reynolds, *The Structure of Labor Markets* (New York: Harper & Brothers, 1951), p. 240.

[7] *Ibid.*, pp. 240–241.

[8] Slichter, *op. cit.*, p. 44.

[9] Although for certain purposes it is meaningful to consider the ability of workers to make job changes without considering their willingness to do so, the converse is not true. The propensity of workers to change jobs in certain directions cannot be divorced from their capacity to make such changes. The willingness of street cleaners to take jobs as physicians has virtually no utility as a measure of short-run flexibility of the labor supply, however valuable it may be in describing the aspirations of street cleaners.

concept in empirical research permits a more precise testing of the theory. According to the theory, the propensity of workers to move in the direction of jobs with the greatest "net economic advantages" results in actual movement until the marginal productivity of labor is equalized among similar employments. Assuming equal marginal productivities, however, it is not necessary for workers actually to move to the high-wage firms in order to equalize the terms of employment for comparable jobs within the labor market. Their propensity to make such shifts will accomplish the same result, for the potential loss of workers to the low-wage firms will constitute a threat forcing those firms to raise their wages in order to maintain the necessary labor supply.

But if mobility is regarded as the propensity to move, there are serious problems involved in measuring it directly, for propensity to move has no operational meaning except in terms of specific circumstances and specific incentives. Determination of the propensity of various groups of workers to make job shifts of certain kinds would necessitate presenting a sample of the labor force with an almost infinite number of specific job offers and noting their responses. Moreover, this experiment would have to be repeated under a variety of economic conditions. An experiment of this type is clearly impossible. As a result, even those investigators who have insisted that labor mobility refers to the propensity of workers to move rather than to their actual movement have had to draw conclusions about mobility by imputation from data on actual movement.[10] Kerr, for instance, after pointing out that mobility differs from movement and is not precisely measured by the actual job shifting of workers, makes the following observation:

[10] In a few studies, answers to hypothetical questions have been used to measure the propensity of workers to move. Reynolds, for example, asked a sample of workers how large a wage increase would be necessary in order to induce them to move into another labor market area (*op. cit.,* p. 78). Such information, if useful at all, must be interpreted with great care, for it is not known whether respondents' reactions to hypothesized situations are valid indicators of what they would actually do should those situations materialize. The validity of workers' expressed attitudes toward making certain types of job changes, as tested by their objective labor market behavior, is an important methodological problem which merits investigation, conceivably in experimental studies. For example, workers might be asked about their "willingness" to take certain kinds of jobs, and then actually be offered jobs similar to those described. Such an experiment would involve numerous practical difficulties, but might be feasible in certain local areas where the cooperation of employers and of the U. S. Employment Service could be secured.

" 'Mobility elasticity' could be measured if data on the degree of response of various sections of the labor force to the same combinations of incentives under similar circumstances could be obtained. Insufficient data are available, however, to permit this measurement. Actual movement, nevertheless, serves as a rough index of the mobility elasticity of various groups in the population, and indicates explanations for the apparently different degrees of elasticity." [11]

Possibly the closest approximation to a measurement of propensity to move that has been made in research is the rather ingenious method used by Makower, Marschak, and Robinson in their study of intercounty differences in the mobility of British workers.[12] Their data, derived from unemployment insurance records, included emigration rates for workers from each county into Oxford. Finding a high correlation between the rate of emigration from a particular county to Oxford and the difference between the rates of unemployment in that county and in Oxford, they developed a formula for the "coefficient of mobility" of a county which eliminates the effect of unemployment differences on the amount of movement. They defined the coefficient of mobility as the number of persons moving per year from a region with 1,000 insured persons to a region with 1,000 insured persons when the unemployment rate in the former region is 100 percent higher than in the latter.[13] This procedure, it will be noted, in effect adjusts intercounty differences in volume of movement for differences in the strength of one of the forces inducing movement (in this case, a greater number of job opportunities in Oxford).

Carrying their analysis a step further, the investigators found, as might be expected, a negative correlation between the emigration rate from a particular county into Oxford and that county's distance from Oxford. Accordingly, they developed a "coefficient of spatial friction," which measures the extent to which migration from a county is reduced for a given increase in distance from Oxford. Introducing the

[11] Kerr, *op. cit.*, p. 151n.

[12] H. Makower, J. Marschak, and H. W. Robinson, "Studies in Mobility of Labour: A Tentative Statistical Measure," *Oxford Economic Papers,* No. 1 (October 1938), pp. 83–123.

[13] The formula is as follows: coefficient of mobility $= \dfrac{Mu_b}{(u_a-u_b)\,ab}$, where M is the number of in-migrants from a given county to Oxford per year, a is the number of insured workers in thousands in the county, b is the number of insured workers in thousands in Oxford, u_a is the percentage of the county's insured workers who are unemployed, and u_b is the percentage of Oxford's insured workers who are unemployed.

coefficient of spatial friction into the original formula, they arrived at a measure of the relative responsiveness of the workers in a county to a standardized incentive to move (unemployment differential), and a standardized obstacle to such movement (distance). Although the investigators do not use the term "propensity" in their report, the concept is clearly pertinent to the analytical techniques they employed.

If mobility is conceived to be the propensity of workers to make job shifts, it must be remembered that this is not an absolute quality that can be abstracted from circumstances and incentives. The disposition of a worker to move is probably a function of his objectives and the degree to which his present situation, as compared with perceived alternatives, satisfies those objectives. Moreover, both the goals of a worker and his evaluation of his present situation are subject to influences external to himself, such as the value system of the culture and the wishes of his family. It follows that the mobility of a worker cannot be considered except in relation to a complex of social and institutional factors.

For the same worker, a given set of objectives might argue for a move in one situation and against a move in another. For example, Myers and Shultz found that the workers who quit their jobs at a New England textile mill after it was announced that the mill would close but before the actual shutdown were not more mobile in terms of their previous work experience than those who waited to be laid off. Indeed, the latter group had made more moves than the former.[14] Superficially these results appear to be paradoxical: workers who have been less "mobile" in the past become more "mobile" when faced with an almost certain layoff. But the paradox may be more apparent than real. It can be hypothesized that the workers who quit valued the prospect of steady working opportunities more highly than the group who remained. If this is true, one would expect the previous work experience of the group that quit to show a greater degree of stability and less movement than that of those who waited to be laid off.[15]

[14] Charles A. Myers and George P. Shultz, *The Dynamics of a Labor Market* (New York: Prentice-Hall, 1951), pp. 25–26.

[15] This hypothesis is illustrated by a comment made by one of the workers interviewed. In commenting on the fact that he had quit his mill job, whereas his wife, who worked in the same mill, remained in her job even after the shutdown notice, he remarked, "That's the difference between the two of us. She's going to keep working there, because I'm the one that's supposed to bring in the money, so I had to quit to get a job before they were all gone." (*Ibid.*, p. 213.)

Thus, considerable care must be used in drawing conclusions about the relative mobility (in the sense of propensity to move) of workers on the basis of the number and kinds of job shifts they have made. Indeed, the very notion of relative propensity to move, divorced from considerations of incentives, aspirations, and circumstances, is suspect. It is in the latter factors that the real key to the reasons for movement is to be sought. The number and kinds of job shifts made by various groups of workers may provide clues, but they must be interpreted cautiously.

Mobility as Movement. Regardless of the concept of mobility preferred by various investigators, it has almost invariably been measured in terms of the actual movement of workers. Conclusions concerning the relative propensities of various groups in the labor force to make job shifts have been deduced from differentials in the amount of movement by these groups and from the circumstances in which such movement has taken place.

Studies of historical patterns of movement not only permit interpretations of past changes in the distribution of the labor force, but, on the assumption that such patterns will be repeated under similar circumstances, permit predictions of the potential future flexibility of labor supply under assumed conditions. However, an analysis of the types of moves made by workers during a given period in the past does not provide a complete measure of flexibility even for that period. At best, it shows only what did take place, when one pattern of institutional influences and certain kinds of incentives prevailed.

The usefulness of data on actual job movement is increased if voluntary and forced job shifts are differentiated. For some purposes, particularly the study of motivation, it is undesirable to include information on job shifts occasioned by layoffs or discharges, for workers are not *motivated* to make such shifts, and their inclusion may produce misleading results.[16]

Reynolds' suggestion for the further differentiation of voluntary movement into two categories, depending on whether the worker quit his job with another one assured or quit an unsatisfactory job in order to look for a new one, also appears to have merit. To say that a worker made a job change because of "working conditions" may mean that he quit one job to take another about which he had learned and in which working conditions were more favorable. On the other hand,

16 See pp. 177n, 181 infra.

it may mean that he quit because of distasteful working conditions and set out to find other work which he hoped would be more attractive. These two situations have quite different implications for understanding labor market behavior.

In noting the desirability of differentiating between voluntary and forced movement of workers, it is not suggested that the latter is less significant than the former with respect to flexibility of the labor force. It is true that a layoff has no volitional elements so far as the employee is concerned, and that his propensities are irrelevant when he is laid off. But it is also true that a considerable amount of the adjustment of labor supply to changes in the patterns and volume of labor requirements occurs through this process, and its neglect would result in an incomplete picture. The *ability* of workers to make job shifts of various kinds is evidenced just as much by involuntary as by voluntary movement.

It is clear that whatever theoretical advantages can be claimed for viewing mobility as the ability or the propensity of workers to change jobs under various circumstances, there is also much to be said for thinking of mobility as actual movement. Indeed, even those who have been most insistent upon differentiating between propensity to move and actual movement have been unable at times to maintain terminological consistency. Thus, although Reynolds objects to the tendency to use the terms "movement" and "mobility" interchangeably and suggests that mobility be reserved to describe willingness or propensity to move, he discusses "patterns of labor mobility" as follows: "Labor mobility is of several sorts: *movement* into and out of the labor force, between employment and unemployment, between employers, industries, occupational levels, and geographical areas." [17]

The difficulty is not simply one of terminological inconsistency, but stems rather from the impossibility of approaching all the problems with which mobility research is concerned in terms of a single concept. It would be possible to develop a new terminology, in which "mobility" would refer only to propensity to move, and in which some other term such as "flexibility" or "adaptability" would be used to embrace the actual processes by which labor supply is adjusted to labor demand. The advantage of such a procedure, however, is not clear. The same difficulties would persist under different names. At present the problem is not whether mobility is most properly conceived as ability to

[17] Reynolds, *op. cit.*, p. 19; italics ours.

move, propensity to move, or actual movement, but how best to measure each of these and to assess its implications with respect to causing or permitting changes in the size and distribution of the labor force. The difficulties, therefore, are not terminological so much as methodological. They may result from erroneously imputing certain motivational influences to an observed volume of movement, or from predicting a given volume and type of movement on the basis of "propensities" abstracted from the institutional influences which alone give such "propensities" operational meaning. These difficulties are not solved by developing new terms.

In the remainder of this monograph, unless otherwise indicated, the term mobility will refer to the actual movement of workers among jobs, between employment and unemployment, or into and out of the labor force. Mobility is thus conceived as embracing all the types of changes in the labor market or job status of a worker that alter either his function or his location in the productive process.

Labor Turnover and Labor Mobility. Some students of labor mobility have suggested a distinction between mobility and labor turnover. Bezanson has used turnover to refer to the horizontal shifting of workers among jobs at the same occupational level, reserving the term mobility for vertical shifts from one occupational level to another.[18] Palmer has suggested a less restricted definition of mobility, including not only changes in occupational assignment, but also industrial and geographic shifts, as well as changes in employment or labor force status. Job changes that involve none of these shifts, however, she regarded as turnover rather than mobility.[19] More recently Palmer has considered "the mobility of workers to include changes of job, of employer, of occupation, of industry, of locality or region, and also changes of status." [20]

The distinction formerly made by Palmer was apparently based on the view that simple interfirm shifts differ from the more complex job changes in purposes and effects. Of mobility, as she defined it in 1947, Palmer said, "it encompasses all the adjustments which workers make

[18] Anne Bezanson, "The Advantages of Labor Turnover: An Illustrative Case," *Quarterly Journal of Economics,* 42:450–464 (May 1928).

[19] Gladys L. Palmer, *Research Planning Memorandum on Labor Mobility,* Social Science Research Council Pamphlet 2 (New York, April 1947), pp. 1–2.

[20] Gladys L. Palmer, *Labor Mobility in Six Cities: A Report on the Survey of Patterns and Factors in Labor Mobility* (New York: Social Science Research Council, 1954), p. 2.

on account of their own needs or aspirations—for a job, a 'better' job, more income, more social prestige, more leisure, or a more acceptable 'way of life'—and on account of changes forced upon them by changes in the economy." [21] But it does not seem that a simple job change between two firms in the same industry and same labor market, without any change in occupational assignment, is necessarily any less an adjustment of the kind described than an occupational, geographic, or industrial change. Workers change employers, as well as their occupations, because of their "needs or aspirations." Moreover, the shifting of workers from a declining to an expanding firm in the same industry is as essential in a free enterprise economy as the shifting of workers from a contracting to an expanding industry or occupation. The problems involved in defining an "industry" make this point particularly significant.[22] It seems desirable therefore to regard the shifting of workers among firms as a kind of mobility, and to recognize that it contributes to a necessary kind of flexibility in the labor supply.[23]

What, then, of the concept of labor turnover? As traditionally used, this refers to the change in personnel that takes place during a given period in the work force of a firm or an industry.[24] Turnover is generally measured as a percentage: the number of workers separated (or hired) per 100 workers on the average payroll during the period covered. Workers who leave the payroll of a particular plant make some kind of shift in job or status. They may take a job with another employer in the same or a different industry. A change in occupation may or may not be involved. They may leave, or remain within, the local labor market. They may be unemployed for a period of time, or leave the labor force. Thus, labor mobility and labor turnover are distinguishable not on the basis of the *kinds* of job shifts that are involved, but on the basis of the viewpoint from which these shifts are

[21] *Research Planning Memorandum on Labor Mobility*, p. 1.

[22] For an analysis of the theoretical problems involved in the concept of an industrial group, see Robert Triffin, *Monopolistic Competition and General Equilibrium Theory* (Cambridge: Harvard University Press, 1940), pp. 78–89.

[23] It is not implied that no purpose is served by distinguishing between simple changes of employer and more complex job shifts that involve occupational, industrial, or geographic changes. Such a distinction, which is important for certain types of analysis, may be preserved by classifying job changes according to the nature of the shift involved. See Palmer, *Labor Mobility in Six Cities*, especially Chapter 4.

[24] See Florence Peterson, *Survey of Labor Economics* (New York: Harper & Brothers, 1947), p. 208.

seen.[25] Analysis of mobility requires a *comparison* of the worker's status before and after a labor market transaction—for example, a change of jobs, a move into or out of employment, or into or out of the labor force. Turnover, on the other hand, is based on a *count* of separations or accessions.

CLASSIFYING LABOR MOBILITY

Since the short-run supply of labor can adjust to changes in the volume or pattern of labor requirements by changes in the size of the labor force, in the volume of employment and unemployment, or in the distribution of employed workers among firms, occupations, industries, or localities, most investigators of mobility have classified the moves of workers in terms of those aspects of flexibility. Thus, the following types of mobility of workers have been commonly recognized:

1. Interfirm movement, from one firm to another or a change of employer.

2. Occupational movement, from one occupation to another.

3. Industrial movement, from one industry to another.

4. Geographic movement, from one local area to another.

5. Movement from an unemployed to an employed status.

6. Movement from an employed to an unemployed status.

7. Movement into and out of the labor force.[26]

These types of mobility clearly do not represent discrete and mutually exclusive categories of labor market transactions. A single job change may involve a combination of several of the kinds of mobility specified. For example, a worker who has been employed as an unskilled laborer in a Pittsburgh steel mill and who takes a job as a panel assembler in a Seattle aircraft plant has made an interfirm, occupa-

[25] Cf. W. S. Woytinsky, *Three Aspects of Labor Dynamics*, p. 1: "Labor turnover statistics are computed from the employer's standpoint, while the statistics of duration of unemployment and of length of service tend to report what happens to individual employees."

[26] Herbert G. Heneman, Jr. has used the terms "employment mobility" and "unemployment mobility," respectively, for the fifth and sixth categories listed, and "entrance mobility" and "exit mobility" for the moves included in the seventh category. ("Differential Short-Run Labor Mobilities: St. Paul, 1941–42," in *Minnesota Manpower Mobilities*, University of Minnesota Industrial Relations Center, Bulletin 10, 1950, pp. 36–37.) Another type of mobility which must be distinguished for certain kinds of analysis is movement of a worker from an employed to a self-employed status, or vice versa.

tional, industrial, and geographic shift in that one transaction. Indeed, when a worker makes either an occupational, geographic, or industrial shift, he generally changes firms at the same time. This, however, is not necessarily the case. Intraplant transfers or promotions may occasion occupational shifts alone. An industrial shift unaccompanied by a change of firm can occur when a worker moves between two plants of a company that is engaged in different industries. Geographic movement may occur without a change in employer, occupation, or industry, as when a worker transfers from one plant of a company to another in a different area.

It is considerably easier to define and classify types of labor mobility conceptually than to give operational meaning to the various terms and to decide how specific job changes are to be classified. To say that occupational mobility involves changes in occupation is meaningless in the absence of a definition of occupation and a suggested occupational classification system. The same is true of the concept of industrial mobility. Likewise, what is meant by geographic mobility depends upon what one conceives a local labor market area to be. Some of these definitional problems will now be examined.

Definition of a Job. Basic to any analysis of the extent and nature of job shifting is the definition of a "job," for the meaning given to this term will affect both the incidence and the pattern of mobility yielded by a given body of data on workers' employment histories. In most of the empirical research on labor mobility a job has been defined as a continuous period of service with a single employer.[27] This definition automatically excludes from the analysis of labor mobility all changes in the occupational assignments of workers within a given firm, thus understating the occupational mobility of workers and the

[27] The most notable exception is the series of studies of Philadelphia workers conducted in the 1930's by Gladys L. Palmer and her associates at the University of Pennsylvania. In these studies a job was defined as "continuous paid service at one occupational assignment for one or more months." The studies are reported in the following publications of the W. P. A. National Research Project in cooperation with the University of Pennsylvania Industrial Research Department: Gladys L. Palmer and Ada M. Stoflet, *The Labor Force of the Philadelphia Radio Industry in 1936*, Report No. P-2 (April 1938); Gladys L. Palmer, *Ten Years of Work Experience of Philadelphia Weavers and Loom Fixers*, Report No. P-4 (July 1938); Helen Herrmann, *Ten Years of Work Experience of Philadelphia Machinists*, Report No. P-5 (September 1938); Gladys L. Palmer and Constance Williams, *Reemployment of Philadelphia Hosiery Workers after Shut-downs in 1933–34*, Report No. P-6 (January 1939).

occupational flexibility in labor supply. The omission is the more significant if, as some observers believe, most upward occupational movement is intra- rather than interfirm.[28]

The definition of a job as an attachment to a particular employer rather than to a particular occupation in a given firm probably results from considerations of expediency and feasibility. It is especially difficult to obtain accurate and complete information on intraplant changes in occupation through interviews with workers. Workers are apt to remember a change in employer much more distinctly than a change in occupational assignment for a given employer, particularly when the change is between two specific occupations within a major occupational category (skilled, semiskilled, unskilled, etc.).

There are other problems in the definition of a job. Anyone who has studied the employment experience of large groups of workers realizes that labor market activities do not always fall neatly into any set of categories that an investigator may establish. A number of specific problems may be illustrated. If a worker leaves a job and within a short period returns to the same employer in the same occupational assignment, without having taken other work in the meantime, are these two jobs or one job? When a worker performs "odd jobs" for numerous employers during a period of, say, two years, is each of his specific assignments with a particular employer to be regarded as a job, or should the entire two-year period be treated as a single job? How does one treat a worker who has held two jobs concurrently? In obtaining work histories, is a part-time job held after school hours to be included? What should be done about temporary jobs held by students during summer vacations before they have completed school? These questions merely illustrate the sorts of judgments required in analyzing work histories.

There can be no general prescription as to how to deal with such problems. Decisions about definitions must take into account the specific objectives of the study and considerations of feasibility, and compromise is often necessary. Two suggestions may be made. First, because the definitions adopted in a study affect the statistical measures of mobility computed, it seems desirable that future investigators use

---

[28] See Reynolds, *op. cit.*, p. 139. Clark Kerr makes the same point in "The Balkanization of Labor Markets," in E. Wight Bakke and others, *Labor Mobility and Economic Opportunity*. According to Kerr's analysis, this type of upward occupational movement within an employing unit is particularly characteristic of the industrial as opposed to the craft type of enterprise.

common definitions, unless there are compelling reasons for deviations in particular cases. Only in this way can comparability of results be assured, and research in this area become truly additive. Second, in order to make such uniformity possible, future publications reporting the results of research on labor mobility should include detailed descriptions of definitions and methodology. Unfortunately, much of the published work in this field is seriously deficient in this regard.

Occupational Mobility. Whatever system of classifying occupations is adopted, an occupational shift is one that involves movement from one category to another. Measures of occupational mobility are therefore predetermined to a large extent by the degree of detail in the occupational classification used.

Most studies of occupational mobility have used the classification system of the Bureau of the Census or that of the Bureau of Employment Security, as given in its *Dictionary of Occupational Titles.* Occasionally these two systems have been used in conjunction with one another, with the occupational descriptions in the *Dictionary of Occupational Titles* serving as guides for the classification of doubtful cases. A brief description of each of these systems will indicate some of the problems involved.[29]

The Census Bureau's classification consists of 11 major groups of occupations,[30] comprising 269 detailed occupational categories. For each decennial census, the Census Bureau prepares for its coders a volume containing an alphabetical listing of specific occupations together with code numbers relating these occupations to the categories of the classification system.[31] This volume is useful for classifying specific job titles, but since it includes only job titles, and no job descriptions, it does not provide detailed occupational information for the use of students of mobility.

[29] For a more detailed description of these and other classifications, and an analysis of the problems involved in using them, see Carroll L. Shartle, *Occupational Information* (New York: Prentice-Hall, 1952), Chapter 4.

[30] The groups used in the 1950 census are as follows: professional, technical, and kindred workers; farmers and farm managers; managers, officials, and proprietors, except farm; clerical and kindred workers; sales workers; craftsmen, foremen, and kindred workers; operatives and kindred workers; private household workers; service workers, except private household; farm laborers and foremen; and laborers, except farm and mine.

[31] U. S. Bureau of the Census, *1950 Census of Population: Alphabetical Index of Occupations and Industries.* The *Index* includes approximately 18,000 occupational titles.

The *Dictionary of Occupational Titles* was prepared by the Division of Occupational Analysis of the Bureau of Employment Security, principally to facilitate the placement and counseling activities of the local offices of the Employment Service. The *Dictionary* was first published in 1940 and has undergone revision since that time. The latest edition consists of three volumes, only the first of which is pertinent to the present discussion. This lists alphabetically more than 21,000 separate jobs or occupations, together with their descriptions and code numbers. The classification structure has three levels of detail: 7 major occupational groups [32] are divided into 579 categories, which are further subdivided into almost 9,000 more detailed classes.

Disregarding for a moment the merits of the classifications themselves, the chief advantage in use of the Census classification is that it makes possible comparison of the findings of a study and data published by the Census Bureau. On the other hand, the advantage in using the *Dictionary* classification is that its occupational descriptions facilitate and increase accuracy in assigning particular occupations to specific categories.[33]

Reynolds, and Myers and Shultz have used the relevant major occupational groups of the Census for classifying job shifts.[34] On the other hand, in the recent survey of patterns and factors in labor mobility in six cities occupational shifts were analyzed in terms of the 269 code items in the 1950 Census occupation code, although tabulations of the current or the usual occupations of workers were made in terms of the major occupational groups.[35] In the studies of Philadelphia work-

[32] Professional and managerial occupations; clerical and sales occupations; service occupations; agriculture, fishing, forestry, and kindred occupations; skilled occupations; semiskilled occupations; and unskilled occupations.

[33] In this section the problem of getting accurate information on occupations is neglected; it is assumed that the data collected are complete and accurate. Only the problems of classifying them are considered. The problems involved in collecting the data are considered on pp. 52–53 infra.

[34] Reynolds, *op. cit.*, Chapter 5. Myers and Shultz, *op. cit.*, p. 32, Table 6.

[35] Gladys L. Palmer, *Labor Mobility in Six Cities*, p. 62. The survey was conducted in 1951 through the cooperation of seven university research centers, the Committee on Labor Market Research of the Social Science Research Council, and the Bureau of the Census, for the Department of Air Force. This survey represents the most ambitious single study of labor mobility ever to be undertaken in the United States. Representative samples of the population in each of six cities (Chicago, Los Angeles, New Haven, Philadelphia, St. Paul, and San Francisco) were selected by the Bureau of the Census. Detailed work histories for the 11-year period 1940–50 were obtained for workers in the sample who were 25 years of age

ers conducted by Palmer and her associates in the 1930's, a relatively detailed classification of occupations was used.[36]

Surprisingly little attention has been given in research on labor mobility to analyzing the problem of classifying occupations. Although many investigators have recognized that the degree of detail in the classification system affects the measurement of the amount of occupational mobility, few have analyzed the relationship between the structure of the classification system and the objectives of their research. At least two recent studies, however, have dealt with this relationship to some extent. In a study of the mobility patterns of skilled workers during the period 1940–51,[37] Myers and Shultz point to the difficulties involved in using either the Census or the *Dictionary of Occupational Titles* classification for skilled workers. Specifically, they note discrepancies between the two systems of classification with respect to whether certain jobs should be regarded as skilled. Some occupations classified as skilled by the *Dictionary* are not so classified by the Census. More frequently, jobs listed as skilled (craftsmen, foremen, and kindred workers) by the Census are considered semiskilled or unskilled by the *Dictionary*. Moreover, in some cases in which the Census and the *Dictionary* agreed that a job was skilled, the data on earnings and previous work experience included in the work histories indicated that the job in question could not realistically be so regarded. The latter problem, however, probably resulted from inadequacies in the data collected rather than from deficiencies in the classification systems.[38]

---

and over at the time of the survey and who had worked at least one month in 1950. The field work and the basic tabulations were done by the Census Bureau, while the data were analyzed and reports were written by members of the staffs of the seven university research centers: Institute of Industrial Relations, University of California at Berkeley; Institute of Industrial Relations, University of California at Los Angeles; Chicago Community Inventory, University of Chicago; Industrial Relations Section, Massachusetts Institute of Technology; Industrial Relations Center, University of Minnesota; Industrial Research Department, University of Pennsylvania; and the Labor and Management Center, Yale University. For the objectives, methodology, and findings of the survey, see Palmer, *Labor Mobility in Six Cities*, a summary report. The unpublished reports prepared by the participating university research centers are listed on pp. 139–141 of that volume.

[36] See p. 25n supra.

[37] Charles A. Myers and George P. Shultz, "Patterns of Mobility of Skilled Workers and Factors Affecting Their Occupational Choice, Six Cities, 1940–51," unpublished manuscript, Massachusetts Institute of Technology Industrial Relations Section (February 1952).

[38] *Ibid.*, pp. 75–80.

Reynolds' objections to the use of existing occupational classification systems in mobility research are somewhat more fundamental. In his study of the work experience of a sample of New Haven manual workers, he classified jobs according to the occupational categories of the Census, using the *Dictionary of Occupational Titles* as a guide in doubtful cases. He concluded that "These categories are rather unsatisfactory for the present purpose"—and they "stand in need of thorough rethinking and revision." [39] As illustrative of the difficulties involved, he cites the following: (1) The Census category of skilled workers (craftsmen, foremen, and kindred workers) groups together members of true craft occupations such as printing and carpentry, skilled maintenance workers in manufacturing, and a diverse list of production workers in manufacturing. These groups, Reynolds thinks, have different mobility characteristics. Moreover, he believes that the *Dictionary of Occupational Titles* "seriously overstates the degree of skill involved in present-day manufacturing operations." (2) He observes that the semiskilled group (operatives and kindred workers) is far too heterogeneous, "ranging all the way from virtually unskilled jobs paying about the same as common labor to jobs which pay (on an output basis) more than many craft occupations." (3) He notes that the service worker category "rests on an *industrial* rather than an *occupational* distinction," and suggests that service workers should be "distributed among the skilled, semiskilled, and unskilled categories, depending on the kind of work they do." [40]

The shifts of workers among occupations must be analyzed with considerably more precision than is permitted by the traditional systems of classification, if mobility research is to serve many of the purposes outlined in Chapter 1. For example, the major occupational divisions in both the Census and the *Dictionary* classifications are much too broad and too heterogeneous to allow occupational flexibility to be analyzed in sufficient detail for the construction of useful labor supply models. On the other hand, the detailed breakdowns in each of these systems are far too numerous, particularly for research based on samples of the labor force.[41] But these two desirable features of a

[39] Reynolds, *op. cit.*, p. 134 and its note 18.

[40] *Ibid.*, note 18.

[41] These remarks are not intended as criticisms of either of the two classification systems per se, but refer only to their suitability for use in labor mobility research. It is a commonplace that concepts, definitions, and classification systems must be formulated with reference to the purposes they are to serve. Neither the Census

system of classification, namely, a limited number of classes and homogeneity within each class, are obviously in conflict: the fewer the categories in any classification system, the less its intraclass homogeneity. However, it should be possible to obtain greater homogeneity even within categories as broad as the major occupational groups of either the Census or the *Dictionary of Occupational Titles*. Both these systems involve, to some degree, mixtures of industrial and occupational differentiation. This is most pronounced in the *Dictionary* where, for example, agriculture, fishing, forestry, and kindred occupations are treated as an "occupational" category. In terms of the major groups, therefore, a job shift from fisherman to farm tractor operator would not be an occupational change, while a shift from farm tractor operator to tractor operator for a construction concern would be regarded as an occupational shift. Similar anomalies exist in the Census classification system. Thus, a person who works as a chef and then becomes a barber would be making no occupational shift in terms of the major groups (both are within the service category); whereas a person shifting from a job as a laundress in a private household to an identical job in a laundry would have changed occupations (from "private household worker" to "operative").

Even if some of the components of the major groups were recombined to provide greater homogeneity, it is doubtful whether a useful analysis of the occupational flexibility of labor supply could be made in terms of such a limited number of broad categories. The problem calls for the development of occupational categories sufficiently homogeneous in regard to function and skill that they may be used for describing specific patterns of manpower requirements, and at the same time not so numerous that they are unmanageable in analyzing the kinds of job shifts that workers make. The functional classification system with which the U. S. Employment Service is presently experimenting [42] may ultimately lead to solution of this problem.

Industrial Mobility. The industrial classification system used in research on mobility affects the measurement and description of industrial mobility just as the occupational classification affects the measurement of occupational mobility. The broader the industrial classes, the

---

Bureau nor the Bureau of Employment Security can be criticized because their classification systems do not meet the specific needs of research workers in a particular area. It is the responsibility of the latter to make whatever modifications are called for by their objectives.

[42] See pp. 14–15 supra.

less "mobility" will there appear to be. Also, the broader the classes, the less homogeneity within each class, and as a result significant types of shifts may escape analysis.

However, as far as mobility research is concerned, the industrial classification is probably less crucial than the occupational classification, for there is some evidence that industrial differentials in mobility are more the result of differences in the occupational compositions of industries than of differences in the type of product or service involved.[43] If this is the case, it should be possible for many purposes to ignore industrial movement per se. In developing labor supply models, for example, the ability and willingness of workers to make occupational shifts of various kinds would be the only relevant factors. Industrial barriers to mobility would be presumed to be nonexistent.

In most studies of labor mobility the Standard Industrial Classification, or an adaptation of it, has been used to classify the industrial affiliations of workers and to measure and describe their industrial mobility.[44] This classification of economic pursuits has 10 major divisions.[45] These are further divided into a total of 78 major industrial groups. In manufacturing, for example, there are 21 such major groups. The major groups are further broken down into about 500 industrial groups which consist of more than 1,500 specific industries.

Although practically all studies have used the Standard Industrial Classification for defining industrial shifts, there is considerable variation in the way in which "industry" has been defined. Some investigators have used the 10 divisions of industry as the basic units, and thus have classified as an industrial shift only a job change from one such division to another (manufacturing, construction, retail trade, etc.).[46] Others have used detailed industry codes for determining what constitutes an industrial shift, although the current or the usual industrial affiliation of the worker has almost invariably been presented in terms of the divisions of industry.[47] Finally, in some cases the divisions are

[43] See p. 86n infra.

[44] U. S. Bureau of the Budget, Division of Statistical Standards, *Standard Industrial Classification Manual* (1945).

[45] Agriculture, forestry, and fisheries; mining; contract construction; manufacturing; transportation, communication, and other public utilities; wholesale trade; retail trade; finance, insurance, and real estate; services; and government.

[46] See, for example, Myers and Shultz, *The Dynamics of a Labor Market*, p. 32; Kerr, "Migration to the Seattle Labor Market Area, 1940–1942," pp. 146–149.

[47] This was true, for example, in the survey of occupational mobility in six cities, and in the studies of the Philadelphia labor market made during the 1930's by Palmer and associates.

used to represent some industries, while finer breakdowns are used with respect to others.[48]

These variations do not result from differences in the preferences of research workers for one concept of an industry as opposed to another, but stem from such considerations as the specific purpose of the investigation, the nature of the sample of workers whose job histories are being studied, and the size of the sample. To illustrate, in a study of almost 2,500 workers who shifted among the major manufacturing and utility firms of Fitchburg, Massachusetts between 1937 and 1939, Myers and Maclaurin used an industrial classification consisting of "public utilities" and nine major industrial groups within manufacturing.[49] Such a classification system was virtually dictated by the data. Again, the fact that Reynolds' study of the New Haven labor market included only manual workers, three fifths of whom were in manufacturing, made it appropriate to use an industrial classification consisting of "construction," "transportation and utilities," "wholesale and retail trade," "service," and six major groups in manufacturing. On the other hand, in the survey of occupational mobility in six cities the samples of workers were much broader in coverage. Moreover, one of the principal purposes of the investigation was to provide detailed information on the volume and the nature of job shifting during a 10-year period. Hence, the three-digit industry code of the Bureau of the Census was used as a basis for tabulating industrial shifts.

Geographic Mobility. Although the problems relating to the concept of geographic mobility are perhaps not so significant as those pertaining to occupational mobility, several questions may be raised with respect to the nature of a geographic job shift. In analysis of the geographic flexibility in labor supply—that is, the extent to which the distribution of manpower resources can adjust to changes in the geographic distribution of manpower requirements—geographic movement should refer to a situation in which a worker changes his residence so as to make himself available for jobs for which he previously would not have been available because of their distance from his home. Not every change of residence, nor every change in location of work,

---

[48] See Reynolds, *op. cit.*, pp. 23–37.

[49] Charles A. Myers and W. Rupert Maclaurin, *The Movement of Factory Workers: A Study of a New England Industrial Community* (New York: John Wiley & Sons, 1943).

is embraced by this concept of geographic mobility. For example, workers may change even the state of their residence (to say nothing of their county) without changing their place of work, or take jobs in another state or county without changing their residence. It requires no greater adjustment for a person who resides and works in Bridgeport, Ohio to take a job in Wheeling, West Virginia (directly across the Ohio River) than for him to make a similar job change within Bridgeport. In other words, since labor market areas, in the sense of areas within which workers with fixed addresses will accept employment, are by definition overlapping, measures of geographic mobility are necessarily somewhat ambiguous.

This point indicates the need for care in drawing conclusions from data on geographic job changes. For instance, if job shifts across county lines are more numerous in a metropolitan area covering two or more contiguous counties than in a metropolitan area contained in one county, this does not necessarily mean that the residents of the former have greater geographic mobility than the residents of the latter.

Analyses of geographic mobility have generally been based either on changes in the location of *jobs* or changes in the place of *residence*. In a study of mobility using Old-Age and Survivors Insurance data, Bogue defined geographic mobility as a change in a worker's county of employment.[50] On the other hand, Census studies of the geographic mobility of the labor force have been based on changes in county of residence. [51] There seems to be no basis for deciding that one of these methods is preferable to the other. The fundamental difficulty, the overlapping of labor market areas, applies in both cases. This difficulty can be avoided if geographic movement is defined as shifts in location in excess of a specified minimum number of miles, rather than as shifts across the boundaries of political units. Although such a procedure significantly complicates the classifying and coding of job changes, it was used by Myers and Shultz in their study of the mobility of skilled workers. Job changes were classified in five categories, according to the distance between two successive places of employment. The investigators arbitrarily established 49 miles as "a

[50] Donald J. Bogue, *A Methodological Study of Migration and Labor Mobility in Michigan and Ohio in 1947*, Scripps Foundation Studies in Population Distribution, No. 4 (June 1952).

[51] U. S. Bureau of the Census, *Current Population Reports: Population Characteristics*, Series P-20, No. 36 (December 9, 1951).

maximum sustainable commuting range" and regarded all shifts in excess of this distance as instances of geographic mobility.[52]

Employment, Unemployment, and Changes in Labor Force Status. A shift from one job to another and a shift from employment to unemployment are not mutually exclusive possibilities. Many, if not most, job separations are followed by a period of unemployment during which the worker is seeking new work, and this is true of voluntary as well as involuntary separations. How should such "transactions" be classified? Should they be treated as two moves—from employment to unemployment and from unemployment to employment—or as a simple job change, ignoring the intervening period of unemployment? The answer depends on the specific objectives of the study. If information on the extent and duration of unemployment is desired, the former procedure may be preferable. In all cases, however, it would seem expedient to disregard any shift in employment status unless the period of unemployment exceeds a certain minimum.[53]

Even when the period of unemployment or absence from the labor force exceeds the minimum established for a particular study, it would seem desirable for many purposes to compare the jobs held prior to and subsequent to the period of unemployment. An occupational, industrial, or geographic job shift after a period of unemployment of several months has implications concerning the flexibility of labor supply fully as important as shifts directly from one job to another. Therefore, if shifts from employment to unemployment (or into or out of the labor force) are to be tabulated, they ought to be tabulated separately in addition to, not instead of, the job shifts involved.[54]

[52] Myers and Shultz, "Patterns of Mobility of Skilled Workers and Factors Affecting Their Occupational Choice, Six Cities, 1940–51," pp. 43–49.

[53] In the studies of the Philadelphia labor market conducted by Palmer and her associates in the 1930's, periods of unemployment or of absence from the labor force that were less than one month in duration were not tabulated.

[54] The procedure followed in the survey of occupational mobility in six cities illustrates the suggestion offered here. Although shifts between employment and unemployment were not tabulated, periods of unemployment or of absence from the labor force were disregarded in enumerating job shifts. The coding instructions read as follows: "A change from one civilian job to another is to be considered a shift. A person may go directly from one job to another, he may spend some time looking for work before he finds a new job, he may go into the armed forces, or leave the labor force between jobs. You will compare each civilian job with the following civilian job, disregarding the amount of time or the type of

COVERAGE OF WORKERS

Most empirical studies of labor mobility have been based on work histories of a segment of the labor force in a local labor market area. Manual workers, or more specifically, manufacturing employees, have commonly been singled out for study. Reynolds' investigation of the New Haven labor market, for example, covered three samples of workers, one of manual workers, one of male manufacturing employees, and one of unemployed workers.[55] Myers and Shultz, in their investigation of the Nashua, New Hampshire labor market, sampled the former employees of a large textile mill which had closed.[56] Myers and Maclaurin's study of the movement of workers in Fitchburg was confined to employees of the major manufacturing and utility firms in the area.[57] The studies of the work experience of Philadelphia workers in the 1930's by Palmer and her associates covered machinists, weavers and loom fixers, and workers attached to the radio and the full-fashioned hosiery industries. More recently, the manpower recruitment problems of the defense industries during World War II have stimulated investigations into the sources of labor supply for manufacturing firms, and many of these studies have analyzed the mobility of the workers involved.[58]

Only a beginning has been made in investigating the mobility and the labor market behavior of nonmanual workers. A recent report by the Bureau of Labor Statistics analyzes the occupational and geographic mobility of scientists from work experience data provided by a sample of Ph.D.'s in chemistry, physics, and biology.[59] In the Colum-

---

activity between civilian jobs. You will code the type of shift on the basis of the name of the employer, the occupation code and the industry code of the two jobs." (U. S. Bureau of the Census, *General Coding Instructions for the Occupational Mobility Survey,* p. 35.)

[55] Reynolds, *op. cit.,* pp. 15–16.

[56] Myers and Shultz, *The Dynamics of a Labor Market,* p. 6.

[57] Myers and Maclaurin, *op. cit.,* pp. 12–13.

[58] See, for example, Kerr, "Migration to the Seattle Labor Market Area, 1940–1942"; Toivo P. Kanninen, "Sources of Labor Supply in West Coast Ship Yards and Aircraft-Parts Plants," *Monthly Labor Review,* 55:926–931 (November 1942); Hilda W. Callaway, "Wilmington Shipbuilders During and After World War II," *Monthly Labor Review,* 62:870–878 (June 1946); U. S. Bureau of Labor Statistics, *Worker Mobility and Skill Utilization in World War II* (1952, mimeo.); and Herbert S. Parnes, *A Study in the Dynamics of Local Labor Force Expansion* (Columbus: Ohio State University Research Foundation, 1951, mimeo.).

[59] U. S. Bureau of Labor Statistics, *Occupational Mobility of Scientists,* Bulletin No. 1121 (1953).

bus, Ohio labor market area, studies have been made of the job attitudes and the mobility of government and private clerical workers.[60]

Studies based on samples of the entire labor force are also infrequent. The most notable example is the survey of occupational mobility in six cities. Two studies involving a cross section of the entire labor force in Minneapolis and St. Paul in the 1940's have been made by Heneman and his associates.[61] One of these studies analyzes the characteristics of 98 "mobile" workers selected from a sample of the entire labor force; the other investigates the patterns of mobility revealed by the one-year work records of a sample of the labor force.

The restricted coverage of most studies of labor mobility seriously limits the conclusions that can be drawn from them. It cannot be assumed, for example, that either the degree or the pattern of mobility of production workers in manufacturing is typical of all segments of the labor force. There are good reasons for believing that the motivational factors in labor market behavior may vary widely among different groups of workers, and particularly between the various classes of white collar workers on the one hand and manual workers on the other.[62] Studies of samples of the entire labor force permit certain comparisons among these various groups of workers. But the more intensive investigations of attitudes of workers that have attempted to explain the "why" of labor market behavior (those by Reynolds and by Myers and Shultz, for example) have been limited to manual workers. Before a comprehensive theory of the operation of labor markets and of the behavior of "labor" can be developed, therefore, there is need for considerably more research on nonmanual groups. Nonagricultural manual work accounts for only half of the total labor force.[63]

Agricultural workers have been neglected by most investigators of

[60] Herbert S. Parnes, "Government Employment in Franklin County, Ohio, and Its Relation to the Local Labor Market" (unpublished Ph.D. dissertation, Ohio State University, 1950); June T. Fox, "A Study of the Clerical Employment at the Ohio Farm Bureau" (unpublished M.A. thesis, Ohio State University, 1950).

[61] Herbert G. Heneman, Jr., Harland Fox, and Dale Yoder, "Patterns of Manpower Mobility: Minneapolis, 1948," and Herbert G. Heneman, Jr., "Differential Short-Run Labor Mobilities: St. Paul, 1941–42," *op. cit.* These studies were by-products of a comprehensive labor market research program reported in Dale Yoder, Donald G. Paterson, and others, *Local Labor Market Research* (Minneapolis: University of Minnesota Press, 1948).

[62] Cf. E. Wight Bakke, *The Unemployed Man* (New York: E. P. Dutton and Company, 1934), pp. 253–255.

[63] Jaffe and Stewart, *op. cit.*, p. 145.

38   RESEARCH ON LABOR MOBILITY

mobility, although several recent studies of the agricultural labor
force made by the Bureau of Agricultural Economics shed some light
on the mobility of farm workers.[64] Since these studies show a rather
substantial amount of movement between farm and nonfarm work,[65]
the mobility of agricultural workers is clearly important with respect
to the flexibility of the industrial labor supply.

It is noteworthy, also, that little is known about the mobility of
workers in small towns. No recent study of mobility in an area with
less than 25,000 population has come to our attention. Since labor
market structure seems to influence both the degree and the pattern
of mobility, and since well over a fourth of the urban population of
the United States resides in communities with populations under
25,000,[66] this would seem to be a serious omission.

No comprehensive national survey of labor mobility in the United
States has been made.[67] The survey of occupational mobility in six
cities is the closest approximation yet undertaken, but the samples
on which the survey was based are not, and were not intended to be,
representative of the national labor force. Many of the gaps in knowledge of labor mobility that have been described could be filled only

[64] See the following mimeographed reports issued by the U. S. Bureau of Agricultural Economics: Louis J. Ducoff, *Migratory Farm Workers in 1949* (Agricultural
Information Bulletin No. 25, 1950); Gladys K. Bowles, Louis J. Ducoff, and Margaret
J. Hagood, *The Hired Farm Working Force—1948 and 1949* (November 1950); Wil-
liam H. Metzler and Afife F. Sayin, *The Agricultural Labor Force in the San Joaquin
Valley, California, 1948* (U. S. Bureau of Agricultural Economics cooperating with
the University of California Institute of Industrial Relations, February 1950); Robert
G. Burnight and others, *Regular Hired Workers on Commercial Dairy Farms in
Connecticut, April 1950–April 1952* (Storrs Agricultural Experiment Station in cooperation with U. S. Bureau of Agricultural Economics, Bulletin 267, January 1953).
The Agricultural Marketing Service (formerly the Bureau of Agricultural Economics)
is currently engaged in a number of other studies dealing wholly or in part with
aspects of agricultural labor mobility.

[65] For example, it is estimated that about a third of the farm wage workers in
1948 and 1949 were in nonfarm employment at some time during each year.
(Bowles, Ducoff, and Hagood, *op. cit.,* p. 2.)

[66] U. S. Bureau of the Census, *1950 Census of Population,* Vol. 1, computed from
data in Table 5b, pp. 1–6.

[67] The Bureau of the Census has made surveys of the geographic mobility of
the population, but although migrants and nonmigrants are classified by major
occupational group (as well as by age, sex, and other characteristics), neither
occupational, industrial, nor interfirm mobility has been analyzed. See U. S. Bureau
of the Census, *Current Population Reports: Population Characteristics,* Series P-20,
No. 36.

by analyses of data obtained in a national survey. Such a survey would be difficult and costly, but the successful cooperation between research agencies and the Bureau of the Census in the survey of six cities suggests the possibilities. Indeed, much useful information could be obtained if the sample now used by the Bureau of the Census for its *Monthly Report on the Labor Force* were interviewed concerning work histories and job attitudes.[68]

In the meantime, more modest studies of mobility might well focus on some of the hitherto neglected groups within the labor force. The labor market behavior of manual workers in nonmanufacturing industries and of various white collar groups might be intensively analyzed, using procedures similar to those used by Myers and Shultz and by Reynolds in their studies of manual workers. Also, research should be directed to the labor market dynamics of small communities and of agricultural areas. For comparability of results such studies should, so far as possible, use the designs and methods that have been used in investigating other groups.[69]

COVERAGE OF TIME

All empirical studies of the degree and patterns of labor mobility are based on employment histories of workers. There is considerable variation, however, in the time span covered by the "histories" collected in these studies. In some, single job transactions are analyzed—most commonly in studies of the sources of labor supply for given plants or industries, where the workers' previous jobs are compared with those for which they have been hired, and the nature of the shifts is determined.[70] Among other types of studies that have used the same

[68] Some work along these lines has been done. See, for example, U. S. Bureau of the Census, "Experience of Workers at Their Current Jobs, January 1951," *Current Population Reports: Labor Force*, Series P-50, No. 36 (December 5, 1951).

[69] Illustrative of these suggestions is an investigation currently being made in the Morgantown, West Virginia area by Gerald Somers of the West Virginia University Bureau of Business Research. According to a preliminary statement, "the survey centers around the impact of the closing and subsequent reopening of a chemical plant in a predominantly coal mining area." Somers points out that most of the previous studies have been made in heavily populated areas dominated by manufacturing industries, and that his study will make it "possible to test and supplement some general conclusions about the structure of labor markets by analysis in another type of industrial environment."

[70] See Kerr, *op. cit.;* Kanninen, *op. cit.;* and Parnes, *A Study in the Dynamics of Local Labor Force Expansion.*

technique is Myers and Maclaurin's analysis of the shifts made by factory workers among the manufacturing and utility firms of a community during a two-year period, which showed that most of the workers involved made only one such shift. In Reynolds' study of the New Haven labor market and Myers and Shultz's study of the Nashua labor market, part of the analysis likewise is based on single job changes made by the sampled workers, although more complete work histories were collected in each case.

In other studies work histories covering a span of years have been collected, and all the job shifts made during the period have been examined. For example, in the survey of occupational mobility in six cities, employment histories covering the period 1940–49 are analyzed. Heneman used a five-year and a one-year period, respectively, in his studies of the mobility of Minneapolis and of St. Paul workers in the 1940's.

Finally, some investigations have involved complete employment histories of the workers from the time they first entered the labor market until the time of the survey. Information of this kind was obtained from the workers in one of the samples interviewed by Reynolds in his New Haven study.[71]

The time span for which work histories should be collected of course depends upon the specific purposes of the investigation. There are certain hypotheses that cannot possibly be tested by data on single labor market transactions. In order to determine the influence of changing economic conditions on the volume and the pattern of mobility, work records over a span of time including a diversity of economic conditions are required. In the survey of occupational mobility in six cities, for example, comparisons are made between the mobility of workers in the periods 1940–44 and 1945–49. Similarly, in the studies of the employment experience of Philadelphia workers made by Palmer and her associates, comparisons are made between the work experience of the sample in the years 1926–30 and 1931–35.

Single job changes are also probably inadequate for a complete study of the motivation of workers. In this connection, Palmer says:

single job transactions do not take place in a vacuum, but usually bear some relation to what the worker has done before and what he expects or hopes to do later. There are, of course, exceptions; in extreme depression, workers'

[71] See also Percy E. Davidson and H. Dewey Anderson, *Occupational Mobility in an American Community* (Stanford University: Stanford University Press, 1937).

aspirations go by the board and "any port in a storm" is accepted. In interviews, older workers, in effect, apologize for the lack of consistency in their records by saying that they are no longer strong enough to do the work they did earlier or that it is hard for an old man to get work other than as a janitor, watchman, elevator operator, etc. Again and again, we see entries on work history schedules to the effect that a man has no skill and hence has to do unskilled work of various kinds. "I have no trade," "This is all I can do," "I have never done anything else" are frequently noted as reasons for being in an unskilled or semiskilled occupation.

All of these expressions . . . reflect accommodation or adaptation of a worker's aspirations to the "economic realities" of the job market. They are, perhaps, a philosophical acceptance of status or a change of status on the part of those who have decided that they cannot look forward to a lifetime of work in a "trade," promotion in a vocational career, or to continuing what they have done in the past. Conceivably these longer-term considerations may be more important in extending or limiting the range of job seeking activities in case of unemployment, for example, than knowledge about job openings, working conditions, and wage rates per se.[72]

Whether such a logic guides workers' labor market behavior is clearly a crucial question in formulating a theory of motivation of workers. It is also clear that data on individual job changes cannot answer the question, whether such data include only the objective characteristics of the jobs or the workers' attitudes toward them as well. For this purpose, the employment records of workers over extended periods of time—ideally, a lifetime—must be explored.

Despite the advantages of long-term work histories for the purposes described above, it should not be concluded that studies of individual job changes have no value. With respect to the ability and willingness of workers to make job changes of various kinds, single transactions probably have just as great predictive value as lifetime work histories. Myers and Maclaurin, for example, were able to reach several conclusions concerning the relative importance of industrial, as compared with geographic, barriers to mobility by tabulating the relative frequency of movement from one category of firms in the labor market to another.[73]

Even for discovering the motivational forces in mobility, data on single labor market transactions are not without value. The extent to which voluntary job changes result in improved earnings, and the

[72] Gladys L. Palmer, letter to the author, August 7, 1952.
[73] Myers and Maclaurin, op. cit., pp. 23–30.

reasons given by workers for making such shifts provide a basis for assessing the frequency with which various incentives are responsible for movement. The difficulty, of course, is that such data tell nothing about the characteristics of the workers who do *not* change jobs and, more important, about the reasons for their immobility. But this deficiency cannot be entirely corrected merely by the collection of long-term work histories. The latter permit analysis of the characteristics of "immobile" workers, but do not shed much light directly on the reasons for immobility unless attempts are made, by the use of attitude questions, to discover why workers have been attached to particular jobs, occupations, or industries. For a comprehensive understanding of labor market behavior, it is just as important to know why workers do *not* change jobs as to know why they *do*.

SOURCES OF DATA ON WORK HISTORIES

Three chief sources of work history data have been used, either separately or in combination. Personal interviews with the workers themselves, or their written answers to questionnaires, are the most obvious and the most commonly used source. In a few cases, principally the surveys conducted by the Bureau of the Census, information is obtained from a member of the worker's household. The worker himself may or may not be interviewed. The personnel records of employers constitute a second source of data on work experience, while records of government agencies administering social insurance systems are a third. Each of these sources has advantages and disadvantages, and each is particularly suited to certain purposes.

Data Obtained from Workers. A large majority of the recent studies of labor mobility have relied exclusively on interviews with workers for information on job histories and attitudes, or have used interviews to supplement data obtained from other sources. The nature of the interviews has varied from study to study. A depth-interviewing technique was used by Reynolds and by Myers and Shultz. Reynolds asked a fixed question, and then respondents were "allowed to talk freely without any prompting by the interviewer." He reports that this technique was "found to be more satisfactory than pinning the worker down to minute, specific answers as is sometimes done in attitude and public opinion surveys. It did mean that respondents spent a good deal of time talking about subjects which were irrelevant to the question asked; but imbedded in the stream of irrelevancies would be solid pieces of pertinent material. This material, when screened out, seemed to give a more spontaneous indication of actual attitudes than would be secured from brief responses to detailed and highly restricted questions." [74]

The interviews used by Myers and Shultz in their study of the mobility of displaced textile workers were apparently even less structured than those used by Reynolds. The investigators report that "the interviews were in the nature of discussions, guided into the appropriate areas by the interviewer. The interviewee was . . . encouraged to talk at length of his or her experiences and opinions. Thus, specific questions to be answered on the reporting forms were not usually asked directly, but were answered in the interviewee's own way and with a minimum of influence from the interviewer." [75]

In contrast to the type of interview in those studies is the enumeration type of interview that was used in the survey of occupational mobility in six cities. Unlike the former, this was designed primarily to obtain objective facts concerning past and present labor market activity rather than information on the attitudes of workers toward jobs; therefore the questions were specific and could be answered concisely.[76]

Use of questionnaires in obtaining information on job mobility from workers has been relatively uncommon, although de Schweinitz used them in her study of the job-finding methods of Philadelphia hosiery workers in 1930.[77] A more recent example is the Bureau of Labor Statistics' study of the mobility of scientists,[78] in which the data were a by-product of a questionnaire designed for use in the preparation of a biographical directory of American scientists.

The advantages of obtaining information on mobility directly from the workers themselves are fairly evident. Neither of the other sources

[74] Reynolds, *op. cit.,* p. 300.

[75] Myers and Shultz, *The Dynamics of a Labor Market,* p. 205. A verbatim reproduction of an interview (pp. 207–213) merits careful study by those planning similar investigations. Reynolds also includes a description and evaluation of his interviewing technique (*op. cit.,* pp. 299–301).

[76] The only attitude questions included in the schedule were those relating to the reason for each job change by the worker during the period covered by the survey and the reason for going into the kind of work (occupation) at which the respondent served longest during the five-year period preceding the interview.

[77] Dorothea de Schweinitz, *How Workers Find Jobs* (Philadelphia: University of Pennsylvania Press, 1932).

[78] U. S. Bureau of Labor Statistics, *Occupational Mobility of Scientists.*

permits direct analysis of the motivational factors in labor market behavior. Moreover, this procedure is the most flexible with respect to obtaining as precisely as possible the information that is desired. When the records of employers or of government agencies are used, the investigator is limited by the nature of the data that happen to be available.

Employers' Personnel Records. Several studies of local labor market operation and labor mobility have used the personnel records of firms as the source of work history data. The earliest major instance was the study by Myers and Maclaurin, who microfilmed the personnel records of 37 manufacturing and utility firms in a New England community for the period 1937–39.[79] From the microfilm records a schedule was completed for each employee, and the workers who had moved from one of the firms to another during the period were identified by matching the names on the schedules. Of almost 16,000 workers for whom records were obtained, over 1,500 had made at least one job change among the 37 firms. The method made possible not only an analysis of the characteristics of the workers who changed jobs and of the types of changes they made, but also comparisons between those who moved and those who were continuously employed by one firm during the period.

Kerr's study of migration into the Seattle labor market area during the early 1940's was likewise based in large part on the personnel records of the shipyards in the area, as well as the records of federal training projects and those of the local Y.M.C.A. and the local housing authority. Parnes used personnel records exclusively to study the characteristics and employment histories of workers hired during selected prewar, war, and postwar years by major manufacturing firms in the Columbus area. A random sample of the employment cards of workers hired in the specified years was chosen, and data on personal characteristics and job histories were transcribed to schedules.[80]

The experience of Myers and Maclaurin and of Parnes indicates that employers are generally willing to allow their personnel files to be used for this kind of research if they are assured that published reports will not identify the data of individual firms. Myers and Maclaurin report that only five of the 42 establishments originally approached were unwilling to make their records available,[81] while in

79 Myers and Maclaurin, *op. cit.*, pp. 80–87.
80 Parnes, *A Study in the Dynamics of Local Labor Force Expansion,* Chapter 1.
81 Myers and Maclaurin, *op. cit.*, p. 80.

the Columbus study five out of 35 firms refused to cooperate. It is true, of course, that even this number of refusals may bias the sample, and efforts must be made to determine whether and to what extent such bias is likely.

The usefulness of personnel records as a source of work history information is reduced by the incompleteness of the data, particularly if work records for past periods are required. In Parnes' study of the Columbus labor market, eight of the 35 firms approached in 1950 did not have adequate records for employees hired in 1940, despite the fact that all the firms were among the largest in each manufacturing group in the area.

There is considerable variation in the information contained in the personnel records of different companies. As would be expected, the larger firms tend to have more complete records than smaller establishments. Hence this method of obtaining data is probably more appropriate for studying the work experience of manufacturing employees than of workers in other industrial groups. With respect to the prior employment history of the worker, the variation in the records of different firms is especially pronounced. Some require remarkably complete information, including all the jobs previously held by the employee, together with their dates and wage rates. More frequently, however, only the past several employers are listed, and it is not at all uncommon to find no dates marking the beginning and termination of each job. For these reasons, personnel records are more useful for studying single job transactions (i.e. from the preceding job to the present one) than for studying long-term work histories.

Personnel records provide few, if any, valuable clues with respect to worker motivation. In the first place, many firms either do not have exit interviews or do not bother to record the reasons for voluntary separations on their employment cards.[82] Moreover, the validity of such information is questionable even where it exists. Although there is no relevant evidence, it is probable that the reason for quitting a job that is given to a personnel manager or a personnel clerk by a worker does not reflect his real motives as accurately as what he might tell an "outsider."

Nevertheless, for certain purposes personnel records are a better

[82] In the Columbus study this kind of information was found to be so rare that no attempt was made to tabulate it. It is also noteworthy that in the study by Myers and Maclaurin, where the reasons for job changes were obtained from employment cards, half of the 2,451 job separations analyzed are tabulated as "reason for leaving unknown" (op. cit., p. 91).

source of data than are personal interviews. In studying the pattern of job changes in a local labor market during some period in the past, it is unsatisfactory to rely on interviews with those persons who are in the area at the time of the survey. The difficulty lies not in the interviewing technique itself, but in locating the appropriate group of workers for whom the information should be obtained. To ascertain the extent, sources, and characteristics of the migration into a particular local labor market during World War II, for example, it may be misleading to study the work histories of a sample of the present population, for many of the wartime in-migrants may have since left the area. Plant records for the period under consideration, however, may indicate not only in what numbers migrants entered the local labor market, but also the areas from which they came, and the kinds of occupational and industrial shifts they made.

Social Insurance Records. The use of social insurance records as a source of work history data has been more common in England than in the United States. The greater age of social insurance in that country, the fact that unemployment insurance is a national system, and the more extensive coverage of the British programs, all probably help to account for this fact. Moreover, the unemployment insurance cards, which are held by all covered workers in Great Britain and which are collected annually by the local employment exchanges, each bear a number identifying the area in which the card was originally issued, thus providing a convenient basis for analyzing geographic movement.[83]

In the United States many studies of mobility in local labor markets have profited immeasurably by the cooperation of the public employment service, particularly in providing statistical information and in facilitating the sampling of unemployed individuals.[84] But relatively

---

[83] See Makower, Marschak, and Robinson, "Studies in Mobility of Labour: A Tentative Statistical Measure" and "Studies in Mobility of Labour: Analysis for Great Britain, Part II," *Oxford Economic Papers*, No. 1 (October 1938), pp. 83–123, and No. 4 (September 1940), pp. 39–62. See also J. Jewkes and H. Campion, "The Mobility of Labour in the Cotton Industry," *Economic Journal*, 38:135–137 (March 1928). An example of a British mobility study using claims units rather than unemployment insurance cards as a source of data is that of Goronwy H. Daniel, "Some Factors Affecting the Movement of Labour," *Oxford Economic Papers*, No. 3 (February 1940), pp. 144–179.

[84] See Yoder, Paterson, and others, *op. cit.;* Reynolds, *op. cit.*, pp. 16, 299; Myers and Shultz, *The Dynamics of a Labor Market*, pp. 96–98.

little use has been made of unemployment insurance records for the actual collection of work histories.[85] Two studies, however, have used Old-Age and Survivors Insurance records to measure labor mobility.[86] In the more recent study, Bogue describes the nature of these data and their usefulness for research on mobility. When a worker first enters employment covered by the Old-Age and Survivors Insurance program he must file an application for a social security account number, giving his birth date, race, sex, and address. Similarly, each employer whose employees are covered by the program must apply for an identification number, specifying in his application the nature and the location of his business. Moreover, each employer must file a quarterly tax return, listing his employees, their social security numbers, and the amount of wages paid to each during the quarter. All wages on which contributions are paid by employers are credited to the accounts of the employees. On the basis of these data a continuous record can be prepared, showing the number of quarters of employment and the earnings of each worker covered by the program, according to the worker's sex, race, age, place of work, and the industry in which he is employed.[87]

Old-Age and Survivors Insurance data have certain limitations for the study of labor mobility. Perhaps the most serious is that the data do not permit any analysis of occupational shifts, since employers are not required to indicate in their tax returns the capacity in which each employee serves. Second, not all employment is covered by the program. This means that there are no records at all for workers continuously employed in noncovered industries, and there are gaps in

[85] Several state employment security agencies have made analyses of unemployment compensation data that shed some light on the extent of interfirm mobility. Such analyses have involved tabulations of the number of base-period employers of claimants for unemployment compensation. For an example, see Ohio Bureau of Unemployment Compensation, Division of Research and Statistics, Table RS 214.A-1 (October 20, 1948), "New Claims Allowed at Initial Determination Under the Ohio Unemployment Compensation Law, by Industry Division and Number of Base Period Employers, October 1, 1947 through September 30, 1948."

[86] Franklin M. Aaronson and Ruth A. Keller, *Mobility of Workers in Employment Covered by Old-Age and Survivors Insurance*, U. S. Social Security Administration, Bureau of Research and Statistics Report No. 14 (July 1946, mimeo.); Bogue, *A Methodological Study of Migration and Labor Mobility in Michigan and Ohio in 1947.*

[87] See Saul D. Hearn and Paul Eldridge, "Old-Age and Survivors Insurance Records and Their Use for Mobility Research," in Bogue, *op. cit.,* Chapter 2.

the records of workers who shift between covered and noncovered employment. For any quarter in which no wage credits are shown for a worker, he may have been unemployed, in noncovered employment, or outside the labor force.[88] The usefulness of the data has been greatly increased as a result of the 1950 and 1954 amendments to the Social Security Act, which substantially increased the coverage of the program.

In spite of these limitations and a few other minor ones, use of Old-Age and Survivors Insurance data has some real advantages in research on mobility. These data probably have a higher degree of validity than work experience data from any other source, for there is no distortion from faulty memory, and willful falsification creates legal liability. Moreover, the data are already collected and need only to be compiled. Perhaps their greatest advantage lies in the possibility of continuous observation of any selected sample of workers. Workers cannot move into and out of the sample, as they can in local population surveys or in studies of personnel records, although "disappearance" from the sample as a result of movement into noncovered employment is possible.

VALIDITY AND RELIABILITY OF WORK HISTORY INFORMATION

The validity of the responses of workers to questions about their work histories is an important methodological question in mobility research. Unfortunately, most studies of mobility have not been actively concerned with testing the validity of their data, but several methodological investigations are pertinent. These have generally measured the degree of correspondence between factual information provided by workers in interviews, and records maintained by employers or government agencies. The assumption has been that the records are accurate, and that discrepancies between the data reported by the workers and those shown by the records are evidence either of faulty memory on the part of respondents or of their unwillingness to give the correct information to the interviewer. A second type of study has dealt with the correspondence between data furnished by a member of a worker's household and by the worker himself. Finally, studies of the *reliability* of response in household enumerations have involved interviewing the representatives of the same sample of households

[88] However, eligible workers who retire at 65 years of age will be identifiable by the receipt of benefits.

twice, and measuring the variation between the two sets of answers to identical questions.[89]

Validity of Information on Number and Duration of Jobs. Measures of mobility based on work histories reported by workers can be only as good as their ability to recall accurately the number of jobs they have held during a given period in the past and the approximate duration of these jobs. Although the relevant evidence is somewhat conflicting, it suggests that workers with the most varied work experience tend to understate the number of jobs held in the past, and to overstate the duration of those reported. If this is true, the conventional measures of mobility understate the actual amount of movement and minimize the differential between the most and the least mobile workers. Myers and Maclaurin compared the work histories reported by 233 interviewed workers with their employers' personnel records and found that the most frequent discrepancy was in the number of jobs held. Over a third of the workers interviewed failed to mention jobs that they were known to have held. Almost 10 percent neglected to mention at least two jobs, and one individual did not account for seven! As might be expected, the omissions were primarily jobs that had been held for only a short time; rarely was a job that had been held for six months or longer not reported.[90]

Similar findings are reported by Creamer and Coulter, who compared the work histories obtained by interviewing 277 unemployed textile workers with data from employers' records for the period 1930–34. Finding that the duration of employment was reported with complete accuracy in less than 15 percent of the cases, and that more

[89] See Gladys L. Palmer, *The Reliability of Response in Labor Market Inquiries,* U. S. Bureau of the Budget, Division of Statistical Standards, Technical Paper No. 22 (July 1942), and "Factors in the Variability of Response in Enumerative Studies," *Journal of the American Statistical Association,* 38:143–152 (June 1943); Elizabeth Keating, Donald G. Paterson, and C. Harold Stone, "Validity of Work Histories Obtained by Interview," *Journal of Applied Psychology,* 34:6–11 (February 1950); Heneman, Fox, and Yoder, *op. cit.,* pp. 23–27; Myers and Maclaurin, *op. cit.,* pp. 84–87; Daniel Creamer and Charles W. Coulter, *Labor and the Shut-Down of the Amoskeag Textile Mills,* W.P.A. National Research Project Report No. L-5 (Philadelphia, November 1939), p. 342; Gertrude Bancroft, "Consistency of Information from Records and Interviews," *Journal of the American Statistical Association,* 35:377–381 (June 1940). For a more extensive bibliography, see Keating, Paterson, and Stone, *op. cit.*

[90] Myers and Maclaurin, *op. cit.,* pp. 85–86.

than two thirds of the discrepancies were in the direction of overstatement, they concluded that work histories obtained from workers
in an industry characterized by intermittent employment will "tend
to minimize the degree of intermittency by understating the number of
jobs and by overstating the total duration of employment by appreciable amounts." [91] Clague, Couper, and Bakke, although in general
expressing confidence in the validity of the information provided by
the workers interviewed, indicate that the respondents seemed to be
less sure of time intervals and job duration than of other aspects of
their work experience. Without presenting statistical evidence, the
authors note a tendency for workers to report the duration of jobs in
"round numbers," ignoring minor interruptions in employment.[92]

Keating, Paterson, and Stone contest the conclusions suggested above
by presenting evidence comparing the duration of jobs as reported by
workers with the duration as indicated by plant records. They report
a validity coefficient of $r = +.98$, and conclude that workers' reports
on duration of employment are highly accurate.[93] Certain differences
between this study and those described above, however, make it difficult to compare their results. First, Keating and her associates appear
to have checked the duration of each job reported by a respondent
with the employer named by the respondent. Thus, if a worker omitted
a job held during the period under consideration, this would not be
revealed. The results described by Myers and Maclaurin, therefore, are
not contradicted by these findings. Second, it may be that the respondents in the study by Keating and her associates were more highly
motivated than those in the other studies. The former study was designed to analyze the occupational competence of unemployed workers, and the respondents were told that the results would be used not
only for research purposes, but also as a basis for counseling them.
If it is true that respondents' ability to recall is influenced primarily
by "experience or interest factors," [94] the appeal to their self-interest
in this study may have been partly responsible for the high correlation
between reported and actual durations of jobs.

A conclusion similar to that of Keating and her associates is drawn

---

[91] Creamer and Coulter, *op. cit.*, p. 342.

[92] Ewan Clague, Walter J. Couper, and E. Wight Bakke, *After the Shutdown* (New
Haven: Yale University Institute of Human Relations, 1934), p. 129.

[93] Keating, Paterson, and Stone, *op. cit.*, p. 10.

[94] See Gladys L. Palmer, *The Reliability of Response in Labor Market Inquiries.*

by Heneman, Fox, and Yoder from a comparison of job dates reported by respondents with the corresponding dates shown by the personnel records of the establishments at which they worked. They report 70 percent agreement as to the month in which the job began for jobs held within the preceding year and 68 percent for jobs held during the preceding five years. Agreement as to the month in which the job ended was found for 63 percent of the jobs held during the last year and 57 percent of the jobs held during the past five years.[95] It is doubtful, however, that this kind of analysis permits a meaningful conclusion regarding the ability of respondents to recall the duration of jobs they have held. No indication is given of the size of the discrepancy when the estimates of the respondents disagreed with the personnel records. Moreover, presenting the data on the beginning of jobs separately from those on their ending probably understates the proportion of jobs whose duration was incorrectly reported.[96]

On the basis of the limited evidence now available it is not possible to quantify, even roughly, the response error of workers on questions relating to the number and duration of jobs they have held. It seems probable, however, that they tend to understate the number of jobs held, and that this tendency is accentuated among workers with intermittent or diverse job experience.

Validity of Information on Wages. A few attempts have been made to check the accuracy with which workers report their earnings by comparing their responses with the wage records maintained by employers. In most comparisons of this kind a relatively high degree of correspondence has been found. Keating, Paterson, and Stone report validity coefficients of $r = +.90$ for the reported wages of men and $+.93$ for those of women in jobs held within the past year, and no consistent tendency toward either over- or understatement.[97] Heneman, Fox, and Yoder likewise found high correlations between reported and actual wage rates, weekly earnings, and monthly earnings—both for jobs held within a year prior to the interview and for those held within the preceding five years. Correlation coefficients were generally

[95] Heneman, Fox, and Yoder, *op. cit.*, p. 25; percentages computed from data shown in Table 6.

[96] For example, if 25 percent of the beginning dates are incorrect and 25 percent of the ending dates are incorrect, it is possible for the duration of as many as 50 percent of the total jobs to have been incorrectly reported.

[97] Keating, Paterson, and Stone, *op. cit.*, p. 9.

above $+.80$.[98] Bowley and Burnett-Hurst, in an early study of poverty in Great Britain, and Clague, Couper, and Bakke, in their study of displaced New England rubber workers, conclude that the reports of their respondents on income had a high degree of validity, although no statistical data are presented to support the conclusion.[99] On the other hand, Myers and Maclaurin found "a frequent discrepancy . . . between the size of the weekly paycheck which the worker claimed to have earned and the amount which his employment records showed he had actually earned. In those cases where a comparison was possible, more than five times as many workers overestimated their earnings as underestimated them. Usually the difference was small, but the tendency was nonetheless important." [100]

Validity of Information on Job Assignments. For analyzing occupational mobility it is especially important that workers be able to recall, and be willing to report accurately, the capacities in which they have served in the various jobs they have held. Two studies of the correspondence between reported and actual job assignments indicate that workers' reports on these are generally valid. Heneman, Fox, and Yoder found that the job assignments reported by their respondents agreed with those shown by personnel records for over 90 percent of the jobs held within the five years preceding the interviews.[101] Keating, Paterson, and Stone report agreement for 94 percent of the jobs held by men within the year prior to the interview and for 96 percent of the jobs held by women. In the small minority of cases of disagreement, they note a tendency for the respondent to report an occupation of higher responsibility and prestige value than the one he actually held.[102]

Neither of these studies indicates the degree of detail with which the worker described his job assignment in the interview, or how close a correspondence between the respondent's report of his job

[98] Heneman, Fox, and Yoder, *op. cit.*, pp. 23–24.

[99] A. L. Bowley and A. R. Burnett-Hurst, *Livelihood and Poverty* (London: G. Bell & Sons, 1915), p. 174; Clague, Couper, and Bakke, *op. cit.*, p. 129.

[100] Myers and Maclaurin, *op. cit.*, p. 87.

[101] Heneman, Fox, and Yoder, *op. cit.*, p. 24.

[102] Keating, Paterson, and Stone, *op. cit.*, pp. 9–10. Similar results are reported for a study of the Auburn, New York labor market area. Although the validity of occupational reporting was high, there was "some slight tendency to inflate one's job status, particularly among group leaders and assistant foremen, who were likely to report themselves as foremen." (Letter to the author from Robert L. Aronson, New York State School of Industrial and Labor Relations, July 1953.)

assignment and that contained in the personnel records was required for "agreement." Moreover, the analyses skirt perhaps the most difficult problem in obtaining occupational information from workers, namely, getting sufficiently precise descriptions of duties to permit the investigator to place the worker in the appropriate category of skill. Because many job titles involve varying degrees of skill, depending upon the exact content of the job, a worker's job title may be reported with perfect accuracy without providing a basis for classifying him with a high degree of confidence.[103]

Validity and Reliability of Response in Household Surveys. Work histories are rarely obtained from interviews with any person other than the worker himself.[104] Information provided by some other member of the household, however, is fairly often the basis of selection of workers to be interviewed. For example, in the study of "mobile" workers by Heneman, Fox, and Yoder, such workers were selected on the basis of the number of jobs held within the previous one- or five-year period, as reported by another member of the household.[105] Similarly, in the survey of occupational mobility in six cities, detailed work histories were obtained from all persons who were reported by a member of the household to be at least 25 years of age and to have worked at least a month in 1950.[106] It is pertinent, therefore, to review briefly the available evidence regarding the validity and reliability of data provided by respondents in household enumerations.

Heneman, Fox, and Yoder state that nonemployed members of households tend to underestimate the number of jobs held by employed members of the same households during specified periods in the past. In about one fourth of the 72 cases studied, the worker was found to have held more jobs in the preceding year than the original respondent had reported; the number held in the five-year period preceding

---

[103] See Myers and Shultz, "Patterns of Mobility of Skilled Workers and Factors Affecting Their Occupational Choice, Six Cities, 1940–51," pp. 78–79. The investigators conclude that "It is difficult to determine whether work is skilled or not on the basis of the brief occupational assignments listed on the work schedules."

[104] The only instances in the studies reviewed in this volume are the analyses of internal migration made by the Bureau of the Census. For these reports, data on the prior residence of all members of the household, as well as on their current employment status and occupation, are obtained from one member of the household.

[105] Heneman, Fox, and Yoder, *op cit.*, pp. 4–5.

[106] U. S. Bureau of the Census, *Occupational Mobility Survey: Enumerator's Manual* (January 1951, mimeo.).

the survey was understated in nearly half the cases.[107] In a Philadelphia study Palmer discovered discrepancies between the occupation and industry reported by the worker and those reported for him by another member of his household in over 10 percent of the cases.[108]

In a study of the reliability of response in household enumerations, Palmer reports the results of two sets of interviews with representatives of 2,686 Philadelphia households containing 8,519 persons. Different enumerators were used in the two visits, but all had been given the same training. The visits were nine days apart on the average, and in no case did more than 23 days intervene. Questions asked in the second interview related to the same time as those in the first. In slightly less than two thirds of the households, the same respondent was interviewed on both occasions. The results of the two surveys were compared with respect to the marital status, employment status, age, and education of the 8,519 persons in the sample households.[109] The variation in response was found to be 1.7 percent for marital status, 9.9 percent for employment status, 12.8 percent for age, and 23.4 percent for education. For age and education the variability in individual responses tended to cancel out when the data were summarized, but this was not true for employment status. The degree of variability did not appear to be significantly affected by the number of days of experience of the interviewers, by the lapse of time between the two interviews, or by the personnel ratings of the two interviewers. Variability was greater, however, in neighborhoods with high proportions of Negro or foreign-born residents than in neighborhoods with large majorities of native-born whites. Also, as might be expected, variability was generally higher when the respondents in the two interviews were different than when the same persons were reinterviewed.[110]

After reviewing the evidence on the reliability of response in labor market inquiries, Palmer concludes that errors from enumerative procedures and response factors may far outweigh sampling errors. She suggests that with continued research on the question it may be pos-

107 Heneman, Fox, and Yoder, op. cit., p. 26.

108 Gladys L. Palmer, Employment and Unemployment in Philadelphia in 1936 and 1937, Part I: May 1936, W.P.A. National Research Project in cooperation with University of Pennsylvania Industrial Research Department, Report No. P-3, Part I (Philadelphia, August 1938), p. 41.

109 Palmer, "Factors in the Variability of Response in Enumerative Studies."

110 Ibid., pp. 144–145.

sible in the future "to state with some degree of precision the range of reliability of response factors." [111]

Some Problems in Analyzing Work Histories

A detailed description and evaluation of all the techniques that have been used for analyzing work histories and workers' attitudes in relation to labor mobility would be excessively long. In the present section the methods that have been used in dealing with some of the major analytical problems in mobility research are described in rather general terms. Since the findings of research must be appraised with reference to the specific methods that produced them, additional comments on methodology are made at relevant points in the following three chapters.

Measuring Mobility. As has been observed, regardless of how mobility has been defined, it has almost universally been measured in terms of the actual job shifts made by workers. Perhaps the most widely used procedure has been a simple count of the number of jobs held, or the number of job shifts of various kinds, by workers during the period under consideration. The results may be presented as average numbers of jobs per worker, or in frequency distributions of workers according to numbers of shifts to permit conclusions as to the proportion of workers who are involved in the total amount of movement.

If mobility is measured by the number of job shifts by workers, and if comparisons are made among groups of workers, account must be taken of differences in their labor force exposure. Otherwise, differences in the mobility of various groups may reflect only differences in duration of labor force attachment rather than in employment stability or job attachment. This is especially important when analyzing age and sex differentials in mobility. For example, if the average number of jobs held during a 10-year period by workers 25 to 34 years of age is compared with that of workers 35 to 44, the result will probably understate the relative mobility of the younger group because a considerable proportion of them would not have entered the labor force in the early part of the 10-year period, and so would have had less time in which to make job changes. With regard to sex differentials in mobility, the situation is similar. Women generally are less permanently attached to the labor force than are men. During any

[111] Palmer, *The Reliability of Response in Labor Market Inquiries*, p. 8.

10-year period the proportion of women continuously working or seeking work will be lower than that of men, and their "potential" for job shifting will therefore be less. Consequently, differences between the average number of jobs held during the period by men and women will not accurately indicate differences in their tendency to shift jobs.

In computing mobility measures, labor force exposure may be taken into account in several ways. One is to classify the respondents according to time in the labor force, and to subclassify them according to other characteristics. This procedure was used to a limited extent in the survey of occupational mobility in six cities.[112] For comparing groups of workers with varying exposure to the labor force, the average number of jobs held per year of exposure can be computed.

Another method of measuring mobility involves comparison of the worker's status at the beginning of a specified period with his status at its end, without regard to all the shifts made in the interim. This procedure permits analysis of the relation between gross and net changes in status during the period. In the survey of occupational mobility in six cities such analyses are made for the periods from January 1940 to December 1944 and from December 1944 to December 1949, as well as for the total period 1940–50. Tabulations show the number of workers who changed major industrial group, major occupational group, employment status, and labor force status between each of these sets of terminal dates.[113] This method of measuring mobility of course understates the total amount of movement occurring during the period under consideration. For example, Bogue measured the extent of inter-county migration from Old-Age and Survivors Insurance records in two ways: (1) by observing the county of employment of all jobs held by his sample of workers during 1947, and (2) by comparing the county of employment in the first and last quarters of the year. The latter procedure produced a count of migrants only about half as great as the former.[114]

For some purposes the number of job or status changes made by workers is not as significant as the periods of time they have spent in various capacities. In analyzing occupational attachment, for instance, the individual whose 50-year work history is approximately equally divided among five occupations is clearly in a different category from

112 Palmer, *Labor Mobility in Six Cities*, pp. 40–42, 54, 78.
113 *Ibid.*, pp. 102–109, 111–113.
114 Bogue, *op. cit.*, cf. Tables III–1 and V–2, pp. 14, 27.

the worker who has spent 45 years in one occupation with brief intermittent periods in four others. The number of changes in occupation, however, does not differentiate between these two situations; the two individuals appear to be equally "mobile" with respect to occupation. To deal with problems of this kind, an interesting method of analysis is used by Palmer and her associates in their studies of Philadelphia workers. Data are presented not only on the numbers of job shifts and status changes of various types, but also on the length of time spent in certain activities during the 10-year period covered by the work histories.[115] This kind of analysis of groups of workers in other labor markets would probably yield valuable results.

Analyzing Patterns of Labor Mobility. Patterns of mobility are generally analyzed by classifying job shifts according to whether they represent changes in employer, occupation, industry, or location. Two methods of tabulation have been used. In one, each type of mobility is treated as a separate category, and a given job shift is tallied once for each type of movement it represents. For example, a job shift entailing a change of employer, industry, and occupation would be counted three times, once under each of these headings.[116] A second procedure uses as categories of job shifts the possible combinations of types of mobility. The categories might be (1) change in employer only, (2) change in employer and occupation, (3) change in employer and industry, (4) change in employer, occupation, and industry, and (5) no change in employer.[117] Thus, each shift is counted only once. Of these two methods of analyzing patterns of mobility, the second seems to be preferable for all purposes, for it reveals more clearly than the former the relative frequency of the kinds of job changes that workers make. Moreover, the first type of tabulation can be readily derived from the second, while the converse is not true.

One important reason for studying the pattern of workers' job shifts is to determine whether job changes among industries and occupations are primarily random, or whether there are "affinities" among certain

[115] For a list of these studies, see p. 25n supra.

[116] For an example of this kind of analysis, see Heneman, "Differential Short-Run Labor Mobilities: St. Paul, 1941–42," *op. cit.*, pp. 35–41.

[117] This system of classification was used in the survey of occupational mobility in six cities. An almost identical system was used by Palmer and her associates in their studies of Philadelphia workers. Bogue, in his study of industrial, geographic, and interfirm mobility, used seven categories which cover all possible combinations of these three types of movement (*op. cit.*, p. 14).

industries and occupations so that movement is more likely to occur among them than among others. In order to throw light on this question, Reynolds uses an interesting method for analyzing the industrial job shifts made by his respondents. He classifies those who have made industrial shifts by their current industrial attachment and by all the other industries in which they have been employed. The unit of calculation is a "man-industry," so that a person who has been employed in two industries other than his current one is represented twice in the table, once under each of the other two industries. By comparing the industrial distribution of the "outside" employment of current employees in each industry with the industrial distribution of all "outside" employment, the existence of "neighboring" industries can be spotted. For example, assume that 20 percent of all the jobs held in other industries by the sample of workers were in industry X. If inter-industrial movement is completely random, one would expect to find that workers currently attached to each industry would have had about 20 percent of their other industrial experience in industry X. However, if workers presently employed in industry Y had, say, 80 percent of their "outside" industry jobs in X, "one would conclude that there is an unusually close relation between employment in these two industries." [118]

Analyses of this kind should be used more extensively in future studies of both industrial and occupational job changes, if the flexibility of the labor supply is to be described more precisely. It is not enough to know which groups of workers are most likely to make job changes and the relative number of occupational and industrial shifts that will probably occur under various conditions. For many purposes, such as the estimation of manpower requirements or the planning of mobilization programs, it is also necessary to know the specific directions in which various groups of workers may be expected to move.

Determining the Correlates of Labor Mobility. Probably more attention has been given to this problem than to any other single problem in mobility research. Practically every study that deals with labor

---

[118] Reynolds, *op. cit.*, p. 31. For a considerably more complicated and more subtle method of analysis which takes into consideration differences in employment opportunities among industries, see Makower, Marschak, and Robinson, "Studies in Mobility of Labour: Analysis for Great Britain, Part II," *Oxford Economic Papers,* No. 4 (September 1940), pp. 39–62.

mobility in any way is concerned to some extent with the question: "Who are the mobile workers?" Generally, comparisons are made of the mobility of workers classified according to such factors as age, sex, marital status, race, education, union affiliation, occupation, industry, length of service, etc. The difficulty, however, is that many of these factors are of necessity, or under certain circumstances may be, inter-correlated. Older workers are more likely than younger ones to be married, to own their homes, and to have dependents. If older workers are found to be less mobile than younger workers, to what extent is this a result of age, and to what extent is it a result of one or more of the other factors? If men are found to be more mobile than women, to what extent does this reflect a true sex differential, and to what extent does it simply reflect differences in the occupational composition of the two groups?

Detailed cross-classifications of the data, which in effect standardize all the relevant variables except the one whose relationship to mobility is being considered, are generally precluded by the small size of samples. Reynolds dealt with the problem of intercorrelation by preparing "three-way tabulations, in which the influence of a particular variable was examined while holding each of the other major variables constant in turn. Thus the relation of mobility to age was examined first with length of service constant, then with occupational level constant, and so on . . . A variable was held to have a significant influence on mobility only if a clear relationship continued to exist in these sub-tabulations, so that the relationship could not be explained by the presence of other variables correlated with the first." [119]

More refined statistical techniques were used by Kitagawa in analyzing and measuring the relationship between mobility and 11 variables for which data were obtained in the survey of occupational mobility in six cities.[120] The methods employed in her study provide answers to three different but related types of questions: (1) How much of the difference between the "crude" mobility rates of two groups of workers can be explained by differences in their composition; for example, to what extent is the mobility differential between men and

[119] Reynolds, op. cit., p. 21.

[120] Evelyn M. Kitagawa and others, "Relative Importance—and Independence—of Selected Factors in Job Mobility, Six Cities, 1940–1949," unpublished manuscript, University of Chicago, Chicago Community Inventory (March 1953). The variables are age, sex, color, education, marital status, occupation, industry, weekly earnings, migrant status, veteran status, and union membership.

women attributable to differences in their ages and occupations? (2) How do "crude" mobility differentials with respect to a given factor compare with the differentials for that factor when one or more other factors are controlled; for example, what is the size and direction of the mobility differential between men and women if the effects of age and occupation are held constant? (3) What proportion of the total variation in the mobility of workers can be explained by variation in age, occupation, length of time in the labor force, etc.? One important advantage of the methods used by Kitagawa is that they permit quantification of the degree to which observed differences in mobility are due to a particular variable.[121]

Another problem in analyzing the correlates of labor mobility arises in measuring occupational and industrial differentials in mobility. The most usual method compares the past mobility of workers classified according to their occupational or industrial affiliations at the time of the survey. There is a logical difficulty in this procedure. Insofar as there have been industrial and occupational shifts during the period under consideration, a comparison of the mobility of workers classified according to their industries and occupations at the *end* of the period does not afford a precise measure of the relative frequency with which workers in the several categories are likely to make job shifts of various kinds. The purpose of such an analysis, after all, is to find out whether there are differences in the rates at which workers in different industries and occupations change their employers, occupations, industries, or locations; and this can be done only by relating the kinds of shifts to the status of the worker *at the time* the shift is made.

The problem is more pervasive than has been indicated, for it applies also to attempts to relate mobility to other characteristics of workers—age, marital status, union membership, home ownership, etc. All these are subject to change during the period for which the work histories have been collected. As in the study of occupational and industrial differentials, therefore, job shifts ought ideally to be related to the status of the worker at the time they are made, rather than at the time of the survey.

[121] Still another method of dealing with intercorrelated variables is the system of successive weighting used by Daniel in his study of the effect of a number of factors (age, marital status, etc.) on the propensity of workers to move in response to the stimulus of unemployment (*op. cit.*, pp. 144–179).

The procedure suggested here has been used in a recent study by the Bureau of Labor Statistics. In analyzing the relationship between the age and the mobility of tool and die makers, data are presented on the number of "shifts per man-year worked at given ages." The method of computing this measure is described as follows:

To isolate the effect of age, the movements of workers were grouped by the ages at which the movement occurred. Thus, of the 2,127 job changes, 145 were made by workers who were 20–24 years old when they moved, 453 by workers who were 25–29 when they moved, and so forth. Following this, the man-years worked at given ages were computed. For example, a worker who qualified as a tool and die maker before 1940, and who was 25 years of age on January 1, 1940, would have worked five man-years in the age group 25–29, five man-years in the age group 30–34, and one man-year in the age group 35–39. After the man-years were accumulated for each age group, they were divided into the number of moves made at those ages. The result, moves per man-year worked at specified ages, describes the mobility characteristic of a particular age.[122]

This approach might well be used in analyzing occupational and industrial differentials in mobility, as well as the effects of such factors as marital status and union affiliation upon mobility. Admittedly, the problems involved in coding and tabulating the work history data would be considerably greater than when the traditional procedure is used, but the results could be interpreted more precisely. It would be desirable, at least, to experiment with a given collection of work histories to see to what extent different conclusions emerge from use of the two methods.

[122] U. S. Bureau of Labor Statistics, *The Mobility of Tool and Die Makers, 1940–1951*, Bulletin No. 1120 (1952), p. 45.

3 EXTENT AND CHARACTER

OF LABOR MOBILITY

What propositions concerning labor mobility may be regarded with some confidence as having been established, and what problems require additional research? In this and the two following chapters an attempt is made to answer these questions and to synthesize and appraise research findings in terms of the basic framework outlined in Chapter 1. The data yielded by various studies are evaluated with reference to the methods used, and conclusions are examined critically in order to determine whether they rest upon sufficient evidence.

The present chapter analyzes evidence relating to five major questions on the extent and nature of labor mobility: (1) What is the extent of labor mobility, in terms of both numbers of job changes and numbers of workers who make such changes? (2) What is the relative importance of voluntary and involuntary job separations? (3) What patterns are involved in job changes, that is, does the movement of workers represent principally a shifting among employers within the same industry and labor market with no change in job assignment, or is there evidence of considerable occupational, industrial, and geographic flexibility in job shifts? (4) Are there occupational and industrial differentials in mobility: do workers in certain industries and occupations appear to be more mobile, or to make different kinds of job changes, than those in other occupations and industries? (5) What are the directions of job shifts between industries and between occupations? Are there groups of related occupations (and industries) among which movement is more likely to occur than among others, or is such movement primarily random?

EXTENT OF LABOR MOBILITY

Amount of Job Shifting. At the close of the 1930's, Slichter observed that although study of the American labor market was only beginning, several propositions concerning the mobility of labor might safely be asserted. Among these were (1) "the majority of the working population are relatively stable and do little moving either between employers or places and probably between occupations," and (2) "the amount of movement in the labor market is large, and, indeed, is much larger than is generally suspected." [1] With respect to the first, he ventured the guess that a fourth or a fifth of the labor force "is mobile and works for more than one employer in the course of the year." [2] In support of the second, he cited data on labor turnover, on business births and deaths, on the movement between agricultural and nonagricultural pursuits, and on the disparity between the number of social security account numbers issued and the number of persons in employment covered by the social security program at any one time.[3]

The statistical evidence that has become available during the past decade tends to substantiate Slichter's general observations, but it is hardly less difficult now than it was then to quantify precisely the amount of job shifting in the economy. No national survey has ever been made of the total number of job changes that occur in any given period of time. Even if such a survey were made its results could not be generalized because the volume of job shifting is sensitive to changes in the level of business activity.

Perhaps the best single indicator of the amount of job shifting is provided by the data on turnover published by the Bureau of Labor Statistics. Turnover rates for the total of all manufacturing industries have been published since 1930, and statistics for selected manufacturing and nonmanufacturing industries and industrial groups are available for more recent periods.[4] These data have a number of limitations as a measure of gross movement of workers,[5] but they suggest the great amount of job shifting that takes place. In 1951, for example, the total separation rate for the Bureau's sample of manufacturing firms ranged between 3.5 and 5.3 percent per month, totaling 53 percent of the average number of workers on payrolls for the year.[6] If the latter figure is taken to represent the average separation rate in all manufacturing industries, there were about half as many job separations

---

[1] Sumner H. Slichter, "The Impact of Social Security Legislation upon Mobility and Enterprise," *American Economic Review*, 30(suppl.):44 (March 1940).

[2] *Ibid.*, pp. 46, 58.

[3] *Ibid., pp.* 45–46.

[4] For a list of the series that are available and the dates covered, see Lucille C. Ursell, "Measurement of Labor Turnover," *Monthly Labor Review*, 69:420–421 (October 1949).

[5] For a discussion of these limitations and the cautions that must be observed in interpreting the data, see *ibid.*, pp. 417–421.

[6] "Current Labor Statistics," *Monthly Labor Review*, 75:223, Table B-1 (August 1952).

by factory workers during the year as there were manufacturing jobs. This, of course, is not the same as saying that half of the manufacturing employees terminated their jobs during the year, for as will be shown below, a large part of the total separations is accounted for by a disproportionately small number of workers.

Actually, the separation rates computed by the Bureau probably understate the volume of separations in manufacturing. The sample of establishments from which turnover data are collected overrepresents the larger firms, in which the greater prevalence of union agreements and of well-developed personnel programs probably causes employment to be more stable than in the smaller firms. Also, some of the most highly seasonal industries, such as fertilizer manufacturing and canning and preserving, have deliberately been excluded from the sample, thus increasing the downward bias in the data.

Although the volume of job shifts is influenced by economic conditions, it is noteworthy that the separation rates reported for 1951 are not abnormally high in relation to those for other years during the past four or more decades for which data are available. Woytinsky reports that during the second decade of the present century separation rates of 10 percent per month, or over 100 percent per year, were usual.[7] During World War I they reached the phenomenal level of about 17 percent per month in a sample of manufacturing firms, which is the equivalent of about 200 percent on an annual basis.[8] During the relatively prosperous years of the 1920's the median separation rate in manufacturing was approximately 4 percent per month, and this rate also prevailed during the depressed 1930's. In the latter decade, however, about three fourths of the separations were initiated by employers, as compared with only about a fourth of the separations in the 1920's.[9] During the 1940's the average monthly rate rose from about 3.4 percent at the beginning of the decade to 8.2 percent in 1945, and then declined to 4.2 percent in 1949.[10]

It should be stressed that the rates just discussed refer to job *separations,* and that not all separations represent a *job change* even though they do indicate some type of change in the worker's status. A considerable part of *turnover* results from the movement of workers into and out of the labor force. In each month of 1950, for example,

[7] W. S. Woytinsky, *Three Aspects of Labor Dynamics,* p. 2.

[8] *Ibid.*

[9] *Ibid.,* pp. 3–4.

[10] Computed from data in various issues of the *Monthly Labor Review.*

an average of almost three million persons entered the labor force and a slightly smaller number left it. The average monthly gross change in the labor force during the year, therefore, was close to six million workers or almost 10 percent of the average size of the labor force. These figures are particularly impressive in view of the fact that less than three tenths of the workers who entered the labor force each month were under 20 years of age, while less than a tenth of those who withdrew had reached retirement age (65 years or older).[11] Thus, only a small part of the changes in labor force status during the year was attributable to the entrance of young persons just out of school, and to the death or retirement of older workers. Another indication of the large number of shifts in labor force or employment status is that in both 1949 and 1950 the number of persons who worked at some time during the year was more than 10 percent greater than the peak employment attained during the year, and in the neighborhood of 6 percent greater than the peak labor force.[12]

Number of Persons Changing Jobs. The large volume of job shifting is not distributed uniformly within the labor force. Every relevant study has produced evidence that a minority of highly mobile employees account for a major portion of the movement. Woytinsky, in his historical analysis of turnover rates, reports sample surveys conducted prior to and during World War I which indicated that an "unstable" group of workers, numbering only about 10 percent of all manufacturing employees, accounted for almost three fourths of total separations. The separation rate among this group in 1913–14 was about 34 percent monthly, as compared with about 2 percent for all other workers.[13] Reynolds, studying a sample of New Haven workers who changed jobs during selected years in the 1940's, found that "While most of the job-changers moved only once or twice during the year, the minority of very mobile people accounted for a dispropor-

[11] U. S. Bureau of the Census, "Annual Report on the Labor Force, 1950," *Current Population Reports: Labor Force,* Series P-50, No. 31 (March 9, 1951), p. 28. For a more extensive analysis of the census data, see A. J. Jaffe and Charles D. Stewart, *Manpower Resources and Utilization,* pp. 151–154.

[12] Data on persons working from *Current Population Reports: Labor Force,* Series P-50, Nos. 24 and 35 (June 16, 1950; October 26, 1951); monthly data on employment and labor force from *ibid.,* Nos. 19 and 31 (March 2, 1950; March 9, 1951).

[13] Woytinsky, *op. cit.,* pp. 23–28. Woytinsky cautions that there is no evidence that the surveyed firms were representative of all manufacturing industries (p. 27).

tionate share of the total movement"; [14] in 1941 only one third of all persons changing jobs had made three or more moves, but they accounted for three fifths of the total number of shifts. A similar conclusion was reached in a recent study of the 1940–51 work histories of tool and die makers. Nearly three fifths of these workers had only one employer after becoming journeymen. On the other hand, one seventh made at least four changes of employer, and these accounted for almost 60 percent of all the job changes during the period.[15]

Another way to approach the question is to relate the number of workers who change jobs during a specified period to the total number of persons at work during the period. It has been seen from the turnover rates cited that if job shifts were distributed uniformly among the members of the labor force, one would expect as many as half the workers employed in a year like 1951 to change jobs. That this is not the case is shown by the proportions of workers who did not change jobs during specified periods, as reported in several studies to which reference has been made: In the survey of labor mobility in six cities, 37 percent of the workers 25 years of age and over who had worked at least a month in 1950 as well as at some time during 1940–49 had had only one employer during the decade.[16] Over the same decade and 1950, 21 percent of the Census Bureau's national sample of persons of the same ages who were employed in January 1951 had been continuously employed by one employer since before January 1940.[17] In the studies of the Philadelphia labor market in the 1930's it was found that 41 percent of 683 machinists, 32 percent of 357 weavers and loom fixers, but only 14 percent of 382 workers in the radio industry had not changed employers during the decade 1926–35.[18]

[14] Lloyd G. Reynolds, *The Structure of Labor Markets*, pp. 27–28.

[15] U. S. Bureau of Labor Statistics, *The Mobility of Tool and Die Makers, 1940–1951*, pp. 32–33.

[16] Gladys L. Palmer, *Labor Mobility in Six Cities*, percentage computed from Table 14, p. 51.

[17] *Current Population Reports: Labor Force*, Series P-50, No. 36 (December 5, 1951).

[18] These figures are from the following reports of the W.P.A. National Research Project in cooperation with the University of Pennsylvania Industrial Research Department: Helen Herrmann, *Ten Years of Work Experience of Philadelphia Machinists*, Report No. P-5 (September 1938), p. 119; Gladys L. Palmer, *Ten Years of Work Experience of Philadelphia Weavers and Loom Fixers*, Report No. P-4 (July 1938), p. 91; Gladys L. Palmer and Ada M. Stoflet, *The Labor Force of the Philadelphia Radio Industry in 1936*, Report No. P-2 (April 1938), percentage computed from Table 40, p. 92.

These percentages of workers who may be considered "immobile" over a decade may be compared with the following percentages of workers who did not change employers during much briefer periods (from one to two years):

Group	Time period	Percent
Bogue's sample of Michigan and Ohio workers who were in employment covered by Old-Age and Survivors Insurance in the first or last quarter of 1947 [19]	1947	66
Aaronson and Keller's national sample of workers with Old-Age and Survivors Insurance wage credits in specified years [20]	1938	77
	1939	74
	1940	73
	1941	67
	1942	62
	1943	63
Census Bureau's national sample of employed persons aged 14 and over [21]	1950	71
Reynolds' sample of 450 manual workers in New Haven [22]	18 mos. following V-J Day	76
Heneman's sample of 600 persons in St. Paul labor force [23]	July 1941–June 1942	95
Myers and Maclaurin's 15,808 workers employed by 37 manufacturing and utility firms in Fitchburg [24]	1937–39	c. 30

[19] Donald J. Bogue, *A Methodological Study of Migration and Labor Mobility in Michigan and Ohio in 1947*, Scripps Foundation Studies in Population Distribution No. 4 (June 1952), Table III-1, p. 14.

[20] Franklin M. Aaronson and Ruth A. Keller, *Mobility of Workers in Employment Covered by Old-Age and Survivors Insurance*, U. S. Social Security Administration, Bureau of Research and Statistics Report No. 14 (July 1946), p. 13.

[21] *Current Population Reports: Labor Force*, Series P-50, No. 36; the percentage computed from data on p. 1 represents persons continuously employed by one employer during the entire year.

[22] Lloyd G. Reynolds, *The Structure of Labor Markets*, p. 20.

[23] Herbert G. Heneman, Jr., "Differential Short-Run Labor Mobilities: St. Paul, 1941–42," in *Minnesota Manpower Mobilities*, University of Minnesota Industrial Relations Center, Bulletin 10 (1950), p. 35; the percentage represents workers having the same employer at the beginning and end of the period.

[24] Charles A. Myers and W. Rupert Maclaurin, *The Movement of Factory Workers*, p. 11; the percentage represents persons remaining in the employ of a single firm for the entire period.

It is difficult to summarize the data on the proportion of workers who did not change jobs during 10-year periods, except to note that apparently a substantial number of workers are highly stable. Only the Census report indicates the proportion of workers who served *continuously with one employer during the entire period.* The other percentages refer to the number of workers employed at the time of the survey *who had not made interfirm shifts* during the period. Thus, workers who took their first jobs after the beginning of the period and any workers intermittently employed by the same employer are included despite the fact that they were not employed continuously during the 10 years.[25]

The difference between the results of the survey of occupational mobility in six cities and the Census survey of the labor force merits some comment. According to the former, over a third of the workers who were 25 years of age in 1951 and who had worked a month or longer in 1950 had only one employer during the decade 1940–49. In the latter only a fifth of the workers were continuously employed by the same employer during the 11 years from 1940 to 1950. Although the coverage of the two surveys differed—one related to the labor force of six industrial cities and the other to the entire national labor force—the difference in the results is probably attributable mainly to differences in definitions and in the time period. Three factors would tend to make the percentage of "stable" workers shown by the Census survey lower than that shown by the six-city survey. First, the former covers one more year. Second, according to the definitions used, a person who was intermittently employed by the same employer during the decade would have been included among those who did not change employers in the six-city survey, but would not be included by the Census among those who held "one job" during the period. Third, workers who entered the labor force after 1940 and who remained with one employer would be included in the former group, but not in the latter.

The effects of the last two factors cannot be precisely quantified, but there is some evidence that they account for most of the difference between the two percentages. In the six-city survey approximately 10 percent of the workers had only one employer during the decade but had been in the labor force less than 115 of the 120 months,

---

[25] For the radio workers the former factor is not relevant, since only those who had entered the labor force prior to the beginning of the period are included.

leaving 27 percent who had only one employer while in the labor force during at least 115 months; this proportion is considerably closer to that shown by the Census. Much of the remaining difference is probably accounted for by workers with only one employer and from 115 to 120 months of labor force exposure.[26]

Summarizing the findings of these two surveys, it appears that as of 1950 about a fifth of all workers who might potentially have been members of the labor force during the preceding decade were highly stable, in that they not only worked continuously during the period but served with only one employer. A larger proportion, amounting to over a third, were stable in the sense that they served with only one employer, although not necessarily continuously during the entire period. The latter group included persons who had not yet entered the labor force in the early part of the decade and also those who withdrew from the labor force for one reason or another. For men, military service was an important cause of interrupted employment. In any case it would be dangerous to generalize on the basis of experience during the 1940's. The extremely high level of economic activity during the war, the reconversion to peacetime pursuits, the existence of manpower controls during several years of the decade, and the induction of millions of men and women into the armed services, all combined to make labor market processes atypical during the decade.

The proportions of various groups of workers who did not change jobs during one-year or other brief periods are somewhat easier to interpret, and there is a remarkable similarity among the findings of the several studies summarized. In all but two, the proportion of workers making no job change is roughly between two thirds and three fourths. In the two studies that show markedly different results, methodological factors can account for the differences.

[26] The percentages of each sex shown as "stable" by the Census and the six-city surveys are as follows:

	Six-city survey			Census
	Workers with 1 employer	Workers with 1 employer, but less than 115 mos. in labor force	Workers with 1 employer and 115 or more mos. in labor force (Col. 1 — Col. 2)	Workers with continuous jobs
Male	37	6	31	25
Female	36	18	18	14

Heneman's finding that 95 percent of his sample of the St. Paul labor force had not changed employers between July 1941 and June 1942 may be accounted for by two factors. First, whether a worker had changed employers was determined by comparing the job held at the beginning of the one-year period with that held at the end; consequently, a person who had changed his job but had returned to the original one before the end of the year would have been counted as having made no job change. More important, however, is the fact that 27 percent of the individuals in the sample of households surveyed at the beginning of the period had moved out of the sample by the end of the year. These persons were not interviewed at their new addresses, and no information on changes in their job status during the year was obtained.[27] Since many persons who changed residence during the year are likely to have made job shifts also, their exclusion from the sample almost certainly leads to a serious overstatement of the proportion of "stable" workers. The difference between the findings of this study and those of others is probably more the result of these factors than of differences between the St. Paul and the national labor force, which Heneman suggests may be influential.[28]

The small percentage of "stable" employees found in Myers and Maclaurin's study is probably attributable largely to the fact that the data relate to a three-year period rather than to a single year as in most of the other studies. The proportion of Reynolds' sample that had not changed employers is somewhat high in comparison with the proportions found by Bogue and by Aaronson and Keller, particularly in view of the 18-month period used by Reynolds as compared with a one-year period in the other studies. However, Reynolds' sample overrepresented older and more skilled workers, among whom mobility tends to be lower than average.[29] Finally, it should be noted that Bogue's and Aaronson and Keller's findings probably somewhat overstate the proportion of workers making no job changes, since Old-Age and Survivors Insurance wage records do not reveal changes between covered and noncovered employment.

Taking all these qualifications into consideration, the evidence suggests that between a fourth and a third of all workers change jobs

[27] Herbert G. Heneman, Jr., "Differential Short-Run Labor Mobilities: St. Paul, 1941–42," p. 35.

[28] Ibid., p. 47.

[29] Reynolds, op. cit., p. 15.

either by choice or by force of circumstance in the course of a year.[30] In periods of dynamic economic change and almost unlimited employment opportunities, such as the World War II period, the proportion changing jobs may even exceed the upper limit of this range. During 1942 and 1943, for example, it is likely that as many as 4 out of every 10 workers made at least one job change during each year.

VOLUNTARY AND INVOLUNTARY SEPARATIONS

Up to this point there has been no attempt to differentiate the job shifts that are voluntarily initiated by the employee from those that are forced upon him by layoff or discharge. The distinction between these two types of movement is important and has both practical and theoretical implications. From the practical standpoint, the relative proportions of voluntary and involuntary job separations indicate the condition of the economy and the magnitude of the adjustments that workers are compelled to make.[31] From the theoretical viewpoint, only the voluntary separations represent *choices* made by workers and consequently are relevant in the development of theories of motivation of workers. It is important to ascertain, therefore, the extent to which job changes are voluntary and the extent to which they are "forced."

The relative importance of voluntary and involuntary job separations is largely a function of the stage of the business cycle. It is estimated that about three fourths of all separations in manufacturing industries during the prosperous 1920's were voluntary. During the 1930's the proportions of voluntary and involuntary separations were approximately reversed. Up to the end of 1940, on the average about 25 percent of all separations were voluntary, 70 percent were layoffs,

[30] To a large extent these are the same workers year after year. Aaronson and Keller report that of workers with wage credits in 1939 and 1940, 14 percent changed jobs in *both* years. Since about one fourth of the workers with wage credits in *each* of the years changed employers at least once in that year, "it is apparent that more than half of the workers who made a change in 1939 also made a change in 1940. On the basis of these data it would seem reasonable to conclude that, at least in normal periods of labor market activity, a large proportion of the workers who change employers in one year are likely to make a change in subsequent years." (*Op. cit.*, p. 14.)

[31] Woytinsky suggests that the ratio of voluntary quits to total separations constitutes "one of the most sensitive indexes of the labor market. It registers not only variations in the demand for labor by industry, but also the changes in the psychological pressure of unemployment on workers." (*Op. cit.*, p. 52.)

and 5 percent were discharges. In February 1933, and again in the autumn of 1937, voluntary quits amounted to only about 10 percent of all separations. Indeed, when allowance is made for the fact that the "quit" rates reported by the Bureau of Labor Statistics during this period included "miscellaneous separations" due to such factors as death and illness, it appears that there was virtually no voluntary job shifting by manufacturing workers in 1932 and "only a feeble trace of it in 1931 and from 1933 to 1935." [32]

Perhaps the best data available on the extent of voluntary and involuntary job shifting in the 1940's are those reported by the survey of labor mobility in six cities. Workers who had more than one employer between 1940 and 1949 are estimated to have made a total of more than 5.6 million job separations during the decade; of these slightly under a fourth were layoffs.[33] All other separations included discharges as well as separations caused by induction into military service. The latter two causes of separations were found to account for about 1 percent and 6 percent, respectively, of all those made by St. Paul workers during the period.[34] It appears, therefore, that about 7 out of 10 job terminations during this period represented voluntary quits.

In a sample consisting entirely of manual workers, Reynolds found that three fifths of those who had changed jobs in the 18 months following V-J Day had done so voluntarily, while the remaining two fifths had been laid off.[35] This somewhat lower proportion of voluntary movement is understandable inasmuch as the particular period was one of heavy layoffs and reconversion to peacetime activities.

Since a substantial majority of job separations in the recent past have been initiated by employees, the kinds of job changes that have been made may be considered to be primarily indicative of workers' choices. This is an important point, for most of the studies that have examined patterns of job changes have not differentiated between voluntary and involuntary job shifts. A priori one would suppose

[32] Ibid., pp. 3–4, 52–54. Although Woytinsky does not say so, the number of voluntary job shifts appears to have been very small in 1938 and 1939, also. (Compare p. 54 with Table 6, p. 49.)

[33] Gladys L. Palmer, Labor Mobility in Six Cities, pp. 59–60.

[34] Harland Fox, Adele H. Osterchek, and Herbert G. Heneman, Jr., "Voluntary Shifts of St. Paul Workers, 1940–44 and 1945–50," unpublished manuscript, University of Minnesota Industrial Relations Center (February 1, 1951).

[35] Reynolds, op. cit., p. 20.

that job shifts occasioned by layoffs might differ in nature from those made by choice, and there is some slight evidence that this is true.[36]

PATTERNS OF MOBILITY

What kinds of job shifts do workers make? What are the relative frequencies of changes in occupation, industry, and local labor market area? Such questions are of great significance in assessing the flexibility of the labor supply. The degree to which it can adjust to changes in the composition of labor demand is a function not only of the volume of job changes, but also of their pattern. Thus, a labor force may be quite flexible with respect to its distribution among employers, but inflexible in its occupational and industrial composition. Or, being occupationally and industrially flexible, the labor supply may be quite insensitive to changes in the geographic distribution of labor demand.

Extent of Occupational and Industrial Mobility. Most studies of patterns of job changes have found evidence of a rather high degree of occupational and industrial flexibility in the work force. Although there are differences among various occupational and industrial groups, large proportions of the job changes made in the labor force as a whole involve a change in industry, in occupation, or in both. Before reviewing the evidence it must again be emphasized that measures of occupational and industrial mobility are influenced by the systems of classification used: the more detailed the classification, the greater the number of shifts that will be tallied.

The six-city survey measured occupational and industrial shifts in terms of the Census Bureau's three-digit codes, in which there are 269 occupational and 146 industrial categories. A few examples of the activities recognized as separate occupations and industries will give some idea of the degree of detail in these classifications. In the professional group, civil and chemical engineers are each a separate category, as are architects, musicians, and lawyers. In the clerical field, stenographers, typists, and secretaries constitute a single occupational cate-

---

[36] Among both men and women covered in the six-city survey complex job shifts involving a simultaneous change of employer, occupation, and industry were somewhat more likely to be associated with voluntary than with involuntary movement. On the other hand, simple interfirm shifts within the same occupation and industry accounted for a larger proportion of the layoffs than of the other separations. See Palmer, *Labor Mobility in Six Cities,* Tables 28 and 29, pp. 74–75.

gory, while bookkeepers and cashiers comprise another. Examples of separate skilled categories are electricians, carpenters, locomotive engineers, and structural and ornamental metal workers. The semiskilled group (operatives) includes such separate categories as deliverymen, welders and flame-cutters, metal heaters, and also operatives classified according to the industry in which they work. Laborers are classified principally in categories defined by the industries to which they are attached. Examples of the industrial categories are agriculture, metal mining, bakery products, miscellaneous chemical industries, electrical machinery and equipment, taxicab service, shoe stores, and insurance. These illustrations indicate that the occupational and industrial categories used are not the narrowest that could be defined. Shifts across these occupational or industrial lines represent a considerable modification either in the duties of the worker or in the product or service that he helps to produce.

About half of all the job shifts made during 1940–49 by workers in the six cities involved simultaneous changes of employer, occupation, and industry. An additional fifth of the shifts involved changes in employer and industry, while 5 percent were changes in employer and occupation. A fifth of all the shifts were changes in employer only.[37] Expressed another way, three fourths of all the interfirm shifts made by the workers during the decade involved a change in industry, and three fifths involved a change in occupation. Since occupational changes made by workers while in the service of a single employer were not recorded in the survey, it is certain that the actual extent of occupational movement is understated by these figures.[38]

An interesting comparison with these findings is provided by the

[37] *Ibid.*

[38] A special analysis of the work history samples of four of the cities showed that somewhat over one fifth of the workers had experienced "upward" occupational mobility during the decade 1940–50, that is, had moved up the scale of occupations ranked according to skill and prestige. Of these, about 40 percent had made their occupational shifts without changing employers. (Albert J. Reiss, Jr., "Patterns of Occupation Mobility for Workers in Four Cities," unpublished manuscript, University of Chicago, Chicago Community Inventory, March 1953, Tables 1 and 21.) In San Francisco, 14 percent of the men and 12 percent of the women with only one civilian job between 1940 and 1949 had *more than one* occupational assignment. (Margaret S. Gordon, "The Relation of Gross to Net Changes in the Inter-Occupational and Inter-Industrial Movements of the Urban Labor Force," unpublished manuscript, University of California Institute of Industrial Relations, Berkeley, March 1953, Appendix Table A-1.)

work history data collected by Palmer and her associates for the Philadelphia labor market during the decade 1926–35. Data are available on the number and kinds of job shifts made by machinists and tool makers, weavers and loom fixers, male and female radio workers, and male and female hosiery workers. For all these groups except the hosiery workers, shifts involving simultaneous changes of employer, occupation, and industry were more numerous than any other category, accounting for over two thirds of the job changes made by radio workers and about half of those made by weavers and loom fixers and by machinists. A majority of the job shifts by hosiery workers were changes in employer alone, with no occupational or industrial movement.[39] These findings are basically consistent with those of the six-city survey with respect to the relative importance of the complex type of job shift, although they indicate that the attachment of workers to certain industries and occupations is particularly great, and that movement from these is consequently less common than from other occupations and industries.

The complex job shift was found to be even more prominent in the 1941–45 work experience of over 2,000 production workers employed in certain war industries in 1945. Of the nearly 4,000 job shifts made by the workers during the war period, 70 percent represented simultaneous changes of employer, occupation, and industry, while only about 10 percent were simple interfirm shifts.[40] The three-digit code of the Standard Industrial Classification was used in this study for measuring industrial shifts. The report of the study does not indicate the occupational classification system used, but several examples cited suggest a more detailed classification than that used in the six-city survey.[41]

Even when very broad industrial and occupational groups are considered, there is substantial movement by workers across their boundaries. Thus, a large majority of the occupational and industrial shifts

[39] Computed from data in Gladys L. Palmer, "Interpreting Patterns of Labor Mobility," in E. Wight Bakke and others, *Labor Mobility and Economic Opportunity*, pp. 47–67. Percentages have been computed on the basis of the total number of shifts involving movement from one employer to another; that is, changes of occupational assignment within a single firm have been excluded from the total number of shifts in order to make the data comparable with those of the six-city survey.

[40] U. S. Bureau of Labor Statistics, *Worker Mobility and Skill Utilization in World War II* (1952, processed), p. 17.

[41] *Ibid.*, pp. 6, 8.

made by San Francisco workers between 1940 and 1949 were *between* major groups of occupations and major divisions of industry. Four fifths of the occupational shifts made by men and two thirds of those made by women were intergroup shifts, while even higher proportions of the industrial changes were from one major division of industry to another.[42] Of the workers covered by the six-city survey who were employed in both 1940 and 1950, over a third of both the men and women had changed *industry divisions* between those dates, while over a third of the men and a fourth of the women had changed their *major occupational groups*.[43] The occupational and industrial flexibility revealed by these figures becomes even more remarkable when it is noted that only 8 broad occupational categories and 12 major industrial divisions were used in the analysis.[44] Moreover, it must be kept in mind that these proportions almost certainly understate the extent of shifting among these categories because all the changes that occurred between the two terminal dates were not included in the analysis.

Reynolds' data likewise show a large amount of shifting among broad occupational and industrial groups. Of the 12 major industrial groups in which his sample of manual workers were currently employed, there were only two in which a fourth or more of the workers had not been employed in at least three other major industrial groups. Moreover, almost two fifths of the workers had been employed in at least three major occupational groups.[45]

Extent of Geographic Mobility. As might be expected, the evidence indicates conclusively that job changes from one local labor market area to another are much less frequent than those from one occupation or industry to another. Reynolds notes that whereas less than a fifth of his sample of New Haven manual workers had never shifted from one major industrial group to another, and an equally small number had never shifted between two major occupational groups, almost

[42] Margaret S. Gordon, *op. cit.*, Tables 11 and 12.

[43] Palmer, *Labor Mobility in Six Cities*, computed from Tables 40 and 41, pp. 106–108.

[44] *Ibid.*

[45] Reynolds, *op. cit.*, p. 30, Table 8, and p. 135, Table 20. See also Seymour M. Lipset and Reinhard Bendix, "Social Mobility and Occupational Career Patterns," *American Journal of Sociology*, 62:366–374 (January 1952). The authors are principally concerned with showing that most workers have unstable occupational careers, and that it is therefore doubtful whether workers' present occupations can be used as a relatively permanent measure of their social status. The data are obviously pertinent also to the present discussion.

three fifths had not worked outside the community, and three fourths had not made more than one geographic shift. Almost half the workers had made at least three industrial shifts and almost a third had made three or more occupational shifts, as compared with less than 15 percent who had made that many geographic moves.[46]

Aaronson and Keller's analysis of job changes by a national sample of workers covered by Old-Age and Survivors Insurance shows that in each year from 1938 to 1943 the number of workers who moved *across state lines* was only between a fourth and a third of the total number who changed employer. In 1938, for example, 23 percent of the employees worked for at least two covered employers, while only 6 percent worked in more than one state. In 1943, the respective proportions had risen to 37 and 11 percent. Moreover, a sizable minority of the multistate workers—between 2 and 4 out of 10—worked for only one employer, indicating that they were "a very specialized group—mostly high-paid full-time workers who are presumably sent to branch establishments in other states by their employers." [47] It should be stressed that these data are not the best indicators of the extent of geographic movement. A great deal of all geographic mobility may, and undoubtedly does, take place within state boundaries. On the other hand, working in more than one state during a year does not necessarily mean that a worker has changed his residence from one local labor market area to another.[48]

Bogue's study of the Old-Age and Survivors Insurance wage records of Ohio and Michigan workers in 1947 indicates that 17 percent of the workers were employed in more than one county during the year. An equal percentage of the workers had changed jobs within a county.[49] This proportion of intercounty migrants is considerably higher than that shown by the Census Bureau's sample for the nation as a whole in 1949–50. In March 1950 only 5 percent of the total labor force resided in a county different from the county of residence in March 1949.[50] These two sources of data on intercounty movement are of course noncomparable in several respects. Not only do they differ in

[46] Reynolds, *op. cit.*, p. 26, Table 4.

[47] Aaronson and Keller, *op. cit.*, p. 7. See also pp. 6, 13.

[48] See pp. 33–35 supra.

[49] Donald J. Bogue, *A Methodological Study of Migration and Labor Mobility in Michigan and Ohio in 1947*, p. 14, Table III-1.

[50] *Current Population Reports: Population Characteristics*, Series P-20, No. 36 (December 9, 1951), p. 12, Table 6.

coverage of workers and of time, but the insurance data relate to place of employment, while the Census data relate to place of residence. Moreover, the Census data compare residence at the beginning and the end of the one-year period, and thus do not include persons who move and then return to the county of origin before the end of the year. Bogue's data, on the other hand, do include such persons. And it is noteworthy that when he compares county of employment in the first quarter of the year with that in the last quarter, the number of multicounty workers drops to 9 percent as compared with 17 percent on the basis of *all* the jobs they held during the year.[51] This result is considerably closer to, but still higher than, the proportion given by the Census data for 1949–50. Although the evidence does not permit a definitive conclusion, it is probable that the volume of intercounty job shifting is greater than the volume of intercounty change of residence. In other words, more workers change the county in which they work without changing their residence, than change their county of residence without making a similar change in employment.

Despite the evidence that workers are generally less mobile geographically than they are occupationally or industrially, both the absolute amount of geographic movement and its importance in relation to other kinds of job changes increase under certain circumstances. That the migration of workers was widespread during World War II is common knowledge. The Old-Age and Survivors Insurance data used by Aaronson and Keller show that the proportion of multistate workers was twice as high in 1942 and 1943 as in 1938, and that the ratio of interstate to interfirm movement was higher in the former years than in the latter.[52]

Additional evidence of the increased geographic flexibility of the labor force during the war period is provided by several studies of workers in war industries. Among over 2,000 such workers employed in various regions of the United States in 1945, more than half had worked in at least two standard metropolitan areas or counties between 1941 and 1945, and as many as one sixth had worked in three or more areas.[53] Kerr estimates that about 50,000 to 55,000 workers migrated into the Seattle labor market area between January 1940 and March 1942; of these about a third came from areas more than 600

[51] Bogue, *op. cit.*, p. 27, Table V-2.
[52] Aaronson and Keller, *op. cit.*, compare Tables 1 and 6.
[53] U. S. Bureau of Labor Statistics, *Worker Mobility and Skill Utilization in World War II*, computed from Table 26, p. 84.

miles away.[54] Parnes estimates that between 40 and 50 percent of the net increase in manufacturing employment in the Columbus, Ohio area during 1943 was attributable to in-migration, a larger percentage than in prewar or postwar years of rising employment.[55] Whether the increased geographic mobility during the war was primarily a response to higher wages, greater employment opportunities, more interesting work, patriotic appeals, or other factors cannot be stated with confidence, but it is clear that certain combinations of circumstances may significantly increase the geographic mobility of the labor force, and also make geographic mobility more pronounced relative to occupational and industrial movement.

Relative Frequency of Occupational, Industrial, and Geographic Job Shifts. From the foregoing review of the evidence relating to patterns of job shifts it may be concluded that the worker's strongest attachment is to his community, that he is considerably less strongly attached to a particular occupation, and even less so to an industry. With rare exceptions—and these in the case of specific occupations or industries [56]—studies of work histories show that workers make more industrial than occupational changes and far more occupational than geographic shifts. What do these findings imply with respect to the attachment of workers to their employers? The fact that interfirm shifts are more numerous than any other type of movement obviously does not mean that the worker's attachment to a particular company is weaker than his attachment to a specific industry or occupation; if a worker makes a job change at all, he necessarily (by most definitions) changes employers.

[54] Clark Kerr, "Migration to the Seattle Labor Market Area, 1940–1942," *University of Washington Publications in the Social Sciences*, 11:129–188 (August 1942).

[55] Herbert S. Parnes, *A Study in the Dynamics of Local Labor Force Expansion* (Columbus: Ohio State University Research Foundation, 1951, mimeo.), p. 50.

[56] See, for example, Gladys L. Palmer and Constance Williams, *Reemployment of Philadelphia Hosiery Workers after Shut-downs in 1933–34,* W.P.A. National Research Project in cooperation with University of Pennsylvania Industrial Research Department, Report No. P-6 (January 1939), pp. 70–72. In the 10-year work histories of both male and female hosiery workers there were fewer industrial than occupational shifts. Heneman, Fox, and Yoder, in a study of 98 "mobile" workers in Minneapolis, found that the number of occupational shifts made by the workers during 1944–48 exceeded the number of industrial shifts. ("Patterns of Manpower Mobility: Minneapolis, 1948," in *Minnesota Manpower Mobilities,* University of Minnesota Industrial Relations Center, Bulletin 10, 1950, p. 7.)

Reynolds suggests, on the basis of interviews with three samples of New Haven manual workers, that "Attachment to a particular employer is normally stronger than attachment to a particular occupation or industry." [57] The evidence presented, however, does not conclusively support this proposition. Reynolds points out that large majorities of his two samples of employed workers expected to continue working for their present employers; that almost nine tenths of the veterans in one of the samples had returned to their former employers after being discharged from military service, three fourths of them without even looking for other jobs; and that about 9 in every 10 unemployed workers said they would like to return to their previous jobs.[58] He explains these responses in terms of the comfort of an established routine, the desire to establish seniority for purposes of security, the fear of losing promotion and pension rights, and the difficulty faced by many workers, particularly the older ones, in finding other jobs.[59] He concludes that "These factors in combination produce virtually a separate labor market in each plant. Even in the good years 1946–48, something like 80 percent of the manual workers in the area were not really available to other employers. Their horizon was bounded by the enterprise." [60]

The evidence presented by Reynolds does indicate a pronounced attachment of workers to their current jobs, and his conclusion that the vast majority of employed workers are not truly in the job market at any given time seems to be warranted. But his data do not necessarily lead to the conclusion that attachment to an occupation is weaker than that to an employer. It is possible that even greater majorities of the respondents would have indicated reluctance to make an occupational change; and it is not known to what extent the particular duties they performed were responsible for their desire to remain with or go back to certain employers.[61] That workers are more reluctant to change employers than to change occupations is a highly interesting hypothesis, but it is doubtful whether it can be satisfactorily tested with the kinds of data now available.

[57] Reynolds, *op. cit.*, p. 79.
[58] *Ibid.*, pp. 80–81.
[59] *Ibid.*, pp. 82–83.
[60] *Ibid.*, p. 83.
[61] In this connection, roughly between a fifth and a fourth of the reasons given by employed workers for satisfaction with their present jobs related to job interest or to the physical characteristics of the job (*ibid.*, p. 293).

Occupational and Industrial Differentials in Mobility

In view of the variety of occupations in the economy, it is perhaps not so meaningful to consider the mobility of "labor" as to describe the mobility of specific groups of workers. A priori, one would suppose that the differences between the research chemist and the janitor in respect to training and socioeconomic status would produce quite different types of labor market behavior. The evidence relating to occupational and industrial differentials in mobility—that is, the extent to which there are differences either in the degree or the pattern of job shifting among workers in different occupations and industries—is reviewed in this section.

In evaluating the evidence a major methodological difficulty, pointed out in Chapter 2, must be kept in mind: Occupational and industrial differences in the incidence and patterns of mobility have invariably been investigated by examining the job histories of workers classified according to their *present* occupational or industrial status. But there is considerable shifting among the major occupational and industrial groups, and workers currently in one occupational category may not have been in that same category during the entire period under consideration. Thus the usual method of analysis does not relate the job shifts made by a worker to his occupational and industrial status *at the times the shifts were made*. This, however, is precisely what must be done in order to ascertain whether job changes are less frequent among workers in some occupations and industries than in others. An illustration may clarify the nature of the problem. A recent study of workers who held skilled jobs at some time during the period 1940–51 shows that such workers were "much less likely to change employers once they got on a skilled job than they had been on their non-skilled jobs." [62] If this is generally true, and if workers shift between skilled and nonskilled work during, say, a 10-year period, it follows that the true mobility characteristics of skilled and nonskilled occupations are obscured or distorted by an analysis that relates the employment experience of workers during a decade to their occupational status at the end of that decade. Since only data of the latter kind are available, they can perhaps be used to describe the general mobility charac-

[62] Charles A. Myers and George P. Shultz, "Patterns of Mobility of Skilled Workers and Factors Affecting Their Occupational Choice, Six Cities, 1940–51," unpublished manuscript, Massachusetts Institute of Technology Industrial Relations Section (1952), p. viii.

teristics of the major occupational and industrial groups, so long as no attempt at precise quantification is made.

Occupational Differentials in Degree of Mobility. Virtually the only comprehensive data on the comparative mobility of workers in the major occupational groups are provided by the survey of labor mobility in six cities. When the workers covered by the survey are classified by their 1950 occupations, measures of mobility during the preceding decade tend to vary inversely with the traditional socioeconomic rank of the various occupational levels (see Table 1). Although differences between adjacent occupational groups are not great, there is a pronounced variation between the top and the bottom ranks of the occupational ladder. Thus, the mean number of civilian jobs held per worker between 1940 and 1949 was 2.4 for managerial and professional workers, as compared with 3.1 for laborers. Service workers constituted an exception to the general pattern, with a mean lower than any of the other manual groups.[63] Occupational differentials in mobility appear to be somewhat less consistent for women than for men.[64]

Whether the mobility differences among the major occupational groups stem from differences in their propensity to make job changes or in the degree of security of jobs is an interesting question. Are laborers highly mobile because they are exceptionally prone to change jobs or because their jobs are exceptionally unstable? The available data do not permit a conclusive answer, but there is some evidence that the higher mobility rates of workers in manual occupations is

[63] Occupation apparently does not exercise a purely independent influence on mobility. Kitagawa discovered that some changes in the ranking of the occupational groups occurred when several combinations of other factors were held constant. The simultaneous control of weekly earnings, percent self-employed, and migrant status produced the most pronounced change in the pattern of occupational differentials. Since controlling different combinations of variables produced different patterns of occupational differentials, Kitagawa concluded that "more factors should be controlled simultaneously in order to isolate occupation differentials per se." (Evelyn M. Kitagawa, "Relative Importance—and Independence—of Selected Factors in Job Mobility, Six Cities, 1940–1949," unpublished manuscript, University of Chicago, Chicago Community Inventory, March 1953, pp. 18–19.) The relatively low mobility of service workers is probably largely a function of age and length of service. In manufacturing industries workers are frequently transferred into service occupations when advancing age prevents them from keeping up with the pace of production jobs. In Kitagawa's analysis, holding age and union membership constant indicated higher mobility for men in service occupations than in any other occupational group except laborers (p. 101).

[64] Palmer, *Labor Mobility in Six Cities*, p. 43.

partly due to the higher *involuntary* turnover in those occupations. Table 1 shows that the ranking of the occupational groups according to degree of mobility corresponds closely to their ranking according to percentage of layoffs. Only about a sixth of the job separations by professional and managerial workers during the decade 1940–49 were layoffs, as compared with more than a third of those by laborers.[65]

TABLE 1. Mean Number of Jobs Held per Worker and Percentage
of Layoffs in Total Separations by Workers in Six
Cities, 1940–49, by Occupational Group

Occupation of longest job held in 1950	Mean number of jobs held per worker	Layoffs as per- cent of total job shifts
Professional, technical, and kindred workers	2.4	17
Managers, officials, and proprietors	2.4	16
Clerical and kindred workers	2.6	20
Sales workers	2.5	17
Craftsmen, foremen, and kindred workers	2.8	31
Operatives and kindred workers	2.8	28
Service workers	2.7	22
Laborers	3.1	36
All occupations	2.6	24

Source: Gladys L. Palmer, *Labor Mobility in Six Cities,* Table 26, p. 72.

Occupational Differentials in Geographic Mobility. The evidence is fairly clear that the geographic mobility of professional and technical workers is greater than that of other major occupational groups. It would be surprising if this were not the case in view of the large number of professional occupations for which the labor market is virtually national in scope. Moreover, professional workers are more likely than other groups to have wide knowledge of job opportunities in other localities, and to be financially able to make geographic moves. For quite different reasons, the geographic mobility of farm laborers is also above average.

[65] Analysis of the 1940–49 work histories of San Francisco workers has shown that occupational differentials in mobility are not entirely explained by differences in the incidence of involuntary separations. Occupational variations in voluntary mobility were found to be less pronounced than in involuntary mobility, but were nevertheless substantial. (Margaret S. Gordon, *op. cit.,* p. 14.)

Between March 1949 and March 1950, 4.9 percent of the employed persons in the United States are estimated to have changed their county of residence. The percentage of such migrants among professional and semiprofessional workers, on the other hand, was 7.9. The only other occupational group among whom more than 5 percent shifted their county of residence were farm laborers (5.6 percent). In both these groups the men were principally responsible for the higher than average proportions.[66] These findings are supported by those in Webb and Westefeld's study of the geographic movement of Michigan workers between April 1930 and January 1935, although it was concerned primarily with industrial rather than occupational differentials. Webb and Westefeld report that workers in extractive industries (including agriculture) were most mobile, and that professional and semiprofessional workers were more mobile than workers in manufacturing.[67]

The extent to which some groups of professional workers make job shifts involving geographic movement is indicated by a recent study of the work experience of over 1,000 men who held Ph.D. degrees in chemistry, physics, and biology. The study shows that such scientists commonly begin their geographic moves even during their training period: more than three fifths of the sample had received their bachelor's and doctor's degrees in different states. Over two fifths had held professional jobs in at least three states, and of those who had held as many as four such jobs, two thirds had worked in three or more states.[68]

The relatively high geographic mobility of farm laborers doubtless reflects the substantial number of migratory farm workers in the country. Although a precise count of this type of worker is exceptionally difficult, Ducoff estimates that there were at least a million migratory farm workers in the United States at some time during 1949, of whom somewhat over half were citizens of this country and the remainder were Mexican nationals.[69] A recent study of the agricultural labor force of the San Joaquin Valley found that less than half of the

---

[66] *Current Population Reports: Population Characteristics*, Series P-20, No. 36 (December 9, 1951), p. 14, Table 8.

[67] John N. Webb and Albert Westefeld, "Industrial Aspects of Labor Mobility," *Monthly Labor Review*, 48:792 (April 1939).

[68] U. S. Bureau of Labor Statistics, *Occupational Mobility of Scientists*, Bulletin No. 1121, p. 4.

[69] Louis J. Ducoff, *Migratory Farm Workers in 1949*, U. S. Bureau of Agricultural Economics, Agricultural Information Bulletin No. 25 (1950), pp. 1–2.

workers had worked in only one county in California during 1948. More than a third had worked either in two nonadjacent counties or in three or more counties in the state. Another fifth of the workers had been employed in at least one other state during the year.[70]

Occupational Differences in Patterns of Mobility. As would be expected from the lengthy training required for most skilled and professional jobs, workers in these two occupational groups show a higher than average attachment to occupation and are consequently less likely than other workers to make complex job shifts involving the simultaneous change of employer, occupation, and industry. Relatively high proportions of their job changes involve movement between two employers in the same industry, with no change in occupational assignment. For clerical workers the six-city survey shows an interesting difference in the patterns of job shifts made by men and by women. A disproportionately high percentage of the shifts made by male clerical workers involved occupational and industrial changes, whereas women made relatively fewer job changes of this type and a disproportionately high percentage of shifts involving a change in employer and industry.[71] Service workers of both sexes were more inclined than most other groups of workers to make job shifts involving only a change in employer. Women in the managerial and sales groups made relatively high percentages of complex job shifts.[72]

Although these differences in mobility patterns are probably indicative of variations among occupational groups in the degree of their occupational and industrial attachments, the preceding analysis should not obscure the fact that the simultaneous change of employer, occupation, and industry was the most common kind of job shift for *all* the major occupational groups in the six-city survey. In no occupational group did this complex type of shift account for fewer than 44 percent of all the job changes made by men during the decade, and the proportion was as high as 63 percent for male clerical workers. Among women the lowest proportion was 35 percent, for professional workers;

[70] William H. Metzler and Afife F. Sayin, *The Agricultural Labor Force in the San Joaquin Valley, California, 1948* (U. S. Bureau of Agricultural Economics in cooperation with University of California Institute of Industrial Relations, February 1950, mimeo.), p. 54, Table 19.

[71] It is probable that this difference is attributable at least in part to the efforts of many men to avoid or delay military service by moving from "nonessential" to "essential" occupations.

[72] Palmer, *Labor Mobility in Six Cities,* pp. 64, 79.

and even in that group the complex job shift was more frequent than that involving a change in employer only. On the other hand, almost three fifths of all the job shifts by female managerial workers involved the simultaneous change of employer, occupation, and industry.[73]

Industrial Differentials in Mobility. The six-city survey found few differences in the mobility of workers in the major divisions of industry.[74] Except for relatively high mobility among men engaged in construction and low mobility among women employed in transportation, communications, and utilities in 1950, there were few if any significant differences in the degree of mobility. The mean number of jobs held during 1940–49 was 3.4 for men in the former group and 2.1 for women in the latter, as compared with 2.6 for all workers in the six cities combined. Each of the other industrial groups showed a mean number of jobs within the narrow range of 2.4 to 2.8.[75]

The proportions of multi-employer workers in various industrial divisions, presented by Aaronson and Keller, point to a similar conclusion. In 1943, when 37 percent of all workers with Old-Age and Survivors Insurance wage credits made at least one change of employer, the corresponding percentages within each of the major divisions of industry except construction ranged between 32 and 41. In construction the proportion was 59 percent.[76] On the other hand, when the major divisions are broken down into their component industrial groups, rather pronounced variation in the proportions of workers who changed employers is discerned. For example, in six industrial groups [77] less than a fourth of the workers made job changes during the year;

[73] *Ibid.*

[74] An intensive analysis of the San Francisco work history sample has suggested, however, that the small differences for the 1940's as a whole may have resulted in part from a "canceling out" process, since "marked shifts in the industrial distribution of employment in the first half of the decade were followed by shifts in more or less the opposite direction in the second half of the decade." (Gordon, *op. cit.,* p. 17.) Nevertheless, Gordon concludes that occupational differentials in mobility are more pronounced than industrial differentials, and that the industrial differentials she found were attributable primarily to differences in the occupational compositions of the various industrial groups, in the stability of employment, and in the relative rates of growth or decline in employment.

[75] Palmer, *Labor Mobility in Six Cities,* pp. 43, 57. Kitagawa found that the industrial differentials in mobility were largely independent of occupation, age, migrant status, and union membership (*op. cit.,* p. 46).

[76] Aaronson and Keller, *op. cit.,* p. 20, Chart 2; p. 80, Table 33.

[77] Anthracite mining; textile mill products; banks and trust companies; telephone, telegraph, and related services; insurance carriers; electric and gas utilities.

in another six groups,[78] at least half of the workers made such changes. It appears that use of the broad divisions of industry in analyzing the degree of mobility conceals rather pronounced differentials among the smaller and more homogeneous industrial groups.

Concerning the *patterns* of job shifts made by workers in the various industrial divisions, perhaps the most noteworthy finding of the six-city survey is that the simultaneous change of employer, occupation, and industry was the most common type of job change in *every* division. In no major industrial division did this complex type of shift account for fewer than 45 percent of the job changes made by men or 41 percent of those by women. However, certain variations among industrial divisions should be mentioned. Male construction workers were more likely to change employers only, and correspondingly less likely to make the complex shift than were men in any other division. Shifts of employer and industry were relatively more common among male manufacturing workers than among other groups. Men in transportation, communications, and utilities had a higher than average proportion of the complex type of shift. Women in manufacturing showed a greater tendency than other groups to make shifts involving employer and industry, while those in wholesale and retail trade had the highest proportion of complex shifts.[79]

Variations in Mobility among Specific Occupations and Industries. The evidence on occupational and industrial differences in mobility thus far reviewed has been based almost entirely on comparisons among major occupational groups and industrial divisions. Although there is no systematic body of data relating to narrower categories, numerous studies suggest that occupational and industrial variations in mobility characteristics are much greater than is indicated by examination of the broader categories. These studies cannot be summarized in detail here, but a few examples may be noted. Among skilled workers those in the textile trades are known to have a particularly high degree of attachment to their occupations and industry.[80] Machinists and tool

---

[78] Water transportation, services allied to transportation, general building contractors, special trade contractors, general contractors other than building, and trucking and warehousing for hire.

[79] Palmer, *Labor Mobility in Six Cities*, pp. 64, 80.

[80] See Gladys L. Palmer, *Ten Years of Work Experience of Philadelphia Weavers and Loom Fixers*, pp. 52–57, and "The Mobility of Weavers in Three Textile Centers," *Quarterly Journal of Economics*, 55:460–487 (May 1941); Gladys L. Palmer and Constance Williams, *Reemployment of Philadelphia Hosiery Workers after*

and die makers are another group whose occupational attachment is apparently greater than that of most other skilled workers. A recent study of the work histories of tool and die makers during 1940–51 showed that after qualifying at their trade, more than 90 percent worked only at that occupation during the 11-year period.[81] On the other hand, a study of all workers in skilled occupations in six cities indicated that as many as a fourth of the workers had been in at least two skilled occupations during the same period.[82] Even within the narrow occupational category of machinists and tool and die makers, mobility characteristics are apparently affected by the particular industry to which the worker is usually attached.[83] Also, among such a relatively homogeneous group as physical scientists, differences in the extent of interdisciplinary movement (occupational mobility) have been found between physicists on the one hand, and chemists and biologists on the other.[84] It must not be thought, therefore, that the major occupational and industrial groups of workers are even roughly homogeneous with respect to their mobility characteristics. Indeed, the intragroup variation in degree and patterns of mobility may be even greater than the variation among groups.

DIRECTION OF INTEROCCUPATIONAL AND INTERINDUSTRIAL JOB SHIFTING

In order to assess the degree to which the existing labor force can adjust to changes in the occupational and industrial structure of labor demand, it is not sufficient to know the mobility characteristics of various occupational and industrial groups of workers. Information is also required on the direction of the job changes they make, in order eventually to make it possible to predict from what industrial and occupational sources workers could most likely be drawn into expanding occupations and industries. In addition to their usefulness for de-

Shut-downs in 1933–34, p. 46; Carrie Glasser and Bernard N. Freedman, "Work and Wage Experience of Skilled Cotton-Textile Workers," Monthly Labor Review, 63:8–15 (July 1946).

[81] U. S. Bureau of Labor Statistics, The Mobility of Tool and Die Makers, 1940–1951, p. 5.

[82] Myers and Shultz, "Patterns of Mobility of Skilled Workers and Factors Affecting Their Occupational Choice, Six Cities, 1940–51," p. 41.

[83] U. S. Bureau of Labor Statistics, The Mobility of Tool and Die Makers, 1940–1951, p. 7; Helen Herrmann, Ten Years of Work Experience of Philadelphia Machinists, p. 66.

[84] U. S. Bureau of Labor Statistics, Occupational Mobility of Scientists, p. 15.

veloping labor supply models, data on the direction of occupational and industrial shifts are pertinent to analysis of the motivation and labor market behavior of workers. If workers in each occupation make random moves into all other occupations, it may be concluded not only that skills are largely interchangeable, but also that the occupational attachment of shifting workers is extremely weak or nonexistent. If, on the other hand, the pattern of occupational changes shows distinct tendencies for movement to take place between related occupations, it may be concluded that occupational attachment is largely an attachment to a rather broad field of work, rather than to relatively specific operations. The evidence on these questions is quite meager, and most of it relates to the movement of workers among major occupational groups and industrial divisions rather than among narrower categories. As a result, the findings reviewed in this section are of more value in illustrating the type of research that remains to be done, using more detailed classification systems, than in pointing to any definite conclusions.

Interoccupational Shifts. Davidson and Anderson have reported that 56 percent of all the occupational shifts made by a sample of gainfully employed workers since they entered the labor force were from one major occupational level to another.[85] When the workers were classified according to the level of their regular occupation, every level was found to include workers who had worked at every other, except that unskilled workers had never held professional jobs.[86] A majority of all shifts, however, were either within a single occupational level or between two contiguous levels.[87] Reynolds likewise found that a majority of his sample of manual workers had spent their careers either within one level of skill or in two adjacent levels; only 10 percent had ever been in supervisory, technical, or managerial positions.[88]

The survey of labor mobility in six cities provides evidence that although none of the major occupational groups is without some movement of workers across its boundaries, there is considerable variation in the extent of such movement. Analysis of the work histories of San Francisco workers indicates that the professional group tends to con-

85 Percy E. Davidson and H. Dewey Anderson, *Occupational Mobility in an American Community*, p. 180.
86 *Ibid.*, p. 88.
87 *Ibid.*, p. 180.
88 Reynolds, *op. cit.*, pp. 134–136.

stitute a relatively "closed" occupational category—that is, compara-
tively few workers moved into this category from other occupational
groups in either the first or the last half of the 1940's. This was true
for both men and women. In the clerical group a similar, but weaker,
tendency prevailed: movement into this group from other occupational
categories was less than what would have been expected had intergroup
changes in occupation been purely random. Among women, the sales
and managerial categories appeared to be relatively "open," since
rather large proportions of women employed in those occupations
in 1944 and 1949 had been in other occupational groups in 1940 and
1944, respectively. Among men, shifts into the laborer category were
relatively numerous in each of the two five-year periods. For all other
occupational groups the evidence for the two halves of the decade is
conflicting. For example, a relatively high percentage of men who were
craftsmen in 1944 had been in other occupational groups in 1940;
but a relatively low percentage of the men who were craftsmen in
1949 had been in other occupational groups in 1944. These differences,
of course, reflect the different economic trends in the war and postwar periods.[89]

Evidence on the *direction* of intergroup occupational shifts is even
more fragmentary than on the relative "porousness" of the walls around
occupational groups. The San Francisco study contains some clues as
to the direction of occupational job shifts made by men during the
1940's. These may be summarized as follows:

1. The managerial group exchanged workers with both manual and
nonmanual occupational groups. The considerable interchange between the managerial group on the one hand and the craftsmen and
operatives groups on the other probably represented movement into
and out of self-employment.

2. The skilled group (craftsmen, foremen, and kindred workers)
drew workers rather widely from other occupational levels, but prin-

[89] Margaret S. Gordon, "The Mobility of San Francisco Workers, 1940–1949,"
unpublished report, University of California Industrial Relations Section (Berkeley,
November 1951), Chapter 3. The analysis in this paragraph is based principally on
data in Appendix Table A-10. For purposes of this analysis the numbers of persons in different occupational groups were converted to percentages of the total
number of workers employed on both dates under consideration. It should be noted
that the conclusions drawn in the report are somewhat more conservative than those
presented here. Only professional workers and female clerical workers are referred
to as constituting relatively "closed" occupational groups (p. 23).

cipally from the operatives. Workers who left the skilled group were fairly widely dispersed among other occupational groups, but a substantial portion of the movement was into the managerial group.

3. During the decade as a whole the operatives drew workers rather widely from, and similarly lost workers to, other occupational groups. In the postwar years, however, an important source of operatives was the group who had been skilled workers during the war.

4. The most common type of intergroup shift was from one manual category to another. Between 1940 and 1944 there were more changes from nonmanual to manual jobs than from manual to nonmanual occupations, but the reverse was true in the postwar period.[90]

Needless to say, a number of reservations must be made in accepting even these limited findings. They are based on an analysis of the status of workers at the beginning and end of two five-year periods and do not reflect whatever shifts may have intervened. Also, they pertain to a single labor market area during a single decade, and it is obvious that the direction of occupational shifts during any period is affected to a large degree by the structural changes that are taking place within the labor market. Indeed, it has been seen that the direction of intergroup occupational shifts in the San Francisco labor market differed between the war and the postwar periods. On the basis of all the evidence for San Francisco during the 1940's, Gordon concludes that "No single occupation group appears to be an outstandingly important 'source' of workers for any other group, although interchange between the craftsmen and operatives groups seems to play a role of some importance. There is also some evidence of interchange between the craftsmen and operatives groups, on the one hand, and the managerial group, on the other." [91]

It is fairly clear that skilled occupations during World War II were filled to a considerable extent by recruiting workers from other manual groups, principally the operatives; and this conclusion is supported by evidence from other studies. Of all the men covered by the six-city survey who were in skilled occupations in December 1944, and who had been employed in January 1940, almost a third had been in other occupational groups on the earlier date.[92] Assuming that the San Francisco experience was representative, the operatives contributed the

---

90 *Ibid.*, pp. 20–21.

91 *Ibid.*, pp. 23–24.

92 Computed from data included in the reports for individual cities. The exact percentage is 31.7.

largest single group of these recruits to the skilled occupations, and somewhat smaller proportions came from other manual groups and from nonmanual occupations.[93] The important contributions of other manual workers to the ranks of the skilled group are also shown by a study of the experience of workers covered by the six-city survey who were in skilled jobs at any time between 1940 and 1950,[94] and by a study of workers employed by war industries in 1945.[95]

The substantial movement between the semiskilled and the skilled categories raises the question of how semiskilled workers acquire the qualifications necessary for the performance of skilled jobs. Several studies have found that formal apprenticeship training plays a relatively minor role in the acquisition of skills. Of the workers covered by the six-city survey who had held skilled jobs at any time between 1940 and 1950, only a fifth had apprenticeship training, compared with a slightly larger percentage who "picked up" their trade either through informal plant training or accumulated experience.[96] Formal vocational education was also found to be uncommon among workers employed in a group of war industries during World War II. Some plants had short, formal training courses for new employees, but for the most part skill was acquired on the job.[97] On the other hand, about two thirds of the tool and die makers employed in representative industries in 1951 had learned their trade through apprenticeship. It is interesting that even among these "aristocrats" of skilled labor, a majority of those without apprenticeship training had "picked up" the trade while working in tool rooms or as machine tool operators.[98]

The foregoing evidence may have important implications for mobilization planning but must be interpreted cautiously in any case.

[93] Gordon, "The Mobility of San Francisco Workers, 1940–1949," Table 11.

[94] Myers and Shultz, "Patterns of Mobility of Skilled Workers and Factors Affecting Their Occupational Choice, Six Cities, 1940–51," p. x.

[95] U. S. Bureau of Labor Statistics, *Worker Mobility and Skill Utilization in World War II*, pp. 11–13, 18.

[96] However, there was variation in the extent to which workers in specific occupations participated in formal training programs. More than half of the printing craftsmen, for example, had served apprenticeships. (Myers and Shultz, "Patterns of Mobility of Skilled Workers and Factors Affecting Their Occupational Choice, Six Cities, 1940–51," p. 61 and Appendix Table XXVI.)

[97] U. S. Bureau of Labor Statistics, *Worker Mobility and Skill Utilization in World War II*, p. 11.

[98] U. S. Bureau of Labor Statistics, *The Mobility of Tool and Die Makers, 1940–1951*, pp. 27–30.

Certainly it cannot be concluded that distinctions in skill are figments, and that manual workers are largely interchangeable. For one thing, the data concern only *numbers* of workers who transferred into skilled occupations without revealing anything about their competence. There is no measure of the extent to which the upgrading during the war was accompanied by a dilution in the quality of the work done. Second, how much of the "upgrading" was more nominal than real, and due to efforts of employers to circumvent wage stabilization restrictions is also unknown. Third, it is likely that the data reflect the great heterogeneity of the skilled categories in both the Census classification and that in the *Dictionary of Occupational Titles*.[99] In the truly highly skilled crafts, formal training programs appear still to be the rule. Finally, the data also reflect the wartime practice of "breaking down" jobs. There were many skilled metal workers during the war who performed a limited range of skilled duties but were not capable of executing the wide variety of jobs within their "trade" that can usually be performed by a highly skilled journeyman.[100] Further research is needed in order to determine the feasibility of staffing skilled jobs by upgrading. Nevertheless, it is not without significance that certain work processes ordinarily requiring the services of skilled workmen can be so engineered that nonskilled workers can quickly "pick up" the necessary degree of proficiency.

Interindustrial Shifts. The fact that workers change their industries more frequently than their occupations suggests that industrial attachment is weaker than occupational attachment. The question remains, however, whether shifts from one industry to another follow any distinct patterns or whether such shifts are essentially random. When workers move from industry A, is there a greater probability that they will move to B than to C? Reynolds has given this question considerable attention in his study of the New Haven labor market. He concludes, first, that when a worker changes jobs, the probability that he will take another job in the same industry is greater than would be expected on a random basis.[101] (Major industrial divisions are used in his analysis, except that manufacturing is divided into metalworking, apparel, and "all other manufacturing.") This conclusion is

99 See pp. 29–30 supra.

100 U. S. Bureau of Labor Statistics, *Worker Mobility and Skill Utilization in World War II*, p. 7, note 6.

101 Reynolds, *op. cit.*, pp. 34, 36.

94   RESEARCH ON LABOR MOBILITY

based on data showing that the percentage of accessions from within each industry is considerably higher than the ratio of employment in that industry to total employment in the area.

Second, Reynolds cites evidence that although expanding war industries drew rather equally on all other industries (relative to their size), nevertheless movement between certain pairs of industries in 1941, 1943, and 1946 was more pronounced than between others. Expressing the gross movement between each pair of industries as a percentage of the aggregate employment in the two industries, he notes that the trade and service industries show a high interchange of labor with each other and with manufacturing. Also, manufacturing industries show more interchange with each other than with nonmanufacturing industries, although the clothing industry "occupies a relatively isolated position." Construction seems to have a greater interchange with transportation and utilities than with other industries.[102]

Third, on the basis of the *lifetime* work histories of a sample of manual workers, Reynolds concludes that movement between industries is primarily random. Among workers who have made such shifts, he finds few distinctive relationships between the industries in which the workers are currently employed and the others in which they have served.[103] This conclusion appears to conflict with the second, but Reynolds reconciles the two by observing that although a worker, in making a single job shift, is more likely to go to certain industries than to others, "when one aggregates the entire past careers of workers in a particular industry their movements will have been so numerous and varied that neighborhood relationships between industries become blurred and indistinguishable. If a worker moves often enough, he will eventually run the gamut of industries; yet each one of these moves may have been influenced considerably by the industry of his last employment." [104]

Myers and Maclaurin, in their analysis of the interfirm movement of factory workers in a New England community between 1937 and 1939, imply that the geographic location of the firms in the labor market area was a more important factor than their industry in determining patterns of movement. Thus, there was more movement among the four industries located in one part of the labor market and among the three industries in another, than there was between

102 *Ibid.*, pp. 35–36; Appendix Tables A-10 and A-11, pp. 288–291.
103 *Ibid.*, pp. 30–32.
104 *Ibid.*, p. 36.

these two neighborhoods. To illustrate, a small woolen mill was separated from other textile firms in the community, and almost no movement occurred between it and the rest of the industry. That mill, however, which was located in the midst of the plastics and apparel industries, was involved in "half the movement between textiles, plastics, and apparel." [105]

Several studies dealing with the industrial "sources" of workers who moved into manufacturing industries during World War II also shed some light on patterns of shifts between industries.[106] In each of these studies, every major industrial division was found to have contributed workers to the war industries. Moreover, while there were variations in the patterns revealed, these were not so great that they could not be accounted for largely by variations in the industrial structures of the communities investigated. In an analysis of the sources of manufacturing employees hired in Columbus during four selected years of the 1940's, Parnes found that with a few minor exceptions each of the nonmanufacturing industries contributed workers roughly in proportion to its share of the total employment in the area.[107]

The evidence is not sufficient to warrant definite conclusions concerning patterns of industrial shifts. It seems probable that there are specific industries, and perhaps also major industrial divisions, among which movement is more frequent than among others, but these cannot yet be confidently identified. In any case, data showing the frequency of various kinds of job shifts are not adequate for the purpose because the patterns shown by such data are intimately affected not only by the industrial structure of the particular labor market area, but also by the relative rates of expansion and contraction of its industries.

Even if industrial movement is not random, its patterns may result from differences in the occupational structures of industries rather than from differences in their products or services (which is the basis for industrial differentiation). For example, if coal miners have a

[105] Charles A. Myers and W. Rupert Maclaurin, *The Movement of Factory Workers*, p. 27.

[106] See, for example, Kerr, *op. cit.*, pp. 146–148; Hilda W. Callaway, "Wilmington Shipbuilders During and After World War II," *Monthly Labor Review*, 62:873–874 (June 1946); Parnes, *A Study in the Dynamics of Local Labor Force Expansion*, p. 43.

[107] *Ibid.*, p. 49. Gordon found that while interindustrial movement in San Francisco between 1940 and 1949 was not entirely random, movement into most of the major industrial groups "did not depart significantly from a random pattern." ("The Relation of Gross to Net Changes in the Inter-Occupational and Inter-Industrial Movements of the Urban Labor Force," p. 42.)

greater propensity to move into the brick-making industry than into the clothing industry,[108] it is reasonable to assume that this is because there are more occupations that coal miners are able (or willing) to perform in the former industry than in the latter. If this is the case, the industrial variable may safely be ignored in many analyses of mobility. That is, if industrial attachment is only a reflection of attachment to employer or occupation, and if the direction of movement between industries is merely a function of their occupational compositions, then the concept of industrial flexibility in labor supply is superfluous. So long as workers are able and willing to change employers and to make specified occupational shifts, their current industrial affiliation becomes immaterial.[109]

SUMMARY

There is a substantial amount of movement into and out of jobs and into and out of the labor force in the United States. The number of job separations in a year is perhaps half as great as the number of jobs in the economy. Not all separations are evidence of the "propensity" of workers to make job changes. Some represent movement out of the labor force rather than between jobs. Moreover, a substantial proportion of separations are not voluntary at all, but result from layoffs and, to a much smaller extent, from discharges. The ratio between voluntary and total separations is intimately affected by economic conditions. During some of the depression years of the 1930's, for example, voluntary movement virtually disappeared. But during periods of business prosperity and expansion such as the 1920's and the 1940's, between two thirds and three fourths of the separations of workers are voluntary.

A major portion of the total movement among jobs is attributable to a minority of workers. Probably a fourth to a third of all workers

108 H. Makower, J. Marschak, and H. W. Robinson, "Studies in Mobility of Labour: Analysis for Great Britain, Part II," *Oxford Economic Papers*, No. 4 (September 1940), p. 50.

109 Gordon reaches a similar conclusion: "in the preparation of manpower estimates, we need to think in terms of the occupational requirements within the various industry groups and of the sources from which these requirements can be met, rather than in terms of inter-industry movement as such." ("The Relation of Gross to Net Changes in the Inter-Occupational and Inter-Industrial Movements of the Urban Labor Force," p. 43.) Cf. Palmer, *Labor Mobility in Six Cities*, p. 94.

change jobs during the course of a year—at least during years such as those of the 1940's—but it is an even smaller minority who make several job changes per year who account for most of the total movement. Moreover, the substantial number of workers who keep the same job for long periods indicates that to a large extent the same workers make job changes year after year.

When workers move from one employer to another they are more likely than not to change both their occupation and their industry, and the probability that they will make at least one of these changes appears to be approximately four to one. Of course, such a statement has meaning only if "industry" and "occupation" are defined. The reference here is to rather narrow, but not the narrowest, categories of occupations and industries, specifically to the three-digit codes used by the Bureau of the Census. If wider industrial and occupational classes are used—such as the major occupational groups and the major divisions of industry—the amount of shifting from one category to another is reduced, but is still considerable.

The findings of past research indicate a substantial amount of occupational and industrial flexibility in the labor supply, and also suggest that many workers do not have strong attachments to particular occupations and industries. However, the proportions that have been cited are based on the shifts made by those workers who *do* change jobs and therefore cannot be used to characterize the degree of occupational and industrial attachment of the work force as a whole. Many workers do not make *any* kind of job change.

In changing from one employer to another, workers tend to change their industry more readily than their occupation; this appears to be true whether one speaks in terms of broad or narrow categories. However, there can be a considerable amount of occupational movement within a single firm, and most studies of mobility have not attempted to measure the importance of this kind of "movement." Even when it is investigated, workers are probably less careful in reporting changes of occupational assignment within a firm than they are in reporting changes of employers. Job changes that involve a change of residence from one labor market area to another are much less frequent than changes of occupation or industry.

What has been said thus far relates to "workers" in the abstract. As would be expected, there is evidence that both the frequencies and the patterns of job shifts are affected by the kinds of jobs that workers hold. The differences in the mobility characteristics of various groups of workers cannot be precisely stated because of certain inadequacies in the methods that have been used in almost all the relevant studies. Comparisons of the past experience of workers have invariably been made on the basis of their *current* occupation and industry, and the amount of interoccupational and interindustrial shifting that takes place makes such an analysis unsatisfactory.

Nevertheless, there seems to be a rough inverse relationship between the socioeconomic status of an occupational group and its relative mobility. Thus, interfirm movement is least among professional workers and greatest among unskilled workers. The proportions of involuntary separations among all separations by the various occupational groups seem to follow the same pattern—professional workers show the lowest proportion and laborers the highest.

Geographic mobility is highest among professional workers, probably because the market for their services is more truly national in scope than it is for the other occupational categories. Farm laborers rank second in degree of geographic mobility. There is no clear evidence of any other occupational differentials in geographic mobility.

There are differences not only in number of job changes by workers in the various major occupational groups, but also in the kinds of changes. For example, professional workers, skilled workers, and female clerical workers are more likely than other groups to remain in the same occupation when they shift from one employer to another.

Industrial differences in mobility are considerably less evident than occupational differences. Construction workers appear to make more job shifts than workers in other major industrial divisions, and also to make more shifts that involve only a change of employer; but there are few, if any, other important differences. It is quite possible that any differences in the mobility of industrial groups result mainly from differences in their occupational compositions or from the atypical kinds of employment relationship that characterize such industries as construction and domestic service.

The variations found among the major occupational groups and among the major industrial divisions give an incomplete picture of occupational and industrial differences in mobility. There is evidence of substantial variation among specific occupations and industries within the larger groups, but these have not been systematically explored.

Probably less is known about the direction of occupational and industrial shifts than about any other facet of mobility. No study of the patterns of job shifts among specific occupations and industries has been made, and even the information on the direction of shifts among the major occupational and industrial groups leaves much to be desired.

4 SOME DETERMINANTS
OF LABOR MOBILITY

Inquiries into the factors that influence the amount and character of movement within and among labor markets have been of two basically different types. One of these attempts to discover whether there is a consistent relationship between the mobility of workers and their personal and status characteristics. For example, are there age or sex differences in mobility? Are there differences in mobility between union and non-union members? Are home owners less mobile than those who rent their homes? Studies of occupational and industrial differentials, discussed in the preceding chapter, constitute another example of this approach.

The second type of inquiry examines the institutional forces at work in a labor market and evaluates more or less deductively their impact on the willingness or ability of workers to make job changes. For example, do union policies appear to affect the volume or the incidence of involuntary job separations? Are seniority provisions in union contracts likely to reduce voluntary movement? What are the usual recruitment policies and the hiring standards of employers, and how do these affect the ability or the willingness of workers to make job changes? Do state unemployment compensation laws have any effect on the amount of voluntary or involuntary movement?

The difference between these two types of study is largely methodological. One might be tempted to assume that the first is concerned with the *personal* determinants of mobility and the second with *institutional* determinants, but there is no valid basis for such a distinction. Variations in mobility according to the personal characteristics of workers may actually reflect the influence of institutional factors. This point deserves elaboration. Unless labor market activity is regarded as essentially random, it must be assumed that a worker's behavior in the labor market—including the number and kinds of job shifts he makes—is determined by the interaction between his abilities and aspirations on the one hand and the environment in which he operates, or his perception of that environment, on the other. The environmental factors are clearly "institutional," but even the ostensibly subjective elements of motives, goals, and aspirations are institutionally conditioned. Each individual plays a number of culturally defined roles, and the situation is complicated by the fact that multiple roles are the rule rather than the exception. A worker may be at the same time a father, a union member, and a technician; or a bachelor and a professional person; or a widow and a factory operative; or a mother and an office worker. These roles may be reinforcing or conflicting in their effect on labor market activity, but the significant point is that each involves a more or less rigidly institutionalized pattern of behavior, and influences attitudes, values, and goals.

If a group of workers with a common characteristic are found to have a distinctive pattern of labor market behavior, there are three possible explanations. Consider the case of skilled workers, whose mobility has been seen to be less than that of unskilled workers. It may be that persons with certain temperaments and attitudes conducive to stability of employment are more likely to be attracted into skilled occupations than into others. Or their roles as skilled workers may instill in them the attitudes and goals that encourage stability. Or, finally, factors quite external to the worker—the way in which the labor market is organized, the personnel policies of employers, the opportunities for applying their skills elsewhere—may make frequent job shifts less feasible or less desirable. These three possibilities are of course not mutually exclusive. Any combination of them may account for particular differentials in mobility. It is possible, for example, that personality characteristics are selective in drawing workers into certain types of employment, and that the "role requirements" of jobs reinforce the characteristics that initially led workers into them.

Of the three sorts of factors described, only the first is in any real sense a *personal* as distinguished from an *institutional* determinant of mobility. Since institutional factors condition the way in which the worker perceives or responds to his environment, or in effect create different environments for different groups of workers, it is not possible to isolate the "personal" determinants of mobility by comparing the characteristics of mobile and immobile workers. Whether mobility differences among various groups of workers are "personal" or "institutional" can only be deduced by relating the observed differences in their behavior to what is known about their roles and about the characteristics of their labor market environment. In this connection it is noteworthy that, although there has been considerable research on the factors that motivate labor force behavior (see Chapter 5), no systematic attempt has been made to determine whether classes of workers with different mobility characteristics have correspondingly different motivational patterns. This is a significant gap in research, for it could at least provide a clue as to whether psychological or institutional factors are more important in explaining differences in the mobility characteristics of workers.

As has been observed, most empirical research on factors affecting labor mobility has involved comparisons of the work histories of employees classified according to readily ascertainable characteristics. The results of such studies are reviewed in the next section of this chapter. Where the evidence indicates that mobility is associated with a particular characteristic, possible explanations are suggested. The subsequent section of the chapter summarizes and evaluates the conclusions of studies concerning the influence of institutional factors on labor mobility.

Characteristics of Mobile Workers

Age. So universally has mobility been found to decline with advancing age that this relationship may be regarded as conclusively established.[1] There is some evidence, however, that workers in their teens may be no more mobile, or perhaps even less mobile, than workers in their early 20's.

Palmer's study of the work histories of Philadelphia weavers and loom fixers during 1926–35 showed that the average number of job separations decreased continuously with increases in the age of workers. Respondents under 30 years of age had about twice as many separations as those 60 and older.[2] During the same decade the proportion of skilled metal workers who made no interfirm shifts increased with increasing age.[3] Among male and female hosiery workers, also, the median number of job separations and interfirm shifts varied inversely with age.[4] In all these studies the age groups used in the analysis were 16–29, 30–44, and 45 and over.

---

[1] Kitagawa reports that age differentials in mobility were more pronounced in the six-city survey than differentials for any of the other ten factors she analyzed. (Evelyn M. Kitagawa, "Relative Importance—and Independence—of Selected Factors in Job Mobility, Six Cities, 1940–1949," p. 15.)

[2] Gladys L. Palmer, *Ten Years of Work Experience of Philadelphia Weavers and Loom Fixers,* p. 49.

[3] Helen Herrmann, *Ten Years of Work Experience of Philadelphia Machinists,* p. 116.

[4] Gladys L. Palmer and Constance Williams, *Reemployment of Philadelphia Hosiery Workers After Shut-downs in 1933–34,* p. 20.

Aaronson and Keller, using a 1 percent national sample of workers with Old-Age and Survivors Insurance wage credits in 1941 and 1942, found that the proportion of workers with more than one employer in each of these years varied inversely with age for both men and women and for both white and Negro workers. For 1942 the major age groups used were "under 25," 25–44, 45–64, and 65 and over. The decline in the proportion of workers with more than one employer during the year was continuous from the lowest to the highest age group. For example, 48 percent of the youngest group of white males worked for more than one employer, as compared with only 22 percent of those 65 and over. When workers under 25 were divided into those under 20 and those 20–24, a curious difference between white and Negro workers became apparent. For both male and female white workers the inverse relationship between age and mobility persisted; but among Negroes of both sexes relatively more workers in the older age group than in the younger had worked for more than one employer.[5] These results call attention to the fact that the age interval used in classifying the data may conceal relationships between age and mobility.

Bogue's study of a 1 percent sample of workers with Old-Age and Survivors Insurance wage credits in Ohio and Michigan in 1947 also found a pronounced inverse relationship between age and mobility. Comparison of the jobs held during the first and last quarters of the year showed that 44 percent of the workers under 20 years of age had made a change, as compared with only 14 percent of the workers over 60. Between these two extremes there was a continuous decline in the proportion of mobile workers as age increased. The pattern was the same for both women and men, except that there was no difference between male workers under 20 and those aged 20–24.[6]

A recent study by the Bureau of Labor Statistics related the number of job shifts made by tool and die makers between 1940 and 1951 to the ages of the workers at the time of the survey, as well as to the ages at which the job shifts were made. Both analyses indicated a decline in mobility with advancing age.[7] The average number of shifts per

[5] Franklin M. Aaronson and Ruth A. Keller, *Mobility of Workers in Employment Covered by Old-Age and Survivors Insurance*, pp. 70–71.

[6] Donald J. Bogue, *A Methodological Study of Migration and Labor Mobility in Michigan and Ohio in 1947*, p. 33.

[7] U. S. Bureau of Labor Statistics, *The Mobility of Tool and Die Makers, 1940–1951*, pp. 34–36. See p. 61 supra for a description of the method of analysis.

man-year was approximately the same for workers in each of the three
5-year age intervals between 20 and 34. In the 5-year intervals over 35
there was a continuous decline in the average number of job changes
made by workers.[8]

In the six-city survey the degree of mobility of both male and female
workers during 1940–49 was found to be negatively correlated with
their age at the time of the survey. For the six cities combined, men
25–34 years old held an average of 3.4 jobs during the decade. This
average dropped continuously for successive 10-year age groups, reach-
ing a low of 1.7 jobs for men 65 and over. Women 25–34 years old held
an average of 3.1 jobs, as compared with 1.6 for those 65 and over.[9]

Not only do older workers make fewer changes of employer than
younger workers, but when they do move their industrial and occupational mobility is lower. Palmer found that all types of shifts by
Philadelphia weavers and loom fixers—between firms, occupations,
and industries—decreased with increasing age.[10] The same result was
obtained in Herrmann's study of Philadelphia machinists.[11] Machinists
45 years old and over were less likely than younger men to make
complex job shifts involving the simultaneous change of employer,
occupation, and industry. In the six-city survey it was likewise found
that the complex job shift was more characteristic of the younger than
of the older workers during 1940–49. Of all the shifts made by male
workers under 55, over half involved a simultaneous change in employer, occupation, and industry; but only 43 percent of the shifts
made by workers 55–64 years old, and an even smaller proportion (38
percent) of the shifts made by workers 65 and over, were of this type.[12]

The geographic movement of workers also declines with advancing
age. Bogue's study of Ohio and Michigan workers showed that the
proportion of workers 60 years of age and over who changed their
county of employment between the first and last quarters of 1947 was
only a third as great as the proportion of workers under 25 who made
similar changes.[13] Comparable results were obtained by Aaronson and
Keller, who found that persons who worked in more than one state

8 *Ibid.*, p. 36.

9 Gladys L. Palmer, *Labor Mobility in Six Cities*, p. 53.

10 Palmer, *Ten Years of Work Experience of Philadelphia Weavers and Loom
Fixers*, p. 50.

11 Herrmann, *op. cit.*, pp. 60–61.

12 Palmer, *Labor Mobility in Six Cities*, p. 76.

13 Bogue, *op. cit.*, p. 31.

were between two and three times as numerous among workers under 25 as among those 65 and over.[14] However, the data in both these studies suggest that workers under 20, and particularly men, are somewhat less likely to make geographic shifts than workers aged 20–29. The results of the Census Bureau's survey of internal migration between March 1949 and March 1950 tend to confirm these findings. For both men and women in the labor force, peak migration rates were found among workers 18–24 years old, 9 percent of whom changed their county of residence between 1949 and 1950. Among workers 14–17 years old, the proportion was about 6 percent for both sexes. From the peak at ages 18–24, migration rates declined continuously to less than 2 percent for workers 65 and over.[15]

The explanation of the inverse relationship between age and labor mobility is probably complex and may involve a number of reinforcing factors. The high mobility of extremely young workers is doubtless attributable in part to part-time and temporary jobs held while attending school. Ten-year work histories for persons, say, 25 years of age would be expected to include at least several years, and perhaps as many as five or six, during which the workers' chief activity was school.

Another reason for higher mobility among younger workers is suggested by Reynolds on the basis of his study of the attitudes, labor market behavior, and work histories of manual workers in New Haven. The early years in the labor market comprise a period of adjustment, according to Reynolds, during which the worker "shops" for jobs by actually trying them. A manual worker's choice of his first job is generally haphazard, at least if judged by the rather rigid standards of rationality imposed by traditional economic theory. Jobs that are satisfactory to the worker are frequently found by a process of trial and error.[16]

The same hypothesis is offered by Ginzberg and others in their study of the process of occupational choice, specifically of professional careers. They conclude that such a choice is not the result of a single decision,

[14] Aaronson and Keller, op. cit., p. 27.

[15] Current Population Reports: Population Characteristics, Series P-20, No. 36 (December 9, 1951), computed from data in Table 7.

[16] Lloyd G. Reynolds, The Structure of Labor Markets, p. 40. For a much earlier but less fully developed recognition of the "job shopping" idea, see Sumner H. Slichter, The Turnover of Factory Labor (New York: D. Appleton and Company, 1919), p. 81.

but rather a "developmental process" which takes place over a period
of perhaps six to ten years. They hypothesize that the "exploration"
phase of this process, which college students experience by being ex-
posed to different fields and courses, is analogous to the job shifting of
young workers: "It is our belief . . . that the early years at work
represent for the lower income group a counterpart of the learning
experiences the upper income group secures from college and post-
graduate studies. The specific parallel is the exploration and testing
during these years—for one group, on the job, and for the other, in
school. Individuals from both groups hesitate to commit themselves
until they have experienced this period of exploration and testing." [17]

The casual labor force attachment of persons of school age and the
job shopping that apparently characterizes early participation in the
labor force are not sufficient explanations of the relationship between
age and mobility, for they fail to account for the continuous decline
in mobility beyond, say, age 30 or 35. Institutional and psychological
factors are also influential. The fact that employers' hiring preferences
make it more difficult for older workers to find jobs is unquestionably
responsible in part for their lower voluntary mobility.[18] The attractiveness of any job currently held is enhanced if the availability of alternatives is limited. Quite aside from this factor, the value that workers
attach to stability and security may increase as they grow older.

The inverse relationship between the likelihood that a worker will
make a voluntary job change and his length of service in his present
job is well established; [19] and older workers are obviously more likely
to have accumulated longer periods of service in their jobs than
younger ones. On the basis of his study of New Haven manual workers, Reynolds concludes that "the propensity to move . . . is slight
after three years and negligible after ten years of work in the same
plant." [20] Of the workers in his sample who had voluntarily changed

[17] Eli Ginzberg, Sol W. Ginsburg, Sidney Axelrad, and John L. Herma, *Occupational Choice: An Approach to a General Theory* (New York: Columbia University
Press, 1951), p. 214.

[18] Kerr emphasizes employers' hiring preferences in accounting for the disproportionate number of young workers among the migrants to the Seattle labor market
area during World War II. ("Migration to the Seattle Labor Market Area, 1940–
1942," pp. 144, 154.)

[19] See Sumner H. Slichter, *The Turnover of Factory Labor*, pp. 44–57; W. S.
Woytinsky, *Three Aspects of Labor Dynamics*, pp. 39–41; Charles A. Myers and W.
Rupert Maclaurin, *The Movement of Factory Workers*, p. 33.

[20] Reynolds, *op. cit.*, p. 21.

jobs between August 1945 and the date of the interview in 1947, more than 4 out of 10 had served less than a year in the job that they left, and more than 7 out of 10 had served less than three years. On the other hand, only about 1 in 20 had served longer than 10 years, and less than 1 percent, longer than 20 years. Among those who had not voluntarily changed jobs during the period, over half had at least 10 years' service, and as many as a fourth had held their jobs for 20 years or longer.[21]

Since age and length of service are clearly related, it is reasonable to conclude that age differentials in mobility reflect differentials in seniority on the job. In other words, to some extent it is the lengthy service, rather than age per se, that reduces the worker's propensity to make a change. There is danger of oversimplification in this kind of analysis, however. Greater length of service is not an *explanation* of *past* immobility, but a *description* or *measure* of it. A worker who has served 20 years in a single job has, by definition, not made a job shift in that length of time. He has been immobile. Conversely, a worker can be mobile during a period of time only by having at least one job and failing to serve continuously in it, and the shorter his length of service in successive jobs, the greater their number, and the more "mobile" he has been. There is a necessary relation between length of service and number of jobs held, and neither can be used to explain the other. Extended length of service can and does explain the reluctance of an employee to leave his *current* job. Thus, the foregoing comments do not refute the conclusion that the probability of a voluntary job separation decreases as an employee's length of service in a particular job increases, nor do they detract from the significance of that conclusion. They do indicate that care must be taken in interpreting data on length of service and degree of mobility.

That the probability of a voluntary separation declines with increasing length of service can be explained by several factors. Regardless of the inherent attractiveness of any job, certain formal and informal prerogatives are concomitants of lengthy service. Job security is perhaps the most obvious of these. Where union contracts with seniority provisions are in effect, the employee with long service is guaranteed greater security than his co-worker with short service. Even in the absence of unionization the seniority principle is rather widely accepted and is more or less rigidly adhered to in sizable sectors of the labor force —particularly among white collar workers. Whether due to contract or

[21] *Ibid.,* p. 22.

custom, the security attached to lengthy service affects mobility of long-service employees in two ways: (1) Involuntary separations tend to be concentrated among short-service workers. (2) The greater "job rights" of long-service workers tend to make them think longer and harder about giving up their jobs, particularly when alternative opportunities are limited or when it is feared that they may become so.

Security is not the only economic advantage accruing from long service. Such perquisites as promotion opportunities, pension rights, and bonus rights frequently depend—again, either by contract or custom—on length of service. Moreover, long-service employees are more likely than those with short service to have reached the top of the ladder of jobs to which they can aspire. Hence, they are less likely than short-service workers to make voluntary job shifts for self-advancement.

In addition to the economic prerogatives associated with long service there are certain noneconomic, relatively intangible, advantages which probably exert an immobilizing influence on the worker. The prestige associated with being an "old-timer" is one of these. The long-service employee is likely to know the job better and to be more familiar with company policies and traditions than his junior colleague, and thus can serve in the ego-satisfying role of teacher and counsellor. Such opportunities for self-expression are generally hard to obtain in a new job, and it would be strange if they did not strengthen the bond between a long-service worker and his job. There is the further influence of habitual activity patterns, which becomes stronger the longer such patterns are uninterrupted. To a person who for many years has gone daily to the same place of work, perhaps at the same time and by the same route, the prospect of a change may be painful. There may be comfort in a familiar routine, a familiar environment, and a familiar circle of friends. In assessing the influence of such factors on the willingness of long-service workers to change jobs, it must be remembered that in most cases such a change would involve substituting the unknown for the intimately familiar.[22]

The positive relationship between age and length of service raises the question whether the differentials in mobility among various age groups may not be wholly explainable in terms of intercorrelations between age and other measurable variables. Is it possible, for example, that age differentials in mobility are simply the combined results of

[22] In most voluntary separations, workers quit jobs and then look for new ones, rather than quitting with a new job already lined up. See pp. 149n, 159–160 infra.

differentials in length of service, income, and skill? Questions of this kind may be raised with respect to any variable whose relation to mobility is investigated. There are no definitive answers to such questions at present, for relatively few studies of labor mobility have done more than recognize the problem of intercorrelated variables; [23] and those that have attempted to isolate the effect of a single variable upon mobility have come nowhere near controlling all the relevant factors. Kitagawa's analysis of the data collected in the six-city survey showed that the inverse relationship between age and mobility remained unchanged when various combinations of the factors of migrant status, marital status, occupation, industry, education, time spent in the labor force, and veteran status were held constant.[24] Similarly, Bogue's study of the job shifts made by Michigan and Ohio workers showed that the age differentials in mobility persisted even when the mobility rates were standardized for annual income and several other factors.[25] Reynolds found an inverse relationship between age and voluntary movement when length of service was held constant, although the relationship was very slight.[26] These findings, together with the wide variety of groups of workers which show the same pattern, suggest that the inverse relation between age and mobility is to some extent independent of other characteristics of workers.

Sex. Mobility rates for men and women have been compared in numerous studies, but the resulting evidence is inconclusive. Most studies have reported higher mobility among men, but the number of investigations that have found no significant difference or have reported higher mobility among women is too large to be ignored. Two important problems which have received insufficient attention complicate any analysis of mobility differentials between men and women. First, pronounced differences in the length of time spent in the labor force by men and women of like ages may result in statistical measures of mobility that are not at all indicative of their relative propensities to change jobs. Second, because of differences in the occupational composition of the male and female labor force, variations in mobility rates and patterns between men and women may be more a function of occupation than of sex.

23 An outstanding exception is the recent study by Evelyn M. Kitagawa, *op. cit.*; cf. pp. 59–60 supra.
24 *Ibid.*, pp. 16–17.
25 Bogue, *op. cit.*, p. 66.
26 Reynolds, *op. cit.*, p. 22.

The 10-year work histories of several groups of Philadelphia workers collected in the 1930's by Palmer and her associates pointed rather strongly to the conclusion that women change their jobs less frequently than men. Among hosiery workers the number of job separations and interfirm shifts during 1926–35 indicated greater job stability on the part of women.[27] In the radio industry, also, women had fewer job separations than men during the decade, and a larger proportion of women had no job separations. On the other hand, the median duration of jobs at the usual occupation was greater for men than for women. Interpretation of these relationships is somewhat difficult, because the men in this industry were older than the women and had considerably longer exposure to the labor force during the period under examination.[28] Among weavers the median number of job separations per worker was higher for men than for women in each of three cities studied. However, the median duration of job was greater for men in one city, greater for women in a second, and about equal for the two groups in the third. These seemingly paradoxical results are probably attributable to the fact that women had more separations followed by time out of the labor force, and more months outside the labor force, than did men.[29]

Bogue's study of the mobility of Ohio and Michigan workers in 1947, which differed from the Philadelphia studies in design, showed no difference between the proportions of women and men who made job changes *within* a local labor market, but a substantially higher proportion of men than of women who made *intercounty* job changes. As a result of their greater geographic mobility, therefore, the proportion of mobile men was higher than that of women, the percentages being 36 and 29 respectively.[30]

Aaronson and Keller's somewhat similar study of a national sample of workers with Old-Age and Survivors Insurance wage credits showed that relatively more men than women worked for more than one employer in each of the years 1941–43. The difference was greatest in 1941, when slightly over a third of the men and about a fourth of the women held more than one job covered by the program. In 1943, on

[27] Palmer and Williams, *op. cit.*, p. 18.

[28] Gladys L. Palmer, "Interpreting Patterns of Labor Mobility," in E. Wight Bakke and others, *Labor Mobility and Economic Opportunity*, pp. 47–67.

[29] Gladys L. Palmer, "The Mobility of Weavers in Three Textile Centers," *Quarterly Journal of Economics*, 55:479 (May 1941).

[30] Bogue, *op. cit.*, p. 14.

the other hand, the percentages of men and women having more than one employer were similar, 38 and 35 percent respectively.[31] With regard to geographic movement, in each year relatively more men than women worked in more than one state, but the difference was least in 1943 when the percentages were 11.5 for men and 9 for women.[32]

The 17-year work histories of government clerical workers employed in the Columbus area in 1948 showed more job shifting among men than among women, although the difference was slight. Many of the job shifts made by women appeared to be incidental to their movement out of and back into the labor force, since women had almost twice as many withdrawals from the labor force lasting six months or longer.[33] The implications of this finding are not entirely clear. It might be argued that many of the job shifts made by women did not reflect a propensity to change jobs, but to move into and out of the labor force, and that were it not for this characteristic of women the difference in the amounts of direct job movement by men and women would be even greater. On the other hand, since men were in the labor force longer than women, it might be argued that their higher mobility reflected a greater *potential* for movement rather than a greater *propensity* to change jobs.[34]

The six-city survey provides the most comprehensive recent data on the relative mobility of men and women: the number of civilian jobs held and the number of interfirm shifts made by men and women between 1940 and 1949 are classified by age, occupation, and length of time in the labor force, so that the effects of the different factors can be taken into account. The differences between men and women in the average numbers of jobs held during the decade were slight. In the six cities combined, men held an average of 2.7 jobs, compared with 2.5

[31] Aaronson and Keller, *op. cit.,* p. 31.

[32] *Ibid.,* p. 26.

[33] Herbert S. Parnes, "Government Employment in Franklin County, Ohio, and Its Relation to the Local Labor Market" (unpublished Ph.D. dissertation, Ohio State University, 1950), pp. 301–304.

[34] A study of the job changes made by a sample of St. Paul workers between July 1941 and June 1942 showed men to be more mobile than women. (Herbert G. Heneman, Jr., "Differential Short-Run Labor Mobilities: St. Paul, 1941–42," in *Minnesota Manpower Mobilities,* University of Minnesota Industrial Relations Center, Bulletin 10, pp. 37–39.) On the other hand, analysis of the one- and five-year work histories of 98 mobile Minneapolis workers produced inconclusive results. (Herbert G. Heneman, Jr., Harland Fox, and Dale Yoder, "Patterns of Manpower Mobility, Minneapolis, 1948," *ibid.,* pp. 6–12.)

for women.[35] This pattern prevailed in each of the six cities covered by the survey. For the six cities combined, the mobility of men was higher in all age groups, and the differential was most pronounced at ages 35–44. In this age group men held an average of 3.0 jobs during the decade, compared with 2.6 for women.[36]

When the respondents are classified according to the major occupational group and the major industrial group of the longest job held in 1950, the sex differential in mobility tends to persist but varies notably in size. In one occupational group—clerical and kindred workers—women held a greater number of jobs than men. Among professional workers there was no difference in the mobility of men and women. Among craftsmen, on the other hand, where the difference was greatest, the average number of jobs held by men was 2.8 as compared with only 2.0 held by women. Men employed in manufacturing in 1950 held an average of 2.6 jobs between 1940 and 1949, while women held an average of 2.5. At the other extreme, the average for men in public utilities and in trade was greater than that for women by almost .5.[37]

Analysis of the relationship between mobility and length of time in the labor force during the decade shows that the higher mobility of men is concentrated almost exclusively among those workers with less than full-time participation in the labor force. Table 2 shows the average number of jobs held by workers in the six cities, by sex and number of months in the labor force. For the six cities combined there was no difference between the amount of job movement by men and women with full-time participation in the labor force—that is, those who were in the labor force for at least 115 of the 120 months in the period. However, among persons who were in the labor force for only part of the period, the average number of jobs held by men was substantially higher than that held by women. This was true of the group with the fewest months in the labor force as well as of the intermediate group.

The proportions of men and women with only one employer during the period 1940–49 show somewhat the same pattern as their

[35] However, Kitagawa found that with age, marital status, and migrant status held constant simultaneously, the size of the differential almost doubled. This resulted mainly from the fact that women were relatively more numerous than men in the younger migrant groups, whose mobility was high. (*Op. cit.*, p. 21.)

[36] Palmer, *Labor Mobility in Six Cities*, p. 53.

[37] *Ibid.*, pp. 56–57.

TABLE 2. MEAN NUMBER OF JOBS HELD BY WORKERS IN SIX CITIES,
BY SEX AND TIME IN LABOR FORCE, 1940–49

| | | | Number of months in labor force | | | | | |
| | Total | | 115–120 | | 60–114 | | Less than 60 | |
City	Men	Women	Men	Women	Men	Women	Men	Women
San Francisco	3.0	2.7	2.6	2.3	4.1	3.4	2.7	2.4
New Haven	2.6	2.3	2.1	1.9	3.6	3.0	2.7	2.2
St. Paul	2.6	2.5	2.1	2.0	3.4	3.2	3.0	2.3
Chicago	2.5	2.4	2.2	2.2	3.4	3.0	2.5	2.0
Los Angeles	3.2	3.0	2.9	2.8	3.9	3.4	2.9	2.4
Philadelphia	2.4	2.1	2.0	2.0	3.3	2.6	2.4	1.8
6 cities combined	2.7	2.5	2.3	2.3	3.6	3.1	2.7	2.1

Source: Gladys L. Palmer, *Labor Mobility in Six Cities*, p. 54.

average numbers of jobs. Among workers with at least 115 months in the labor force during the decade, equal proportions of men and women worked for only one employer (48 percent of the men and 47 percent of the women). On the other hand, of those with less than full-time participation in the labor force, two fifths of the women and only one fourth of the men had only one employer.[38] As might be expected, a much larger proportion of women than of men spent less than full time in the labor force. Only a tenth of the men and as many as a fourth of the women were in the labor force less than 60 months during the decade, while two thirds of the men and only two fifths of the women were in the labor force 115 months or longer.[39]

The foregoing data illustrate the difficulties involved in attempting to interpret measures of the relative mobility of women and men. Because men have much greater continuity of labor force participation, their higher mobility cannot be assumed to indicate a greater propensity to change jobs. So far as propensity to shift jobs is concerned, the six-city survey provides a reasonable basis for assuming that mobility does not differ between women and men, since women

[38] Gladys L. Palmer, "The Mobility of Workers in Six Cities, 1940–1949," unpublished manuscript, University of Pennsylvania Industrial Research Department (January 1952), computed from Appendix Table 19.
[39] *Ibid.*

continuously attached to the labor force during the decade made as many job changes as men, and since there was no appreciable difference between the incidence of layoffs among women and men.[40]

The fact that considerably more job shifts were made by men with less than full time in the labor force than by women in this category is probably attributable to differences in their ages, and to the circumstances accounting for their being in the labor force less than full time. For example, of the women in the San Francisco sample who were in the labor force for fewer than 60 months during the decade, 63 percent were 35 years of age and over in 1951, as compared with only 26 percent of the corresponding group of men.[41] In other words, three fourths of the men with less than 5 years in the labor force during the decade were young men whose full-time participation was prevented either by military service or by their being still in school at the beginning of the decade, or by both of these factors. Almost two thirds of the women, on the other hand, were well beyond school age at the beginning of the decade, and half of these had only one employer while in the labor force. The men and women in this category thus do not appear to be comparable either in age or in the strength of their attachment to the labor force. Many of the jobs reported by the men were undoubtedly part-time or temporary, while attending school; others were held during the period of "job shopping "that ordinarily characterizes the early years in the labor force; still other job shifts were occasioned by the interruption of work by military service. The women in this category typically appear to have entered the labor force for relatively brief periods, when already well past youth, under the stimulus of the high

[40] Layoffs accounted for 25 percent of the job separations of men and for 23 percent of the separations of women. (Palmer, *Labor Mobility in Six Cities,* pp. 68–69.) There is additional evidence that some of the differences in the mobility characteristics of men and women can be explained by differences in labor force exposure. Palmer and Miller found that a much larger percentage of the men than of the women in the six-city survey were "career" workers, i.e., had strong attachments to a particular occupation or field of work. But considering only persons who had been in the labor force more or less continuously throughout the decade, men and women had almost identical proportions of "career" workers. (Gladys L. Palmer and Ann R. Miller, "Work-Attachment Patterns in Six Cities," unpublished manuscript, University of Pennsylvania Industrial Research Department, June 1953, p. 5.) For a fuller discussion of this study, see pp. 172–174 infra.

[41] Margaret S. Gordon, "The Mobility of San Francisco Workers, 1940–1949," unpublished manuscript, University of California Institute of Industrial Relations (Berkeley, November 1951), computed from data in Table A-16.

levels of employment during the 1940's. If this interpretation of the data is valid, the differences in the mobility of men and women with less than full time in the labor force probably would disappear if the measures were standardized for age and veteran status, but the available tabulations do not permit the testing of this hypothesis.[42]

The *patterns* of mobility of men and women do differ, whatever may be true of their relative propensities to make job changes. Women make considerably more changes in labor force status than do men. The number of women who enter the labor force each month and the number who leave it are considerably higher than the corresponding numbers of men, despite the more than two-to-one preponderance of men in the total labor force.[43] It is also probable that male workers make more geographic job shifts. In studies based on Old-Age and Survivors Insurance wage records, both interstate and intercounty moves were found to be consistently more frequent among men than among women (pp. 110–111 supra). Census surveys of the migration status of a national sample of the labor force point to the same conclusion, although the Census Bureau has been somewhat guarded in drawing definite conclusions from its data because the differences between the migration rates of men and women have not been statistically significant.[44] The persistence of slightly higher migration rates for men in numerous Census surveys, however, provides a basis for the belief that there are real though perhaps slight differences in the geographic mobility of men and women, and that if the Census samples were larger the differences would prove to be statistically significant.

Results of the six-city survey show that women were less likely than men to change their occupations when they shifted from one employer to another, but were about as likely as the men to change industries. Men made relatively more shifts involving the simultaneous change of occupation, industry, and employer, while women had a higher proportion of shifts involving a change of employer and industry, with

42 Cf. Palmer, *Labor Mobility in Six Cities,* pp. 46–47. She concludes that "differences in labor force exposure operate to reduce observed differentials in mobility between men and women, if not to eliminate them."

43 "Gross Changes in the Labor Force," *Current Population Reports: Labor Force,* Series P-59, Nos. 18–29 (August 25, 1950 – July 20, 1951).

44 *Current Population Reports: Labor Force,* Series P-50, No. 10 (October 22, 1948), p. 1; No. 20 (March 17, 1950), p. 1; *Current Population Reports: Population Characteristics,* Series P-20, No. 36 (December 9, 1951), Table 6; No. 47 (September 27, 1953), Table 4.

no occupational change. There were no pronounced differences between men and women in the proportion of shifts of employer only or of simultaneous changes in employer and occupation.[45]

Race. Few studies have investigated the relationship between race and mobility, largely because samples of workers usually have been too small to permit reliable estimates of mobility by race. The available data, however, suggest that Negroes make more job shifts than whites, at least so far as male workers are concerned.

On the basis of a comparison of job status in the first and last quarters of 1947, Bogue found that Negro workers in jobs covered by Old-Age and Survivors Insurance in Ohio and Michigan were more mobile than non-Negroes. Two fifths of the former and one third of the latter held different jobs in the first and last quarters of the year. The difference between the two groups was due exclusively to the higher mobility of Negro men. Negro women were slightly less mobile than non-Negro women, while 44 percent of Negro men and only 34 percent of non-Negro men made job changes. Furthermore, the former were more mobile than the latter with respect to every type of movemen that could be investigated with the data. Higher percentages of Negroes than of non-Negroes made intracounty changes of employer, intracounty changes in industry, and job changes between counties.[46]

Very similar results were obtained by Aaronson and Keller in their study of a national sample of workers covered by the same program. In both 1941 and 1942 larger proportions of Negro than of white workers had more than one employer, and as in Bogue's study the differences were due entirely to the greater mobility of Negro men. In 1942, 53 percent of the Negro men worked for more than one employer, compared with 40 percent of the white men. The differential was found in all age groups but was more pronounced toward the middle of the age distribution than at the extremes. Among women, on the other hand, and particularly those under 45, a larger proportion of whites than of Negroes had more than one job.[47] It must be borne in mind in interpreting these results that domestic service is more common among Negro than among white women, and that prior to 1951 no domestic servants were covered by the social security program. Since the war and postwar years saw considerable movement

[45] Palmer, *Labor Mobility in Six Cities,* pp. 74–75.

[46] Bogue, *op. cit.,* p. 26.

[47] Aaronson and Keller, *op. cit.,* pp. 30–31.

from domestic service into other types of employment, the data used in this study probably understate appreciably the current mobility of Negro women relative to that of white women.

Aaronson and Keller found approximately the same racial differential in geographic mobility as in interfirm movement. In each of the years 1941–43 larger proportions of Negro men than of white men were in covered employment in more than one state, and the reverse was true of women. It is significant that the difference in geographic mobility of white and Negro men was far greater in 1942 and 1943 than in 1941. In the latter year 10.7 percent of the Negro men and 10.4 percent of the white men worked in more than one state. In 1943 the corresponding percentages were 16 and 11.[48] This suggests that the unprecedented employment opportunities of the World War II period affected white and Negro workers differently, providing the latter with financial means well above normal as well as unusual inducements to make long-distance moves.

The evidence furnished in these two studies is too scanty to permit definite conclusions as to racial differentials in mobility. The data include only shifts between jobs covered by Old-Age and Survivors Insurance, and that is a serious limitation, particularly in view of the possibility of a racial differential in the extent of coverage. Moreover, neither study throws any light on the relative amount of occupational shifting by white and Negro workers, and Aaronson and Keller's study does not even deal with industrial mobility. There is little indication of the extent to which the differentials found in the two studies are a product of factors that are correlated with race. In Chapter 3 mobility was shown to be inversely related to level of skill. Since Negroes are employed in disproportionate numbers in unskilled occupations, the higher mobility of Negroes may be simply a reflection of occupational differentials.[49] Finally, it should be cautioned that higher interfirm movement among Negroes than among whites cannot be interpreted to mean that there is greater "stability" of employment among the latter. In view of the discrimination against Negroes in many kinds of employment, it seems reasonable to assume that the

[48] *Ibid.*, p. 26.

[49] Nonwhite workers included in the six-city survey had mobility rates that were 19 percent higher than the rates for white workers. At least three fourths of the difference between nonwhite and white men, however, was due to differences in their occupations and migrant status. (Kitagawa, *op. cit.*, p. 52.)

incidence of involuntary separations is greater among them than among white workers.

Marital and Family Status. A priori, one would expect the mobility of workers to be influenced by their marital and family status. For example, married men presumably are less likely to make voluntary job changes than unmarried men because of the greater responsibilities of the former and the consequently greater value they attach to security. Differences in the mobility of various marital status groups have been found in several studies, but the results hardly permit confident generalizations. Most of the studies have reported lower mobility for family heads than for other family members, but to what extent this is due to age differentials and to what extent to differences in family status is not known.[50]

In the six-city survey mobility measures for the decade 1940–49 were computed for family heads, other family members, and unrelated individuals. The latter two groups were combined into a "secondary worker" category. For the Los Angeles sample the median number of jobs held during the decade was slightly lower for male heads of families than for other male workers, and this was true in all age brackets except 35–44, where the rates were equal for the two groups. For all age groups combined, male family heads held an average (median) of 2.7 jobs during the decade, as compared with 2.9 jobs for male secondary workers. There were no consistent differences for female heads and female secondary workers when they were classified by age.[51]

In New Haven, also, male family heads appeared to be less mobile during the decade 1940–49 than secondary workers. The former had a smaller median number of jobs and a longer average length of service than the latter. As in Los Angeles the differences, although small, tended to prevail in all age groups. Unlike the situation in Los Angeles,

[50] Kitagawa reports that single men in the six-city survey had slightly higher mobility than married men or men who were widowed, divorced, or separated. With age and migrant status held constant, however, single and married men had approximately equal mobility rates, while those for widowed, divorced, or separated men were higher. (*Ibid.*, p. 54.)

[51] Philip Neff, Gregory Barlous, Tibor Fabian, and Olive Reeks, "The Mobility of Los Angeles Workers, 1940–49," unpublished manuscript, University of California Institute of Industrial Relations (Los Angeles, November 1951), p. 27; Tables XVIII and XIX.

female family heads in New Haven were somewhat less mobile than secondary workers.[52]

In Chicago family heads of both sexes were found to have held fewer jobs per person than other family members or "unrelated individuals" (those living alone or with persons to whom they were not related). When age was taken into account, the difference between family heads and other family workers tended to vanish, but the difference between family heads and unrelated individuals persisted. Kitagawa and Reiss concluded that "Apparently age is more important than family status in job mobility, since very similar age differentials are found in all family status groups, while family status differentials tend to disappear with increasing age." [53]

Male family heads and secondary workers in San Francisco had the same median number of jobs during 1940–49, but there were differences between these groups when classified according to age. In the age groups between 45 and 64, male heads of families had a much lower average number of jobs and a considerably higher average length of service than did secondary workers.[54] The situation was somewhat similar in Philadelphia where male family heads held relatively fewer jobs between 1940 and 1949 than male secondary workers, but the difference between the averages (1.9 and 2.4 respectively) resulted almost exclusively from the much lower mobility of family heads aged 45 to 64. In this age group the median length of job was almost twice as great for family heads as for secondary workers.[55] The data for St. Paul did not point to any consistent differences in mobility of male family heads and secondary workers.[56]

In drawing conclusions on the relationship between family status

[52] Robert M. Macdonald, "The Mobility of New Haven Workers," unpublished manuscript, Yale University Labor and Management Center (November 1951), p. 9; Tables 21, 22.

[53] Evelyn M. Kitagawa and Albert J. Reiss, Jr., "The Mobility of Chicago Workers, 1940–1949," unpublished manuscript, University of Chicago, Chicago Community Inventory (November 1951), p. 33; see also pp. 34–35 and Tables 24 and 25.

[54] Margaret S. Gordon, "The Mobility of San Francisco Workers, 1940–49," p. 30; Tables A-13, A-14.

[55] Gladys L. Palmer, "The Mobility of Philadelphia Workers, 1940–49," unpublished manuscript, University of Pennsylvania Industrial Relations Department (November 1951), Appendix Tables 18–22.

[56] University of Minnesota Industrial Relations Center, "The Mobility of St. Paul Workers, 1940–1949," unpublished manuscript (November 1951), p. 30.

and mobility from the results of the six-city survey, it must be kept in mind that they were almost certainly influenced by one aspect of the methodology. Mobility was measured in terms of the mean number of jobs held during a 10-year period, but individuals were classified by their family status at the time of the survey. At best this could indicate only imperfectly the effect of a particular family status on the degree of job movement. If it is assumed that family heads by virtue of their responsibilities are less mobile than secondary workers, then the kind of analysis used in the six-city survey will understate the extent of this differential in the younger age groups, and possibly in the older groups as well, because the tabulations include among family heads many relatively young workers who during part of the decade—that is, prior to their marriage—were secondary workers. Among young workers such changes in status during a decade are not likely to be counterbalanced by changes resulting from divorce or from the death of dependents. In the older age groups the opposite situation may prevail: some workers who were family heads in the early part of the decade may become secondary workers by its end. If this reasoning is valid, it may partly explain the finding in several cities that the mobility differential between family heads and secondary workers was greatest in the middle age brackets.

With respect to geographic mobility, there is some evidence that married men living with their wives are somewhat less likely to make intercounty changes of residence than men in other marital status categories. A Census Bureau survey comparing the 1949 and 1948 residences of a national sample of the labor force found that only 5 percent of employed married men living with their wives had migrated across county lines during the year, in contrast with 7.5 percent of single men, and 10 percent of men who were divorced, widowed, or "married, spouse absent." [57] The much higher proportion of migrants in the latter category should be interpreted cautiously, for it is possible that many married men spend some time in a new area before sending for their families; such married men, if enumerated by the Census prior to the arrival of their wives, would be classified as "married, spouse absent."

Kerr, in his study of migration into the Seattle labor market area during the early years of World War II, did not find unmarried work-

[57] *Current Population Reports: Labor Force,* Series P-50, No. 20 (March 17, 1950).

ers disproportionately numerous among the migrants,[58] nor a pronounced relationship between marital status and distance migrated, except for those moving the longest distances. Among those moving 2,400 miles or more, 43 percent were single, as compared with 34 to 37 percent of those who moved shorter distances.[59]

On the basis of the available evidence, the most reasonable conclusion is that there is a slight relationship between the marital status and the mobility of male workers, married men making somewhat fewer shifts than nonmarried. It seems certain, however, that the influence of marital status on mobility is not nearly so strong as that of age.[60]

Other Characteristics of Workers. The influence of several other factors, such as union membership, home ownership, and education, on mobility has been investigated to a limited extent. The following brief description of the meager findings shows that they are insufficient for even tentative generalization.

Although much has been written about the effects of trade union policies on labor mobility, only a few studies have compared the mobility of union and non-union workers. A priori there are grounds for supposing that union membership may reduce mobility or may have the opposite effect. Seniority rights and pension plans in many union contracts, together with the social cohesiveness that a union may produce among employees, can be expected to reduce the propensity of union members to change jobs. On the other hand, union members are likely to have a better knowledge of the labor market than non-union workers, and to be better informed about alternative employment opportunities.[61]

Palmer found that although union hosiery workers in Philadelphia made more changes of employer, occupation, and industry in the decade 1926–35 than non-union workers, these mobility differences

[58] Kerr, "Migration to the Seattle Labor Market Area, 1940–1942," p. 154.

[59] *Ibid.,* pp. 144, 184.

[60] In a study comparing the employment status of St. Paul workers in July 1941 with their status in June 1942, Heneman found that family heads were more mobile occupationally and industrially, while secondary family members made more shifts from unemployment to employment, and into and out of the labor force. There were no pronounced differences in interfirm mobility. (Herbert G. Heneman, Jr., "Differential Short-Run Labor Mobilities: St. Paul, 1941–42," *op. cit.,* p. 40.) The methods used for classifying and measuring mobility in this study, however, prevent a meaningful comparison with the results of the other studies.

[61] See pp. 165–174 infra.

were not significant when the workers were classified by occupation. She suggests that "occupational differences outweigh considerations of union membership as a factor in the mobility of workers in a given industry." [62] An alternative explanation, which she recognizes, is that the atypical turnover in hosiery manufacturing establishments in the period 1926–35 may have created a situation in which the average length of service of hosiery workers did not differ materially between union and non-union mills, despite greater protection of the seniority rights of union workers.[63] If this is the case, her findings may not be valid for other periods or other industries.

In his study of the New Haven labor market in the post-World War II period, Reynolds found that non-union workers made relatively more voluntary job changes than union workers. Among the former, 22 percent had changed jobs between August 1945 and the time of the interview in 1947, as compared with only 6 percent of those who had been union members for more than four years and 16 percent of those who had been members for four years or less. These findings, however, were attributable primarily to differences in length of service; when this factor was taken into account, the negative relationship between union membership and voluntary movement was notably reduced.[64]

It should be noted that Reynolds' sample included a cross section of manual workers, and that the analysis of the relation between union membership and mobility was made without regard to the occupational or industrial affiliations of the workers. It is doubtful that this approach can lead to meaningful conclusions regarding the influence of unionism on mobility, for reasons pointed out in the next section, where the effects of trade union policies on mobility are considered and a more promising research design is suggested.

An investigation of the relationship between formal education and the mobility of 98 "mobile" employees in Minneapolis during a one-year and a five-year period in the 1940's produced inconclusive results. The number of interfirm shifts made by these workers between 1947 and 1948 suggested an inverse relationship between mobility and years of schooling. But during 1943–48, workers with high school or college training made more changes of employer than did those with eight or fewer years of school.[65]

---

62 Palmer, "Interpreting Patterns of Labor Mobility," *op. cit.*, p. 65.
63 Communication to the author.
64 Reynolds, *op. cit.*, p. 22.
65 Heneman, Fox, and Yoder, *op. cit.*, p. 8. In the six-city survey "crude" mobility

The 17-year work experience of over a thousand government clerical employees in Columbus in 1948 showed a positive correlation between mobility and the number of years of high school and college training. Workers with less than two years of high school held an average of 2.3 jobs during the 17-year period, as compared with an average of 3.3 jobs for those with three or more years of college. Well over a third of those who had not finished high school were in one job during the entire 17-year period, as compared with less than a fourth of the college graduates. On the other hand, one fifth of the college graduates and only 1 out of 17 of those with less than three years of high school had six or more jobs during the period.[66]

A similar relationship between mobility and educational level was found in a study of the 1940–51 work experience of tool and die makers. Workers who had not gone beyond the eighth grade averaged less than one job change during this period, while those with some college training had an average of almost two shifts. The averages for men with partial or complete high school education fell between these extremes. When years of schooling were standardized by age, the positive relationship between education and mobility persisted.[67]

Home ownership has frequently been suggested as a factor reducing the mobility of workers, but few attempts have been made to measure its effects. Heneman's study of the shifts made by St. Paul workers between July 1941 and June 1942 found that mobility had a more consistent and pronounced relationship to type of home tenure than to any other characteristic according to which workers were classified. Although home owners constituted almost half the labor force, less than a fourth of each of the various types of movement analyzed was attributable to those who owned their homes.[68] When Reynolds asked a sample of 450 New Haven manual workers how great a wage increase would be necessary to induce them to move to a job in another area, tenants indicated a greater willingness to move than did home own-

---

rates for men were inversely related to level of education, except for men with only grade school education, who were least mobile. With age and migrant status held constant the relationship persisted, and the exception in the case of men with grade school education became less pronounced. (Kitagawa, *op. cit.*)

[66] Parnes, "Government Employment in Franklin County, Ohio, and Its Relation to the Local Labor Market," pp. 304–308.

[67] U. S. Bureau of Labor Statistics, *The Mobility of Tool and Die Makers*, p. 36.

[68] Herbert G. Heneman, Jr., "Differential Short-Run Labor Mobilities: St. Paul, 1941–42," *op. cit.*, p. 38.

ers.[69] It is easy to suggest logical explanations for lower *geographic* mobility among home owners than among renters, but difficult to explain why home ownership per se should restrict movement among firms, occupations, or industries within a local labor market. A problem of intercorrelated variables may be involved. Home owners are likely to be older than renters. Also, there is likely to be a relationship between type of home tenure and occupational level. Variations in mobility according to type of tenure may therefore simply reflect the influence of these other factors. On the other hand, although home ownership probably would not seriously restrict job movement within a local labor market, a possible personality difference between home owners and renters may be reflected in different patterns of labor market behavior by these two groups. It might be hypothesized that home owners place a higher value on security and stability than renters do, and that these same factors contribute to a lower propensity of owners to make job changes.

SOME INSTITUTIONAL INFLUENCES ON LABOR MOBILITY

Up to this point attention has been concentrated on the characteristics that seem to differentiate relatively mobile from relatively immobile workers. It has been emphasized that differences in mobility cannot be assumed to reflect "personal" factors that are unaffected by external influences, but may result from institutional forces which create dissimilar environments for different groups of workers or necessitate different responses to the same environment. To be specific, higher job movement among Negroes than among whites does not necessarily imply greater "instability" among the former than the latter, or a greater propensity to move in response to given stimuli, or any different motivations. On the contrary, higher mobility of Negroes might as easily be explained by such "external" factors as discriminatory hiring and personnel policies, less extensive unionization, or an occupational distribution different from that of white workers. Similarly, it has been seen that the decline in mobility with advancing age need not mean that workers inherently become less "flighty" or more security conscious as they grow older, but may be related to a complex of institutional influences which create essentially different labor market environments for old and young workers.

The conclusions of studies concerning institutional influences on

[69] Reynolds, *op. cit.*, pp. 78–79.

labor mobility, which are reviewed in this section, have generally not been reached through empirical research, but have been deduced from examination of the structure and functions of certain institutional or environmental factors that appear to be closely related to the ability or willingness of workers to make various kinds of job changes. The elements of the social milieu that may influence the volume or character of labor mobility are both numerous and diverse, being coextensive with the totality of the culture.[70] The values and basic attitudes of a society, the nature of its technology, and the role and characteristics of family organization are illustrative of the basic cultural elements that affect and are affected by the size, composition, and behavior of the work force. Although a beginning has been made in analyzing the effects of fundamental factors of this kind on participation in the labor force and on relatively long-run changes in its composition,[71] there has been little or no attempt to relate them to the short-run mobility of labor. In the following discussion, those institutional or environmental determinants of short-run labor mobility that have been most extensively treated in the literature are examined under one or more of the following headings: trade unionism, employers' personnel policy, government policy, level of business activity, and industrial structure of the labor market.[72]

Trade Unionism. Although the empirical evidence concerning the relative mobility of union and non-union workers is inconclusive, there seems to be a consensus among students of the labor market that the net effect of trade unionism has been to diminish labor mobility.

Shister, for example, believes that although trade union policies have little influence on the volume as distinguished from the incidence of involuntary movement, they play an important role in reducing voluntary movement.[73] He observes that the extent of involuntary mobility is determined principally by the level of business activity. On the assumption that the effects of union policies on general business conditions are relatively insignificant, he concludes that while the seniority principle determines the *incidence* of layoffs,

---

[70] Cf. A. J. Jaffe and Charles D. Stewart, *Manpower Resources and Utilization,* p. vi.

[71] See *ibid.,* Part III, "The Working Force in Its Social and Economic Context."

[72] See Joseph Shister, "Labor Mobility: Some Institutional Aspects," *Industrial Relations Research Association Proceedings of Third Annual Meeting . . . 1950,* pp. 42–59. The first four of these "institutional forces" are suggested by Shister.

[73] *Ibid.,* pp. 43–48.

the *amount* of involuntary movement is largely unaffected by union policies. He concedes that unions are influential through the grievance procedure in discharge cases, but points out that discharges are an almost negligible component of total involuntary mobility. Finally, he admits the possibility of the emergence of union policies that would profoundly affect involuntary mobility and cites the guaranteed annual wage as an example. Curiously, Shister refers to union policies on equal division of work as a factor influencing the incidence of job separations, without recognizing that such policies also reduce the number of layoffs.

Shister thinks that the effects of trade unionism on voluntary job shifting are conflicting, even though those tending to reduce mobility are much the stronger. He mentions two factors that might tend to increase voluntary movement. One is the greater knowledge of labor market conditions which union members are likely to gain through formal (union journal) or informal (oral information) channels. But Shister is doubtful that such information encourages movement. If it does, he suggests that the movement will be restricted to the trade or industry in question, and will involve geographic shifts rather than shifts within one labor market. The second aspect of trade unionism that might be regarded as a stimulus to mobility is the general practice of fixing wages for a specified period of time, frequently a year. In a "tight" labor market, individual workers under such a contract may move to other plants where wage scales are higher, whereas in the absence of a union agreement the employer would be likely to raise individual wage rates in order to retain the necessary work force. Shister counters this line of reasoning, however, by pointing out that even under union contracts employers have done precisely this same thing.

According to Shister many policies and characteristics of trade unionism operate to reduce the voluntary movement of labor. Seniority in promotions and layoffs provides an inducement to workers to build up their length of service with a given firm. Negotiated pension plans have a similar effect, particularly for older workers.[74] The removal of the sources of job dissatisfaction, which Shister regards as perhaps the

[74] Arthur M. Ross, "The New Industrial Pensions," *Review of Economics and Statistics,* 32:137 (May 1950). But for a different conclusion based on a study of the operation of 11 pension plans in New York State, see Michael Puchek, *Pension Plan Policies and Practices,* New York State School of Industrial and Labor Relations Bulletin 21 (Cornell University, July 1952), p. 49.

principal function of American unionism, reduces the force of unsatisfactory job conditions in causing voluntary separations. Moreover, to the extent that unions standardize wages and working conditions throughout the competitive market, differentials in the "net advantage" of alternative jobs are narrowed, thus reducing the incentives to interfirm movement. The effect of unionism, in other words, is to render less potent the "pulls" as well as the "pushes" toward voluntary moves by workers. The tendency toward more uniform wage and job standards may operate to reduce mobility in an even more subtle manner, according to Shister. Standardization of wage rates may contribute to increased industrial concentration by forcing marginal firms out of existence and encouraging the stronger firms to grow. Since the opportunities for advancement are greater in large than in small organizations, the result would be a reduction in that part of interfirm movement occasioned by workers' dissatisfaction with their progress or with their prospects for promotion within the firm. This, of course, would not represent a net decrease in movement, but rather a substitution of interfirm occupational movement for movement from one firm to another. Union policies impose still another limitation on mobility in those cases where a closed shop agreement is accompanied by a restrictive admission policy on the part of the union, as in some craft unions. This situation obviously restricts the movement of workers into these skilled occupations.[75]

Unions are not merely economic institutions but political organizations as well, and in this facet of trade unionism Shister also sees influences tending to reduce labor mobility. The various administrative offices in a local union "enable many a worker to attain a gratifying status which he would lose if he were to leave the plant." [76] Moreover, because of the turnover in these local offices, the *expectations* of holding office also constitute a deterrent to voluntary movement. Shister fails to mention a related factor which may be of even greater importance in reducing mobility, if only because it affects a considerably larger number of workers. This is the sense of "belong-

[75] This point, while not invalid, probably requires some qualification in the interest of realism. When job opportunities in a particular craft are abundant, even unions that restrict membership commonly grant "work permits" to nonmembers. On the other hand, if the demand for workers is being met with the supply of available union members, there would not be much movement into the trade even in the absence of the restrictive policy.

[76] Shister, *op. cit.*, p. 46.

ing" to the union group which may strengthen the attachment of a union member to his job, irrespective of his ambitions to hold union office. A voluntary job separation in any case requires the worker to overcome a certain inertia, to be willing to forego the comforts inherent in a familiar physical and social environment. From this point of view, union membership may create an additional bond which a worker must be willing to sever in order to make a job change.

Kerr [77] agrees with the conclusion that the "institutional rules" developed by trade unionism have probably tended to reduce mobility, but he cautions that the effect of unions on mobility cannot be determined without differentiating between the institutional rules characteristic of craft unionism and those characteristic of industrial unionism. The former is the "communal ownership" system of rules: "The craft union asserts proprietorship on behalf of its members over the jobs falling within a carefully defined occupational and geographical area." [78] The latter is the "private property" system: "In the industrial enterprise, the central rule is to each man one job and to each job one man." [79] These two different complexes of "rules" have different effects on the movement of workers: "The craft worker moves horizontally in the craft area and the industrial worker vertically in the seniority area. Interoccupational movement is reduced for the former and employer-to-employer movement for the latter. Thus they are both captives, albeit ones who surrendered voluntarily or even enthusiastically, of the rules which guide their working careers. Job rights protect but they also confine. Reduction of insecurity also brings reduction of independence." [80]

More specifically, Kerr suggests that while craft rules greatly increase interfirm mobility, they generally reduce occupational mobility and movement between employment and unemployment and into and out of the labor force. Industrial and geographic mobility are also usually decreased. On the other hand, industrial unionism tends to reduce all types of movement except occupational movement within a firm, and this it tends to increase. Not only is the mobility of union-

---

[77] Clark Kerr, "The Balkanization of Labor Markets," in E. Wight Bakke and others, *Labor Mobility and Economic Opportunity*, pp. 92–110; see also Kerr, "Labor Markets: Their Character and Consequences," *American Economic Review*, 40(suppl.):278–291 (May 1950), especially 289–290.

[78] Kerr, "The Balkanization of Labor Markets," p. 97.

[79] *Ibid.*, p. 99.

[80] *Ibid.*, p. 104.

ized workers reduced by these rules, but that of non-union workers as well. Because of the job rights of union members, some jobs are not open to non-unionists, at least under certain circumstances. Moreover, to the extent that union members are reluctant to forfeit their security by leaving their jobs, there will be fewer jobs into which other workers can move.

The kinds of generalizations that have been summarized above require empirical testing. Practically all of them should be regarded as hypotheses rather than as established propositions. It is true that most of the deductive analysis leading to the conclusion that unionism restricts mobility is perfectly logical, and that the immobilizing effects of union policies seem almost self-evident. But there are dangers in accepting "self-evident" truths. The effect of negotiated seniority rules on mobility has been "explained" so repeatedly that it has become virtually an axiom in textbooks on labor economics. But these effects may have been overstated. For one thing, the seniority principle, in layoffs as well as in promotions, is not unique to unionized establishments despite the greater likelihood of its being formalized in such organizations. For another, the psychological and sociological deterrents to job shifting by long-service employees may be so strong even in the absence of seniority rules that the addition of such rules would make little difference.

Even if it is granted that union policies and characteristics "tend" to reduce voluntary movement, the very significant question of this tendency's actual strength remains to be answered. With respect to Kerr's differentiation between the effects of the craft and the industrial unions, how much of this difference results from their rules, and how much from inherent differences in the work done by their members? With or without unions, one would expect fewer occupational changes among skilled craftsmen than among semiskilled production workers.

The testing of these hypotheses requires more than mere comparison of measures of mobility of union and non-union workers. Workers move into and out of union membership as well as into and out of jobs, and knowledge of a worker's union status as of a particular time is no assurance that he was in that status during the entire period for which his work history has been obtained. Moreover, nonmembers of a union in a bargaining unit covered by a union agreement are also subject to many of the influences on mobility that stem from the presence of the union. Consequently, in order to examine the impact of unionism as an institution it is necessary to use a technique of analysis that takes cognizance of the commonality of these influences on the work force. Finally, more than the employment histories of workers must be studied in order to reach judgments as to which aspects of trade unionism have the greatest effects on mobility. Attitudes toward jobs and toward the union, the extent of active participation in the union's business meetings and social affairs, and the extent to which the union has handled individual grievances for the workers are illustrative of other types of information required.

All these considerations point to the desirability of studying the relationship between unionism and mobility on the basis of a sample of establishments rather than of workers. An experimental study might be designed, with a sample of unionized firms and a control sample of nonunion firms, matched for such factors as industry, size, and condition of equipment. Within each firm, work histories and also information on the prospective plans and the attitudes of a sample of workers might be obtained. With a design of this kind, most of the hypotheses concerning the influence of unionism on mobility could be tested.

Employers' Personnel Policies. The importance of the influence of employers' personnel policies on the volume and pattern of mobility has been recognized by most research workers in this field. It is clear that the incidence, if not the amount, of voluntary movement is affected by employers' hiring preferences.[81] Discrimination against racial, religious, or other minorities in hiring and layoffs will tend to reduce the voluntary mobility of these groups,[82] but perhaps to increase their involuntary movement. Maximum age limits in hiring almost certainly tend to reduce the mobility of older workers, as has already been observed. Kerr concluded from his study of wartime migration to the Seattle labor market that the hiring policies of employers in the area were the most important single factor explaining the characteristics of in-migrants.[83] An analysis of the interregional recruitment program of the U. S. Employment Service during World War II also points to the importance of this factor. In 1944 local public employment offices interviewed, selected, and referred 529,605 workers to jobs in other areas in an attempt to fill 371,195 openings. Only about half the referrals, however, resulted in placements. Workers refused to accept the jobs for a va-

---

[81] For a study of hiring preferences, see E. William Noland and E. Wight Bakke, *Workers Wanted* (New York: Harper & Brothers, 1949).

[82] Shister, *op. cit.*, p. 51.

[83] Kerr, "Migration to the Seattle Labor Market Area, 1940–1942," p. 154.

riety of reasons, but the War Manpower Commission reported that "Inordinately high job specifications and extremely unrealistic selectivity [among employers] have persisted." [84] It is noteworthy that the period was one of extreme manpower shortages.

"Anti-pirating" agreements among employers are another factor influencing the amount of voluntary movement of workers.[85] To the extent that employers tacitly or explicitly agree not to hire workers currently employed in other establishments in the community, voluntary movement of workers is discouraged. At best, this practice means that workers desirous of changing jobs must quit their present ones before looking for others.

Shister observes that the promotion policies of employers influence the amount and the incidence of voluntary interfirm movement. Most firms, particularly the larger ones, follow a policy of filling vacancies as far as possible by promotion from within the firm. The greater intra-firm occupational mobility resulting from this practice will reduce the volume of interfirm movement, since workers will be able to satisfy their desire for progress without changing employers.[86] However, to the extent that this is true, the result is not so much a reduction in mobility as a change in its pattern. That is, simple occupational shifts are substituted for more complex shifts involving a simultaneous change of employer and occupation (and perhaps industry, as well). But it must be remembered that simple occupational shifts without a change in employer have not often been defined as job changes, and the vast majority of the studies of labor mobility have not dealt with these intrafirm occupational shifts at all. It may be, therefore, that the long-run decrease in mobility that some students have noted results at least in part from an increase in the relative importance of a type of mobility not shown by their data.[87.]

To the extent that differentials in the "net advantage" of alternative jobs produce voluntary movement, and to the extent that wage and other job characteristics are amenable to control by employers, their policies concerning these factors will have important effects on mo-

[84] "Interregional Recruitment of Workers in 1944," *Monthly Labor Review*, 60:291 (February 1945).

[85] Myers and Maclaurin, *op. cit.*, p. 39; Shister, *op. cit.*, p. 51; Reynolds, *op. cit.*, pp. 51–52.

[86] Shister, *op. cit.*, p. 52.

[87] See Shister, *op. cit.*, p. 53; Gladys L. Palmer, "Social Values in Labor Mobility," in E. Wight Bakke and others, *Labor Mobility and Economic Opportunity*, pp. 111–116.

bility. Considering all employers collectively, this is true whether voluntary job changes are explainable principally in terms of the "push" exerted by unsatisfactory conditions in the present job or the "pull" exerted by more favorable opportunities elsewhere. Employers' techniques of selection are also significant in this connection. If aptitude testing is used, for example, workers who are hired are likely to be better "fitted" to their jobs in terms of abilities, interests, and personality characteristics; and poor initial selection is less frequently responsible for either voluntary or involuntary separations.

Appraisal of the net effect of employers' policies on labor mobility is difficult, both because of the large number of variables involved and because of the great diversity of policy concerning each of them. It is reasonable to assume, however, that employers' policies are at least *directed* toward reducing interfirm movement of workers. To the individual employer labor mobility (excepting intrafirm occupational mobility) appears as labor turnover, and it is an axiom of personnel administration that labor turnover is costly and should be minimized.[88] It may be concluded, therefore, that labor mobility will be reduced to the extent that employers' personnel policies are successful.

Government Policies. The types of government policies and programs that might logically be expected to influence the volume, incidence, or pattern of labor mobility are too numerous to be listed here. Government functions as diverse as municipal road building, on the one hand, and federal attempts to stabilize the economy through fiscal and monetary policy, on the other, can affect the willingness of workers to make voluntary job changes or their opportunities to do so. In this section, only those governmental influences that have been dealt with in the literature on mobility are discussed; no attempt is made to analyze extensively the impact of government practices and policies on mobility.

Shister suggests that, except in wartime when manpower controls are consciously designed to govern the amount of movement by workers and to channel its direction, the principal governmental influence on mobility "is exerted through the indirect impact of its fiscal and monetary policy on the state of business activity."[89] Since it has been

---

[88] See Sumner H. Slichter, *The Turnover of Factory Labor.* For a more recent discussion of "what the employer can do to reduce turnover," see Kenneth Lehmann and C. Edward Weber, *Workers on the Move,* University of Illinois Institute of Labor and Industrial Relations Bulletin Series, Vol. 6, No. 1 (September 1952).

[89] Shister, *op. cit.,* p. 50.

established that involuntary movement by workers varies inversely, and voluntary movement directly, with the level of business activity (see pp. 135–138 infra), it follows that government policies that influence this level are among the significant determinants of different kinds of labor mobility.

In discussing the relationship of the social security program to labor mobility, Slichter states that the Old-Age and Survivors Insurance program tends to encourage mobility both because it stimulates earlier retirement and because movement among covered employers and industries does not endanger the worker's eligibility for retirement benefits.[90] Shister agrees that mobility is increased by this program. He suggests that in its absence some employers would keep older workers on the payroll longer than they now do. As it is, involuntarily retired workers turn to other jobs (when they can find them) and thus increase the amount of movement.[91]

Slichter and Shister also agree that unemployment compensation has had little if any effect on the amount of labor mobility. Shister believes that voluntary movement is not affected at all, on the assumption that not many workers will quit their jobs more readily because unemployment benefits are available. A worker who voluntarily leaves his job cannot be sure that he will qualify for benefits, since he may not be able to show that he quit for a "just cause." On the other hand, Shister admits the possibility that unemployed workers, particularly in seasonal industries, may be encouraged by the receipt of unemployment compensation to delay seeking work elsewhere. If this occurs, interfirm mobility is somewhat reduced, but Shister considers the evidence on the subject too scanty to permit a definite conclusion.[92]

The study by Myers and Shultz of the experiences of workers disemployed by the shutdown of a textile mill sheds some light on the way in which an unemployment compensation program may affect mobility. Of the 144 persons in the sample who had been laid off, 56 percent were drawing unemployment compensation. Although more than two fifths of these recipients of benefits admitted they were not looking for work, their responses to the interviewers indicated that most of them had left the labor market and apparently regarded unemployment benefits as a kind of severance pay to which they were

90 Sumner H. Slichter, "The Impact of Social Security Legislation upon Mobility and Enterprise," *American Economic Review,* 30(suppl.):48 (March 1940).

91 Shister, *op. cit.,* p. 50.

92 *Ibid.,* p. 48.

entitled as a result of the wage credits they had accumulated while employed. This group apparently would not have looked for other jobs even in the absence of unemployment compensation. Only four workers of the 34 who were receiving benefits but not looking for work said that they were waiting for their benefit rights to expire before they sought other jobs. Another four said that they were waiting for the Employment Service to find them jobs, and it is possible that this group might have been more active in their own behalf in the absence of compensation. Finally, there was evidence that the existence of the compensation program allowed some workers who were actively seeking "suitable" work to avoid taking jobs substantially less desirable than those held prior to the layoff.[93] In evaluating these results, it must be kept in mind that the workers had been displaced not by a seasonal layoff, but by a permanent plant shutdown, and that alternative employment opportunities were distinctly limited. While the evidence suggests that the existence of an unemployment compensation program in this situation may have restricted certain types of movement to a limited degree, it is not certain that the same pattern of behavior would prevail in other circumstances.

The experience rating feature of unemployment compensation laws is relevant to a discussion of *involuntary* mobility. Slichter predicted in 1940 that experience rating provisions might convert some casual employment into regular employment.[94] However, Shister observes that employment stabilization, which experience rating was designed to encourage, has not developed to any considerable extent. In establishments where stabilization has occurred, it has generally involved only part of the work force, at the expense of less employment for other workers.[95]

The state employment services, which help administer the unem-

---

[93] Charles A. Myers and George P. Shultz, *The Dynamics of a Labor Market*, pp. 87–95. Bakke, in a study of the effect of the British Unemployment Insurance System on "the willingness . . . of workers to support themselves," concluded that unemployment insurance acts as one of a number of deterrents to certain types of movement. Specifically, he found that it reduced the readiness of unemployed workers to take odd jobs, and was one among many factors discouraging them from going into self-employment. It was only a "minor element in the factors which root the British worker to his home locality." (E. Wight Bakke, *The Unemployed Man*, pp. 261–263.)

[94] Slichter, "The Impact of Social Security Legislation upon Mobility and Enterprise," p. 48.

[95] Shister, *op. cit.*, p. 49.

ployment compensation programs, clearly operate to increase the mobility of workers by making registrants aware of available jobs and by finding workers for employers. There is abundant evidence, however, that the *potential* stimulus to mobility inherent in the existence of a national network of public employment offices has actually not been realized. Neither employers nor employees have made full use of the facilities of the public employment services.[96]

One of the few empirical studies of the relationship between a government policy and labor mobility investigated the effect of the relief program on geographic mobility in the 1930's. The hypothesis tested was that such mobility was restricted by the residence requirements for eligibility under the relief program (generally at least a year of self-supporting residence). Analysis of the work and relief experience of almost 150,000 Michigan workers between 1930 and 1935 showed relatively more recipients of relief among those who made geographic moves than among those who did not. Moreover, of all workers making geographic moves, recipients of relief tended to make more moves than did those not receiving relief. The investigators concluded that relief was responsible for some of the movement of Michigan workers during the period studied, but that the amount of movement directly attributable to the relief program was not sufficient to alter the general assumption that relief programs tend to discourage mobility.[97] Partly on the basis of the evidence produced by this study, Slichter concluded that the mobility of persons on relief is above average—not because relief programs encourage mobility, but because persons on relief tend to be those whose attachment to the labor force is marginal, and who consequently are highly mobile.[98]

Level of Business Activity. A priori, the volume of voluntary job shifting would be expected to vary directly with changes in the level of business activity. A given propensity to move would produce more movement in prosperity than in depression simply because of the

[96] See Reynolds, *op. cit.*, pp. 56–60; Myers and Shultz, *op. cit.*, pp. 75–81; Murray Edelman, *Channels of Employment* (University of Illinois Institute of Labor and Industrial Relations, 1952); Shister, *op. cit.*, p. 50.

[97] John N. Webb and Albert Westefeld, "Labor Mobility and Relief," *Monthly Labor Review*, 48:16–24 (January 1939).

[98] Slichter, "The Impact of Social Security Legislation upon Mobility and Enterprise," p. 50. A few students of labor mobility have suggested that the nature of the public education system is one of the "frictions" impeding the adjustment of labor supply to labor demand. See Dale Yoder, Donald G. Paterson, and others, *Local Labor Market Research*, p. 118; and Reynolds, *op. cit.*, pp. 275–280.

greater opportunities for movement, that is, the greater availability of jobs. In addition, even the propensity to move might be higher during prosperous periods, since plentiful opportunities for employment mitigate the security problem which makes "a job in the hand" so valuable when work is scarce.

This relationship between employment opportunities and voluntary mobility has been amply demonstrated. On the basis of the 10-year work histories of several groups of Philadelphia workers for the decade 1926–35 Palmer concluded that "mobility responds to opportunity." [99] In all the occupations studied, the workers made more voluntary job shifts during the prosperous years 1926–30 than during the depression years 1931–35. Also, more of the shifts during the first part of the decade were "successful," that is, resulted in economic improvement.

The positive correlation between the amount of voluntary mobility and the level of business activity is also clearly shown by data on labor turnover. According to Woytinsky, the average monthly separation rate in manufacturing industries was about 4 percent of the employees on the payroll, both during the depressed 1930's and the prosperous years prior to 1929; but in the latter period about three fourths of the separations were initiated by the employee, while during the 1930's only one fourth were voluntary.[100] During the prosperous 1940's voluntary separations were much higher than during the preceding decade.

The volume of geographic movement also responds to changes in economic conditions. The proportion of workers covered by Old-Age and Survivors Insurance who made interstate job moves was considerably higher in 1942 and 1943, as the peak of the war effort was approached, than in 1938–40.[101] A study of migration into San Francisco during the decade 1940–50 yielded the conclusion that "short-run fluctuations in migration are influenced primarily by short-run changes in relative employment opportunities in the various regions." [102] Webb and Westefeld concluded from a study of the geographic movement of Michigan workers during the early 1930's that the number and

[99] Palmer, "Interpreting Patterns of Labor Mobility," in Bakke and others, *op. cit.*, p. 62.

[100] Woytinsky, *Three Aspects of Labor Dynamics*, pp. 3–4, 47, 52. Cf. pp. 71–73 supra.

[101] Aaronson and Keller, *op. cit.*, p. 6.

[102] Margaret S. Gordon, "The Mobility of Migrants and Nonmigrants, 1940–1949: San Francisco," unpublished manuscript, University of California Institute of Industrial Relations (Berkeley, February 1952), p. 11.

direction of geographic moves were influenced by seasonal changes in employment opportunities.[103] In a study of labor mobility in Great Britain, Makower, Marschak, and Robinson found that differences in intercounty migration rates were correlated with differences among the counties in economic opportunity, as measured by unemployment rates. Moreover, for a particular pattern of differentials in unemployment, mobility appeared to vary directly with fluctuations in business activity.[104]

Shister, after noting the "obvious" short-run variations in labor mobility related to the "40-month" business cycle, points out that there are long-run differences in voluntary mobility. He observes, for example, that despite the prosperity of the 1940's, the amount of voluntary movement did not reach the level of the 1920's, even after the wartime manpower controls were abandoned. A number of institutional factors are cited to explain this long-run trend, but Shister believes that "a very crucial element has been the change in the workman's conception of employment opportunities and employment security." [105] Thus, "long-run changes in employment opportunities—traceable ultimately to the rate and pattern of innovation growth—are a very important force in explaining long-run variations in horizontal labor mobility." [106] Employment opportunities, however, are not a completely independent variable. They influence and are influenced by other institutional forces which affect mobility.

The relationship between employment opportunities and labor mobility has important theoretical implications. The traditional theory of labor allocation and wage determination is based on an assumption of full employment.[107] Whatever the merits of the theory in terms of this assumption, it is clear that full employment—in the sense of the existence of a sellers' market for labor—has not prevailed continuously in our economy. The fact that mobility declines significantly when job opportunities decrease lends support to Reynolds' contention that

---

[103] John N. Webb and Albert Westefeld, "Industrial Aspects of Labor Mobility," *Monthly Labor Review,* 48:800–801 (April 1939).

[104] H. Makower, J. Marschak, and H. W. Robinson, "Studies in Mobility of Labour: Analysis for Great Britain," *Oxford Economic Papers,* No. 2 (May 1939), pp. 70–97, and No. 4 (September 1940), pp. 39–62.

[105] Shister, *op. cit.,* p. 54.

[106] *Ibid.,* p. 55.

[107] More accurately, full employment is a necessary result of the assumptions on which the theory is based.

the weaknesses of traditional wage theory as a description of actual labor market processes result chiefly from the chronic underemployment that characterizes the economy.[108]

Industrial Structure of the Labor Market. Both the pattern and the amount of labor mobility within a local labor market area appear to be affected by the industrial structure of the market. The influence of industrial structure on the kinds of job shifts made by workers is obvious. The proportion of shifts involving the simultaneous change of employer, occupation, and industry would be expected to be higher in an industrially diversified community than in a town with only one industry. This influence was clearly shown by Palmer's study of the 10-year work histories of weavers in three textile centers. In Manchester, New Hampshire, where one large textile firm dominated the labor market, a large majority of the weavers worked for only one employer during the entire decade. In Paterson, New Jersey, on the other hand, where there were many small textile plants, job shifts involving a change of employer only were more common than in the other cities. Finally, Philadelphia, with a more diversified industrial structure than either of the other cities, had the largest proportion of job shifts involving changes in occupation and industry.[109]

Bogue's study of the mobility of Ohio and Michigan workers covered by Old-Age and Survivors Insurance in 1947 points to the same conclusion. Industrial shifts were more prevalent in metropolitan than in nonmetropolitan areas. About 14 percent of the workers in metropolitan areas changed industries between the first and last quarters of the year, as compared with 11 percent of those in nonmetropolitan areas.[110] The former communities, of course, are likely to be more diversified than the latter.

It is probably also true that the labor supply adjusts to changes in labor demand more readily in a diversified than in a specialized labor market area. On the basis of British experience, Allen contends that diversified areas will have less unemployment than specialized areas for this reason. In the former, declining industries will decline more rapidly because new entrants into the labor market, as well as presently employed workers, have *other* industries into which to move. In a

[108] Reynolds, *op. cit.,* pp. 246–247. See pp. 182–185 infra for further discussion of this point.

[109] Palmer, "The Mobility of Weavers in Three Textile Centers," *Quarterly Journal of Economics,* 55:460–487 (May 1941).

[110] Bogue, *op. cit.,* p. 27.

highly specialized labor market, on the other hand, workers have no place to go, and new entrants to the labor market add to the labor reserve, causing wage rates to fall and giving the dying industry an extended lease on life. Moreover, an area that is already diversified has an advantage in attracting new industries because of the variety of labor and technical skills already in the community. Finally, Allen believes that employers in diversified areas are probably more flexible and "less inclined to regard their present activities as settled by laws of nature." [111]

These conclusions not only appear to be logically sound, but can claim the support of at least some empirical evidence. Palmer's study of the work experience of weavers in three cities during 1926–35 showed that the proportion of weavers in the declining textile industry who had entered the labor force during the previous 10 years was smaller in Philadelphia—the most diversified of the areas—than in either of the other two cities.[112] There is also evidence that during the same decade the expanding radio industry in Philadelphia drew young workers from declining industries—particularly women from textiles.[113] On the other hand, the findings of the six-city survey were inconclusive with respect to the effect of industrial structure on labor mobility. Among the six cities, measures of mobility during the 1940's were not closely associated either with the extent of employment diversification or with rates of change in the industrial distribution of employment. Palmer suggests that "The inclusion of more cities or of cities with greater variety of economic structure and employment trends would have provided better tests of these relationships." [114]

The amount of movement into and out of the labor force is clearly influenced by the industrial structure of the labor market area. It has been seen that this kind of movement is much more common among women than among men. Moreover, it appears that the extent of labor force participation by women is significantly influenced by the industrial structure of the labor market. Belloc correlated labor force participation rates for women in 91 cities of 100,000 or more population with certain other labor market characteristics of the

111 G. C. Allen, "Labour Transference and the Unemployment Problem," *Economic Journal*, 40:242–248 (June 1930).

112 Palmer, "The Mobility of Weavers in Three Textile Centers," pp. 460–487.

113 Palmer and Stoflet, *The Labor Force of the Philadelphia Radio Industry in 1936*, p. 20.

114 Palmer, *Labor Mobility in Six Cities*, p. 91.

areas. High rates of participation in the labor force were found to be associated with either or both of two conditions: a concentration of an industry with a relatively large proportion of jobs suitable for women—textiles, apparel, electric machinery, or tobacco manufacturing—or a social tradition favorable to female employment, usually accompanied by a large Negro population accustomed to employment in domestic service.[115] It follows that in communities where the industrial structure encourages labor force participation by women, movement into and out of the labor force will be greater than in communities where the employment of women is less common. This would be particularly true where the industries with large female employment are seasonal.

The influence of industrial structure on labor mobility thus operates largely through the employment opportunities provided. High rates of participation in the labor force by women exist when job opportunities for women are great. Industrial diversification affects the pattern of mobility and the rapidity of the adjustment of labor supply to demand largely because of the wider range of employment opportunities accompanying diversification. Finally, to the extent that rapidly rising levels of employment in an area stimulate mobility, the role of employment opportunities is clearly paramount. The relationships that have been described in this section are additional evidence that the rate and pattern of job movement are, to a large degree, functions of the extent and the nature of the opportunities for employment.

SUMMARY

Mobility rates are not uniform among all groups of workers. Certain characteristics of workers, as well as certain aspects of their status, appear to be related either to the frequency with which they change jobs, the kinds of shifts they make, or both. Of all the characteristics studied, the most clearly associated with mobility is age. The rate of job movement declines with advancing age, at least between the ages of 20 and 65. This is true of all types of job change—interfirm, occupational, industrial, and geographic. There are also differences between the *kinds* of job changes made by younger and older workers. When the latter do change jobs, they are less likely than the former to make

[115] Nedra B. Belloc, "Labor-Force Participation and Employment Opportunities for Women," *Journal of the American Statistical Association*, 45:400–410 (September 1950).

complex shifts, involving changes of occupational and industrial affiliation.

Although men have generally been found to be more mobile than women, there is reason to believe that this may be due to differences between the labor force exposure of men and women and to the measures of mobility used. When women who have been in the labor force continuously for a 10-year period are compared with a similar group of men, there appears to be no difference in the degree of job movement. Nevertheless, there are differences between men and women with regard to the frequency of certain kinds of movement. The most obvious of these is the greater tendency of women to shift into and out of the labor force. It is also probably true that women make fewer occupational and geographic job changes than men.

Relatively few studies have compared the mobility of white and Negro workers. Those that have, however, show greater job movement among the latter. The differences generally exist only for men. To what extent these racial differentials in mobility are simply reflections of differences in the occupational compositions of the white and Negro labor forces and of greater involuntary movement on the part of the latter as a result of discriminatory employment practices is not known.

Marital status, extent of formal education, type of home tenure, and union membership are additional factors whose relationship to mobility rates has been investigated. The evidence, however, has been so scanty as to permit very few generalizations of even a tentative nature.

The institutional or environmental forces most frequently recognized by investigators as impinging on labor mobility are trade unionism, employers' personnel policies, government policies, the level of business activity, and the industrial structure of labor markets. Conclusions as to the effects of all but the last two of these have been largely deductive.

There appears to be general agreement among labor economists that trade unionism has tended to reduce labor mobility, although this proposition has not been empirically established. The "system of rules" established by trade unionism, as well as the sociological implications of union organization, would appear to strengthen the ties of workers to the jobs they hold. Further research is needed, however, in order to determine both the strength of this tendency and the aspects of unionism that most influence mobility.

Numerous personnel policies of employers can affect mobility. Hiring preferences, techniques of recruitment and selection, and promotion policies affect either the incidence or the volume of mobility, or both. In view of the multitude of pertinent variables and the diversity of policy with respect to each, it is difficult to assess the net effect of employers' policies on labor mobility. It can be concluded that the policies of each employer are generally *designed* to reduce his own labor turnover, and that to the extent that these policies are successful, inter-firm mobility is discouraged.

Numerous government programs influence labor mobility either directly or indirectly. Perhaps the most potent influence of government on mobility is indirect. Since the amount of voluntary job shifting varies directly with changes in employment opportunities, government fiscal and monetary policies influence mobility through their effect on the level of economic activity.

That the amount of voluntary labor mobility varies directly with the extent of employment opportunities is amply substantiated by data on labor turnover as well as by studies of work histories for periods including both prosperous and depressed economic conditions. Although voluntary movement increases during prosperity and decreases during depression, the amount of involuntary movement varies in the opposite direction.

Certain characteristics of a local labor market appear to condition the pattern of job changes, as well as the degree of movement. As would be expected, industrial and occupational job changes are relatively more numerous in an industrially diversified than in a highly specialized area. It is also probable that labor supply adjusts to changes in labor demand more rapidly in a diversified than in a specialized area.

On the basis of the findings reviewed in this chapter, the volume and nature of employment opportunities are of paramount importance in conditioning the extent and incidence of labor mobility. Many, if not most, of the mobility differentials among various groups of workers are explainable at least in part by differences in the employment opportunities available to them. Also, most of the institutional forces which have been examined affect mobility, if at all, largely by influencing either the extent or pattern of job opportunities. For example, the limited employment prospects of older workers undoubtedly help to explain their low mobility; and many of the facets of trade unionism that have been regarded as restricting mobility are related, perhaps subtly, to employment opportunities. If seniority arrangements are significant in producing job attachment this is largely because of the actual or feared absence of alternative employment.

The importance of employment opportunities in conditioning mobility has significant theoretical implications. Traditional wage and labor allocation theory is cast in a framework that assumes full employment. To the extent that employment opportunities are limited, the theory may only imperfectly describe or explain actual labor market processes. This question is examined in the next chapter.

5 MOBILITY AND THE PROCESS

OF LABOR ALLOCATION

The reasons why workers shift jobs and the economic effects of that shifting are closely related questions that bear directly on fundamental issues in economic theory. It was pointed out in Chapter 1 that for flexibility a dynamic, free enterprise economy must rely on the mobility of labor. For optimum efficiency, the movement of workers into and out of the labor force and among various occupations, firms, and geographic regions must take place so as to assure the distribution of workers in accordance with the relative need for them. But so long as job choices remain free, to say that labor mobility contributes to the flexibility of the economic system implies that the economy somehow evaluates the differential social importance of possible activities, and that individuals respond to such valuations in making their decisions about whether, where, and in what capacity to work.

It is important to note that two conditions must exist if this functional relationship between labor mobility and economic flexibility is to prevail. First, the employment decisions of workers or potential workers must be rational; that is, they must be made in terms of ascertainable criteria.[1] Second, these criteria must involve either directly or indirectly the factors that measure the relative social importance of alternative activities. If workers' job choices are completely random and lacking in purposiveness, it is meaningless to consider mobility as facilitating the adaptation of the labor force to the changing requirements of a dynamic economy. On the other hand, if such job choices, however rational, are made in terms of objectives that are unrelated to the needs of the economy, there is again no assurance that labor mobility will perform its economic function.

Prevailing economic theory resolves this problem by identifying the

[1] See George Katona, *Psychological Analysis of Economic Behavior* (New York: McGraw-Hill Book Company, 1951), p. 49. Katona says that "the psychologist does not acknowledge the occurrence of behavior that is not eventually understandable. The only meaning he can give to the concept of rational behavior is based on its description as the weighing of different alternative courses of action and of choosing deliberately among them, according to some principle."

factors that measure the relative "need" for labor with those that determine workers' job choices and induce them to move from one job to another. In a free market, differentials in the wages and other economic perquisites of similar jobs reflect differences in the demand for labor. And it is precisely these differentials that produce movement of workers from job to job. Such movement continues, moreover, until the differentials are eliminated. It is noteworthy that in this conception mobility plays a dual role, providing individual as well as social benefits. Not only does it operate to assure society of the "proper" allocation of the labor force, but it also provides the individual with the maximum opportunities for self-improvement.

With respect to jobs that are not alike, the theory proceeds along similar lines. The inherent attractiveness of jobs varies. Some are heavy and dirty, others are light and clean. Some involve great responsibility for the care of expensive materials or for the supervision of workers; others are almost completely free of such responsibility. Some require skills that can be gained only by lengthy training; for others, little or no preparation is needed. But whatever the differences among jobs, there is implicit in traditional economic theory the notion that they can be and are compensated by differentials in wages. Consequently, wage differentials among *different* occupations do not necessarily stimulate the movement of workers. Only when the differentials more than counterbalance the differences in the nonwage attractiveness of jobs will movement occur, and it will continue until the wage differentials are once again only "normal." In each occupation wages are constantly gravitating toward the level at which they are just high enough to attract the required number of workers. Needless to say, "movement" between occupations requiring prolonged training periods is conceived as a long-run process which occurs principally as a result of changes in the rates of entry into various occupations by workers entering the labor force.

The size of the labor force itself, or more precisely the number of man-hours of labor that is "offered" by workers, is also a function of the wage rate in traditional economic theory. Work is regarded as being essentially "painful," or as involving a "disutility" which increases as the number of hours is increased. Workers are conceived to weigh the disutility involved in additional work against the utility of the reward (wages) which they get for that work. Consequently, an increase in wage rates increases the supply of labor in two ways. Persons already in the labor force are willing to serve longer hours, and some of the persons who had been out of the labor force are attracted into it as the higher wage rate overcomes their reluctance to work.

The foregoing statement is obviously a grossly oversimplified version of the theory of labor allocation. Economists are generally careful to point out that the results suggested by the theory are products of a set of rather rigid assumptions, and that there are wide departures from these assumed conditions in the real world. Indeed, some economists caution that economic theory is not intended to describe actual economic behavior, even imperfectly, but rather to provide one kind of model in terms of which the efficiency of a given economic system can be evaluated.[2] Nevertheless, a number of empirical studies of labor market processes, and of labor mobility in particular, have had as either a primary or an incidental objective the testing of some of the premises of traditional allocation theory. Among the problems that have had the attention of investigators in this field is the validity of the assumption that workers make rational job choices and decisions in terms of the economic advantages (principally wages) of alternative jobs, and that the resultant movement of workers in the direction of higher paying jobs tends to reduce or eliminate differentials in the terms of employment.

Investigation of the validity of this assumption has involved four related sets of questions, which are all directed at establishing the interrelationship between the labor market behavior of workers on the one hand and the process of labor allocation on the other. (1) What are the criteria by which workers decide to take, keep, or change jobs? Identification of these criteria throws some light on the extent to which job decisions are "rational," and also on the relative importance of wages and other economic characteristics of jobs in accounting for the mobility of workers. (2) In what ways do workers find jobs, and how much do they know about alternative job opportunities? Since differentials in the attractiveness of jobs can induce movement of labor only insofar as they are known, the operation of the labor market is intimately affected by the amount and kinds of labor market information that workers have. (3) To what extent does movement of workers within local labor markets take place from low-wage to high-wage firms, and how much do individual workers improve their earnings by changing jobs? (4) Is actual or potential movement of workers effec-

---

[2] See, for example, Frank H. Knight, "Economic Theory and Nationalism" in *The Ethics of Competition and Other Essays* (New York: Harper & Brothers, 1935), pp. 277–283.

tive in reducing differentials in wages and in other terms of employment for comparable jobs?

MOTIVATIONAL FACTORS IN JOB DECISIONS

Studies of the motivational factors in labor mobility have almost
invariably proceeded on the assumption that the important influences
on job choices can be ascertained by asking workers why they have
made certain job changes or what they consider important in evaluating
jobs. The latter type of question has been asked both with reference
to actual jobs the worker has had or knows about and to "a job" in
the abstract.[3] Percentage distributions of the responses have been relied
upon to indicate the relative importance of various factors in explaining the labor market behavior of workers.

Limitations of Available Data. The reasons given by workers for
quitting certain jobs and taking others provide some insight into the
nature of labor market behavior and permit some conclusions as to
the factors most frequently responsible for voluntary job changes;
but certain limitations in the data collected in past studies must be
noted before attempting to summarize and interpret their findings.

In the first place, the reasons given by workers for making certain
job choices can indicate motivational influences on labor market behavior in only a very restricted, and perhaps superficial, sense. If
motivation has reference to the deep-seated drives that govern human
activity, then the criteria by which workers make decisions about jobs
—even assuming that they can be discovered—are only reflections or
behavioral manifestations of the motivational forces involved.[4] For

---

[3] The literature relating to the elements in job satisfaction is voluminous. Most
of it, however, is oriented to personnel administration, being concerned with discovering the characteristics of jobs and of personnel policy that bear most directly
on employee "morale." In most studies of this kind, employees have been provided with check lists of job characteristics and have been asked to indicate, in one
manner or another, how important they think these factors are. The results have
been so diverse as to defy generalization, and no attempt to describe them is made
in this section, in which attention is given to attempts to relate workers' attitudes
toward their jobs to their actual labor market behavior. For bibliographies of
"morale studies," see *Occupations,* 16:662–664 (April 1938); 19:27–28 (October 1940);
21:462–463 (February 1943); 23:414–415 (April 1945); 26:431 (April 1948). For a critical analysis of some of the techniques used in these studies, see Arthur Kornhauser,
"Psychological Studies of Employee Morale" in Schuyler D. Hoslett, ed., *Human
Factors in Management* (Parkville, Mo.: Park College Press, 1946), pp. 297–322.

[4] See Else Frenkel-Brunswik, "Motivation and Behavior," *Genetic Psychology*

example, even if it were empirically established that workers' job choices are governed principally by the wage factor, we still would not know *why*. The quest for the highest possible wage might be motivated by a desire for ego recognition, for security, or for physical comfort, to mention only a few possibilities. This is an important point, for a particular drive may manifest itself in different patterns of overt behavior, depending on environmental circumstances. In some situations either the desire for physical comfort or for ego recognition might cause workers to evaluate jobs principally in terms of wages; in others, workers' reactions to wage differentials might depend on which of these two drives predominated.[5] It follows that an adequate theory of labor market behavior requires a knowledge of the identity and relative strength of the basic motivating forces, and of the way in which their manifestations in overt behavior are affected by environmental factors.

No study of labor mobility has attempted to relate the mobility characteristics of workers to these deeper levels of personality, or to discover the basic drives that explain job changes.[6] Although this is a serious omission from some points of view, it does not prevent the testing of labor allocation theory, for the theory is not concerned explicitly with the kind of motivational influences just described,

---

Monographs, 26:121–265 (1942). "The terms motivation and behavior refer to different levels of the personality which are not equally accessible. Behavior can be observed directly; motivation is inferred and has the character of an explanatory construct" (p. 125). In the study reported by Frenkel-Brunswik, motivational drives were conceived as relating to a "level of personality which stands behind the surface of overtly displayed social techniques but which is not as remote from behavior as the psychoanalytic concepts" (pp. 144–145).

[5] For example, in normal times either the desire for physical comfort or the desire for ego recognition may cause workers to emphasize high wages, in the one case because of the greater material well-being, and in the other because of the greater prestige, inherent in a high plane of living. During a war period, on the other hand, the drive for ego recognition might cause wages to assume less importance because of the existence of other means of achieving prestige, as by employment in a war industry. The fact that such "high-prestige" jobs have also generally been high-wage jobs would of course make the foregoing hypothesis very difficult to test.

[6] For an interesting study which illustrates the possibilities for this kind of research, see Jeannette G. Friend and Ernest A. Haggard, *Work Adjustment in Relation to Family Background*, American Psychological Association, Applied Psychology Monographs, No. 16 (Stanford: Stanford University Press, 1948). Among other things, this study sought to determine whether the basic personality traits and the family backgrounds of workers are related to the degree of adjustment and achievement in their jobs.

but merely assumes that workers make job decisions in such a manner as to maximize their net economic advantage. In other words, it assumes a kind of behavior rather than a pattern of motivational forces, and this assumed pattern can be compared with actual patterns of behavior, ignoring the fundamental forces which explain either pattern.[7] For convenience the term motivation is used throughout this chapter, but the restricted meaning should be kept in mind.

The usefulness of available information on the reasons for job changes is further limited by the failure to differentiate among several situations which are quite dissimilar. There are at least three different circumstances in which workers voluntarily terminate employment. A worker may quit a job because he has found another which is more attractive to him; because of dissatisfaction with his present job and the hope that he will find a more satisfying one; or with no intention of seeking other work. Only separations of the first type are clearly relevant in research intended to test empirically the premises of traditional economic theory relating to labor mobility. The basic notion in the theory is that workers choose among alternative jobs in terms of their "net attractiveness." The worker who gives up a job in order to take another about which he already knows can have made the kind of comparison between the two jobs that the theory assumes he will make, and in these circumstances it is appropriate to investigate the characteristics of the jobs compared.

The worker who quits a job with no prospect of another is in a different position. Whether he will succeed in finding a better one cannot be predicted at the time. The reasons for leaving jobs under these circumstances may indicate the conditions that are so onerous to workers that they are willing to risk unemployment in order to avoid them, but do not disclose the characteristics in terms of which alternative opportunities are compared. There is a considerable difference between exchanging a job for unemployment because of dissatisfaction with wages, and exchanging one job for another to obtain better wages. Yet tabulations of reasons for voluntary quits have not distinguished between these two situations. Future studies of the reasons for job separations should differentiate between persons in these two categories.[8]

[7] Cf. Katona, *op. cit.*, p. 74: "for purposes of understanding economic behavior the difficult task of discovering the hidden motives may not be necessary."

[8] Although Reynolds does not classify reasons for leaving jobs in the manner suggested, he does recognize the desirability of distinguishing between the two types

There is a third limitation on the usefulness of available data on reasons for making job changes. Although the reasons given by workers may suggest specific factors responsible for movement, they shed no light whatsoever on the strength of these factors relative to others which induce the worker not to move. For understanding the motivational factors involved in labor mobility, the latter reasons are at least as significant as the reasons for decisions to change jobs. A frequency distribution of the reasons for voluntary job changes may show the relative importance of various factors in accounting for movement that *has occurred,* but does not indicate the power of any of these factors to produce movement.

Finally, in addition to these theoretical limitations, practical difficulties in analyzing and comparing the findings of research on reasons for voluntary job changes result from the great diversity of design and methodology in past studies. Different types of workers have been investigated in varying economic and social environments. Furthermore, the data have been collected in different ways—some in extended semi-guided interviews with workers, some in briefer interviews of an enumerative type, and in one case in the exit interview by company personnel officers. The most complicating factor, however, is the lamentable lack of uniformity in the classification systems used by different investigators. Even where the categories of reasons for job changes have been the same, there is no assurance that identical responses have been classified in the same way by different observers.

Reasons for Voluntary Job Separations. Table 3 is an attempt to reduce this lack of comparability as far as possible and to show the nature of the differences that cannot be eliminated, by applying a standardized classification system to data from recent mobility studies of the reasons for voluntary job separations. The choice of the categories shown in the table was dictated largely by the categories used in the original studies which are summarized. Some of them have

---

of job separations (*The Structure of Labor Markets,* pp. 240–241). Of the more than 60 workers in one of his samples who had voluntarily changed jobs since the end of World War II, about two fifths had found a new job before quitting, while the other three fifths had quit without having first lined up other work (p. 215).

In the University of Minnesota Industrial Relations Center's unpublished study, "Voluntary Shifts of St. Paul Workers, 1940–44 and 1945–50" (1952), the raw data did not distinguish between these two types of job separations. However, an attempt was made to tabulate separately those cases in which it *appeared* from the work histories that workers had left jobs after first having located new ones. For a description of this study, see pp. 158–160 infra.

TABLE 3. PERCENTAGE DISTRIBUTION OF VOLUNTARY JOB SEPARATIONS BY MAJOR REASON
GIVEN BY WORKER, SELECTED STUDIES

		Reasons for voluntary separations					
	Wages	Other economic factors	Intrinsic nature of job	Human relations factors	Personal reasons	Other	Total
New Haven: separations from last job before interview, 1947–48							
Manual workers randomly selected	24	0	31	30	–	15*	100
Male mfg. workers changing status 1946–47	27	0	31	23	–	19†	100
Minneapolis: separations by mobile workers drawn from representative sample							
1947–48	11	0	51	10	18	10‡	100
1943–48	15	0	45	9	14	17§	100
Fitchburg: separations by workers shifting between mfg. and utility firms, 1937–39	4	11	7	2	29	47¶	100
St. Paul: separations by sample of workers 25 and over, working 1 mo. or more in 1950							
1940–44							
Men	15	27	23	2	19	14#	100
Women	13	16	23	1	40	7	100
1945–50							
Men	13	27	29	3	22	6**	100
Women	9	12	23	2	51	3	100
6-city survey: separations 1940–50 by sample of skilled workers 25 and over, working 1 mo. or more in 1950	14	26	7	7	19	27	100

Source: Data for New Haven from Reynolds, *The Structure of Labor Markets;* for Minneapolis, from Heneman, Fox, and Yoder, University of Minnesota Industrial Relations Center Bul. 10, pp. 1–28; for Fitchburg, from Myers and Maclaurin, *The Movement of Factory Workers;* for St. Paul, from University of Minnesota Industrial Relations Center, "Voluntary Shifts of St. Paul Workers, 1940–44 and 1945–50"; for six cities from Myers and Shultz, "Patterns of Mobility of Skilled Workers and Factors Affecting Their Occupational Choice," unpublished manuscript, Massachusetts Institute of Technology Industrial Relations Section.

* All 15 percent satisfied with job but "left to take a better one."

† Includes 17 percent satisfied with job but "left to take a better one."

‡ Includes 2 percent leaving to enter military service.

§ Includes 4 percent leaving to enter military service.

¶ Includes 16 percent giving no reason, 16 percent leaving to take another job, and 14 percent leaving to take a former job.

Includes 10 percent leaving to enter defense work.

** Includes 4 percent leaving to enter defense work.

presented more detailed classifications than that in Table 3, and their categories have been consolidated to make them comparable with the broader classes used in other studies. In a few instances, categories have been not only combined but also regrouped.

Classified under "wages" in Table 3 are those responses of workers that emphasize compensation as the factor responsible for the decision to quit a job.[9] This category is not as homogeneous as it might appear, however. Both Reynolds, and Myers and Shultz report that when a worker expresses an attitude toward wages, he may have in mind either or both of two quite different things. He may be considering the *adequacy* of his wage to cover his cost of living, or he may be evaluating the *fairness* of his wage relative to wages paid for other jobs in the plant or for similar jobs in other plants.

The principal components of "other economic factors" are "steadiness of employment" and "chance for advancement or improvement." These factors have been classified in different studies under such headings as "better future," "steadier work," "to better myself," "to go into business for myself," and "chance for improvement."

Included under "intrinsic nature of the job" are workers' reactions to the physical characteristics of the job and their interest in and capacity for the type of work involved. Such considerations as whether the job is relatively clean or dirty, light or heavy, safe or dangerous, are among its physical characteristics. Physical plant conditions, type of machinery, and hours of work are also included. Job interest and capacity are self-explanatory, including such responses as "I like (or don't like) that kind of work," "I can't stand indoor work," and "that's the only thing I know how to do."

The "human relations" factors might be called the psychological and social satisfactions or dissatisfactions on the job. For example, the

---

[9] Most of the studies have, in effect, involved asking the worker the chief reason for a given job separation. But Reynolds, and Myers and Shultz used semi-guided interviews, and workers sometimes mentioned more than one factor in accounting for a particular decision. These investigators, therefore, tabulated the *frequency* with which various factors were mentioned by workers. As many as three reasons given by a single worker were coded. Reynolds reports, however, that he experimented with the alternative method of tabulating the single most important element in each worker's response, and that the results of this procedure differed very little from the tabulations that he presents. (*The Structure of Labor Markets,* p. 91, note 12.) It appears to be permissible to ignore this difference in methodology, therefore, and to regard all the distributions in Table 3 as showing the principal reason for the job separation.

"degree of independence and control" is one of the categories used by Myers and Shultz and by Reynolds that is included here. As defined by Reynolds, it involves freedom from too close supervision and the opportunity to offer opinions on how the job should be done. Fairness of treatment and congenial relations with fellow workers are also included among the "human relations" factors.

The "personal" reasons for job separations differ from the others in that ordinarily they imply no dissatisfaction with the particular job, but rather a decision to cease working entirely, either temporarily or permanently. Such specific factors as poor health, pregnancy, family responsibilities, continuing in school, retirement, and "moving out of city" are included in this category.

With reference to the assumptions of economic theory, perhaps the most interesting conclusion to be drawn from Table 3 is that wages are not the predominant factor in explaining voluntary job separations. Indeed, the evidence justifies an even stronger statement. Wages are the decisive factor in only a minority of the voluntary separations reported by the various studies—ranging from 4 percent in Myers and Maclaurin's study of Fitchburg factory workers in the late 1930's to about 25 percent in Reynolds' study of manual workers in New Haven in the postwar period. In the other three studies the wage factor accounted for approximately 10 to 15 percent of the voluntary separations.

The marked variation in the relative importance of the wage factor, shown in Table 3, invites investigation. Much of it unquestionably results from differences in the samples of job separations. In Reynolds' study apparently all the job terminations involved fairly direct shifts from one job to another without intervening periods out of the labor market, since no reasons for separation are classified as "personal," which would include such factors as illness, retirement, education, and household duties. On the other hand, in all the other studies substantial proportions of the job terminations were of the "personal" variety, resulting in temporary periods of no labor force activity. Separations of this kind, of course, are not pertinent to an investigation of the factors that motivate job *changes,* and their inclusion in the total necessarily results in understating the importance of the various considerations (including wages) that induce workers to move from one job to another.

The extremely low proportion of voluntary separations ascribed to wage considerations in Myers and Maclaurin's sample has several probable explanations. First, the reasons for almost half the separations are unknown. If the cases for which reasons are not known were distributed in the same proportions as the other cases, wage considerations would account for twice as high a percentage of voluntary quits as that shown. Second, an unusually high percentage of the separations were for "personal" reasons, representing departures from the labor force, and this necessarily reduces the percentage attributable to wages. Third, the reasons tabulated in Myers and Maclaurin's study were obtained from exit interviews recorded on the workers' personnel cards. There is reason to suspect that such information is less valid than that reported by the worker in an informal interview with an "outsider," although there is no evidence as to either the extent or the direction of whatever bias may be involved.

There is some evidence that wages are relatively more important in motivating job changes during periods of high employment than during periods when the labor market is looser. Reynolds emphasizes the fact that an extremely low rate of unemployment characterized the local labor market during the period covered by his survey; and he reports a higher percentage of voluntary separations due to wages than any other investigator. On the other hand, Myers and Maclaurin's study, in which the wage factor appears to be less important than in any other, was conducted in the depressed period of the late 1930's. The substantial differences in the design and methods of these two studies make it dangerous to conclude that the varying results are attributable even in part to differences in economic conditions. However, the University of Minnesota study of St. Paul workers points to the same conclusion, inasmuch as slightly higher percentages of all voluntary separations resulted from wage considerations in the 1940–44 period than in 1945–50. Moreover, the difference is probably understated in Table 3, for a substantial proportion of the separations made for "other" reasons during the earlier period were "to go into defense work," and the wage consideration was undoubtedly important in those changes. Heneman, Fox, and Yoder's data on "mobile" workers in Minneapolis also suggest a positive relationship between the level of employment and the relative importance of the wage factor in motivating job changes. Wage considerations accounted for a larger proportion of separations in 1943–48 than in 1947–48; the former period, which included the wartime peak, had higher average levels of employment than the latter.

Far more important than wages in accounting for voluntary job separations are characteristics of the job itself—its physical characteristics and its interest for the worker. In all but two studies these factors accounted for between a fourth and a half of the total number of separations, and were more important than any other single factor. It is noteworthy that among the skilled workers covered in the study by Myers and Shultz, the "intrinsic nature of the job" was considerably less influential in causing job changes than among other groups of workers. This would be expected in view of the likelihood that skilled craftsmen will remain in the same occupation when they change jobs. Furthermore, the physical conditions in which skilled work is done are likely to vary less from one employer to another than is true of semiskilled or unskilled jobs.

The extreme differences among the studies in the apparent importance of "other economic factors" and of "human relations" factors in motivating workers to leave jobs are not easily explained. While over a fourth of the job separations reported by the University of Minnesota study and by Myers and Shultz were prompted by economic factors other than wages—chiefly "steadiness of work" and "chance for advancement"—none of the separations reported by Reynolds or by Heneman and others was made for these reasons. And while Reynolds reports that between 20 and 30 percent of the separations by members of his two samples were due to "human relations" factors —chiefly "independence and control" and "fairness of treatment"— such reasons accounted for only about 10 percent of the separations reported by Heneman and others and well under 10 percent in the remaining studies.

It is difficult to avoid the suspicion that the results of studies of this kind are influenced considerably by subjective factors in the analysis and coding of interviews and by differences in the meaning of various concepts to individual investigators. It does not seem reasonable, for example, that a fourth or more of the job separations by a cross section of New Haven manual workers should have occurred because of "unfair treatment" and lack of "independence and control," and that only 2 or 3 percent of the job changes by a cross section of men in St. Paul should have had such causes. It is true that two quite different labor markets are involved, and that there are differences in the workers sampled and in the time periods covered. One might conclude therefore that the pattern of motives for job changes is peculiarly related to time and place. This is doubtless true to a degree, and it may be the major explanation for the varying results, but an equally tenable hypothesis is that the variation is attributable to differences in the ways in which the responses of workers were interpreted and classified by investigators (as well as in the way the responses were obtained). It would be an interesting, although time-consuming, experiment for each research staff that has investigated this problem to trade its raw schedules with another staff so that the entire editorial and coding process for each study could be subjected to an independent check. Only in this way could a confident judgment be reached as to how much of the variation in the findings exists in the data and how much is a product of the varying orientations of the observers.[10]

Reasons for Taking Jobs. The reasons given by workers for taking certain jobs, as reported in three independent studies, are presented in Table 4. At first thought, one might presume that the reasons for taking jobs would be correlatives of the reasons for leaving other jobs, and that consequently, at least for a given group of workers, the motivational pattern indicated by the two sets of data would be similar. This is not so, principally because workers frequently leave jobs without having lined up others, and because many workers are separated from jobs involuntarily. Moreover, there are always workers who are entering the labor force and taking their first jobs. Consequently, among the reasons for taking jobs are "unemployment" and "chance," which have no counterparts in the reasons for voluntary separations. The first refers to cases in which the worker's only explanation for taking a job is his inability to find any other or simply being "out of work." The second, which is usually relevant only to the choice of the first job, indicates that the worker "drifted into a job" more or less fortuitously.

For a theory of job choice it is most significant that of a sample of 144 workers employed by a Nashua textile mill, fully a third had not "chosen" the job in any real sense, but had either drifted into it or had taken it because they could find no other. Of those who were laid off when the mill closed and who found other jobs, about half explained their "choice" of these jobs also in terms of their inability to find any others. A large proportion even of those who had voluntarily quit the mill in anticipation of the shutdown took other jobs

[10] Most investigators have been aware of the problem described here, and in a few cases careful efforts have been made to cope with it. Thus, Myers and Shultz, in their investigation of the Nashua labor market (*The Dynamics of a Labor Market*), studied copies of the coded schedules used in Reynolds' study of the New Haven labor market in order to insure the comparability of the two studies.

TABLE 4. PERCENTAGE DISTRIBUTION OF JOBS BY REASONS GIVEN BY WORKERS FOR TAKING JOBS, SELECTED STUDIES

	Reasons for taking jobs							
	Wages	Other economic factors	Intrinsic nature of job	Human relations factors	Unemploy- ment	Chance	Other	Total
Nashua: random samples of workers								
Workers laid off when textile mill closed								
First jobs	9	9	18	18	16	26	4	100
Jobs at textile mill	16	15	23	9	15	19	3	100
Present jobs of workers quitting before mill closed, who found new jobs	4	14	24	2	38	-	18	100
Present jobs of workers laid off who found new jobs	4	23	18	2	49	-	4	100
Minneapolis: mobile workers drawn from representative sample								
All jobs 1947–48	12	10	18	-	53	-	7*	100
All jobs 1943–48	14	7	21	-	53	-	7†	100
St. Paul: all jobs taken 1940– 50—by sample of workers 25 and over, working 1 mo. or more in 1950— for which reasons for taking could be inferred								
1940–44								
Men	21	59	1	-	19	-	-	100
Women	19	59	1	-	21	-	-	100
1945–50								
Men	13	50	2	-	35	-	-	100
Women	21	43	6	-	29	-	1	100

Source: Data for Nashua from Myers and Shultz, *The Dynamics of a Labor Market;* for Minneapolis and St. Paul, see Table 3.
* Includes 4 percent who took job because of "better salary, hours, working conditions, and future."
† Includes 5 percent who took job because of reasons specified in preceding note.

principally out of necessity rather than because of their attractiveness. Almost two fifths of this group said they took their subsequent jobs because they were unemployed. The same pattern was found for 98 "mobile" Minneapolis workers. Of the 370 jobs taken by this group during 1943–48, over half were explained in terms of the unemployment of the worker rather than the attributes of the job.

The data examined up to this point suggest that much of the voluntary mobility of workers is haphazard in the sense that workers do not appear to be making choices on the basis of the characteristics of alternative jobs.[11] But workers frequently do move directly from one job into another already lined up, and the considerations involved in these direct job shifts deserve attention.

The findings in a study of the job shifts made by St. Paul workers during the 1940's are pertinent and are the only available data on reasons for shifts from jobs currently held into others that have been offered. Although these workers were not asked the reasons for changing jobs, they were asked to explain each job termination that occurred during the decade. Some of the reasons given for leaving jobs, however, implied that the respondent had already found another job that was better in some respect. Consequently, the reason for leaving one job and the reason for taking the next one were the same.

This kind of evidence provides an empirical test of the assumptions of economic theory, for the worker is making a comparison between a job that he holds and another that he knows he can have. Furthermore, the St. Paul study has particular value for such a test because the data, collected as a part of the six-city survey, covered a cross section of all St. Paul residents who were 25 years of age and over and who had worked at least one month in 1950. All the job changes made by this group between 1940 and 1950 were analyzed. Thus, the data indicate the pattern of voluntary job changes for virtually the total labor force of an industrially well-diversified city during a decade that included both war and peacetime conditions. Moreover, the wartime and postwar patterns can be compared. The data on reasons for changing jobs have several limitations, however, primarily because they were derived from a schedule that was not designed to produce them. The cases in which the worker had quit a job in order to take another *which he had already lined up* had to be editorially

---

[11] This does not mean that the process is "irrational." A worker who takes a job because no other is available is clearly making a rational decision. In many voluntary job changes the worker simply is not in a position to make a conscious comparison of the advantages of alternative jobs.

determined. There is no assurance that all such cases were included, or that all the cases included were of this kind.[12] Furthermore, reasons for job changes were obtained not from "depth" interviews but from answers to direct questions. With these limitations in mind, the patterns of reasons for direct job shifts in the war and postwar periods can be examined (Table 5).

TABLE 5. NUMBER AND PERCENT OF DIRECT SHIFTS FROM ONE JOB TO ANOTHER BY ST. PAUL WORKERS, 1940–50, BY REASON FOR CHANGE

Reason for change	1940–44		1945–50	
	Men	Women	Men	Women
	Number of direct job shifts*			
Better working conditions	157	51	314	354
Better wages	2,666	759	2,300	1,315
Better future	2,352	708	2,509	506
General improvement †	5,228	1,668	6,640	2,275
Miscellaneous	–	–	52	51
Total	10,403	3,186	11,815	4,501
	Percent			
Better working conditions	1.5	1.6	2.7	7.9
Better wages	25.6	23.8	19.5	29.2
Better future	22.6	22.2	21.2	11.2
General Improvement †	50.3	52.4	56.2	50.5
Miscellaneous	–	–	.4	1.1
Total	100.0	100.0	100.0	100.0

Source: Adapted from University of Minnesota Industrial Relations Center, "Voluntary Shifts of St. Paul Workers, 1940–44 and 1945–50."

* Respondents were asked the reason for *leaving* each job held between 1940 and 1950. In many cases, however, the reason given by the respondent for leaving a job implied that he had already found another job that was better in some respect. Only such jobs are tabulated here.

† Includes some combination of better wages, better working conditions, and better future.

It is noteworthy first that only in a fourth of all the voluntary separations between 1940 and 1950 had the worker given up his job to take

12 In a letter dated June 17, 1952, Herbert G. Heneman, Jr., Assistant Director of the University of Minnesota Industrial Relations Center, writes: "Despite valiant efforts in editing, I am sure you will realize it has been impossible to . . . [determine] which items are intended as reasons for leaving and which are intended as reasons for taking."

another which he had already found.[13] In about one out of four of
these cases, better wages was the reason for the shift, while a "better
future" accounted for a somewhat smaller proportion. Better working
conditions figured in a very small minority of the shifts—less than
5 percent. However, "general improvement," which involves some
combination of the three factors previously mentioned was the motivating influence in about half of all the job changes.

The importance of economic factors in explaining these job shifts
is striking. Comparison of Tables 3 and 5 shows that wages are considerably more significant in accounting for a direct change of jobs
than in explaining all voluntary job separations. Working conditions
per se, on the other hand, seem to be much less important in the
former than in the latter case, although such conditions in combination with some economic factor may loom large in the "general improvement" category. These data suggest that when workers do seize
an opportunity to leave one job for another already found, the decision to make the change is most frequently influenced by the economic
characteristics of the two jobs—wages, and the prospects for the
future. If this is so, traditional economic theory errs less in assuming
the strength of the wage factor as a motivational influence than in
assuming that workers are generally in a position to compare the wages
of jobs. Additional evidence on the latter point will be examined in
subsequent sections of this chapter.

Factors in Job Satisfaction. In addition to approaching the problem
of motivation by asking workers to explain certain "operational" job
decisions they had made, both Reynolds, and Myers and Shultz attempted to discover the factors that produce satisfaction or dissatisfaction with jobs by asking workers to evaluate certain jobs they had
held or heard about. The job characteristics most frequently men-

---

[13] A total of 86,223 "reasons for leaving" jobs are reported, and a total of 41,366
"reasons for taking" jobs. Among the latter, however, are 11,461 cases in which
"unemployment" is listed as the "reason for taking." The Minnesota research
staff included these cases in order to make the tabulation of reasons for taking
jobs comparable with previously reported data on this subject. Since unemployment
obviously cannot figure in voluntary job changes, these cases have been subtracted
from the total "reasons for taking jobs." The remainder, 29,905, represents the
number of cases in which workers voluntarily left their jobs with other jobs already
lined up. This is 25.8 percent of the total of 116,128 voluntary separations reported.
(University of Minnesota Industrial Relations Center, "Voluntary Shifts of St. Paul
Workers, 1940–44 and 1945–50," computed from data in Appendix Tables 2a–2d.)

tioned are regarded by the investigators as the important influences in workers' job choices.[14] The results indicate that money income, the physical nature of the work, whether it is interesting or uninteresting, the degree of independence on the job, the nature of supervision, the fairness with which the worker feels that he is being treated, and the cordiality of relations with fellow workers are among the principal criteria by which workers evaluate jobs. There is no basis, however, for generalizations concerning the relative importance of these factors in producing job satisfaction. Myers and Shultz conclude that "There is simply no one fixed scale of job factors, listed in order of importance, that is held by most workers at all times. Rather, the importance that particular workers, or a group of workers, attach to any given job factor is a product of *the total situation in which they find themselves at a particular time.*" [15]

It does not seem possible to give operational meaning to the concept of "relative importance" of various job elements in producing satisfaction. As Reynolds points out, the only realistic sense in which one may speak of the relative importance of particular job characteristics in affecting workers' decisions is in terms of their marginal rates of substitution.[16] A worker can hardly be expected to say whether he regards higher wages or greater security as more "important" in the abstract. The question is unanswerable unless he knows the range of variation in these two elements in two actual or hypothetical jobs. Nor can the student probe very deeply into the motivational influences in labor market behavior without considering the entire context in which specific job decisions are made and job attitudes are created. Tabulations of the number of workers who do or do not like certain jobs for specified reasons do not provide this context.

One cannot be satisfied with what is presently known about the factors motivating labor market behavior, for their study has only begun. The evidence does not justify thinking of wages as the only explanation of the job choices made by workers. Many other factors, some of which can be more influential than wage considerations in certain circumstances, have to be taken into account. The evidence also indicates that a good deal of voluntary movement—perhaps most of it—is not the product of deliberate and careful comparison of

[14] See Reynolds, *op. cit.*, pp. 87–101 and Myers and Shultz, *The Dynamics of a Labor Market,* Chapter 6.

[15] *Ibid.*, p. 132.

[16] Reynolds, *op. cit.*, p. 88.

alternative job opportunities, but rather the result of workers' leaving jobs that are distasteful in order to cast around for others which they hope will be more satisfactory. There is need, through the combined efforts of psychologists, economists, and sociologists, and with improved research planning,[17] for more intensive investigation of the factors that motivate the labor market decisions of workers.

PROCESS OF JOB FINDING AND JOB CHOICE

How Workers Find Jobs. In contrast to the empirical evidence on *why* workers quit jobs to take others, the results of recent research relating to *how* workers find jobs are clear and unambiguous. Table 6 summarizes the evidence from six studies of this question, for 10 different groups of workers, and a total of 16 sets of jobs.

It is apparent that manual workers most often learn about jobs either through friends or relatives, or by direct application at the gate. These methods of finding jobs account for between about 50 and 85 percent of the cases in all the studies except that by Kerr.[18] The latter study involves only workers who migrated into the Seattle labor market area during World War II and took jobs in the aircraft industry or in the shipyards there. For this reason, it is not surprising that no workers are classified as having learned of the jobs by applying at the gate. Even under these circumstances, however, the influence of friends and relatives was important. About half of the private shipyard workers and a third of the aircraft and government shipyard employees learned of their jobs in this way.

Returning to work for a former employer is another relatively common method of getting jobs, either as a result of being recalled by the employer or at the initiative of the worker. The latter represents a special case of "applying at the gate," but the process is somewhat less random than other gate applications because the worker presumably has a firsthand knowledge of the jobs in the establishment.

In contrast with these techniques for finding jobs, the more formal

[17] It is doubtful whether valid information on motives can be obtained by relying exclusively on the answers to direct questions about the reasons for job decisions. The attitudes of workers expressed in such answers must at least be related to and analyzed in the light of their objective behavior in the labor market. The work done in the field of consumer motivation by the University of Michigan Institute for Social Research may suggest techniques and designs for research on labor market behavior. See Rensis Likert, "The Sample Interview Survey," in Wayne Dennis and others, *Current Trends in Psychology* (Pittsburgh: University of Pittsburgh Press, 1947), pp. 196–225. See also Katona, *op. cit.*, pp. 63–85.

[18] Clark Kerr, "Migration to the Seattle Labor Market Area, 1940–1942."

methods are surprisingly little used. Although the findings vary, in general the studies show that not more than a tenth of the workers find their jobs through public employment offices, that similarly small proportions learn about jobs through advertisements, and that even fewer find work through private employment agencies or unions. An exception to this pattern appears in the case of migrants into the Seattle labor market area during the war; because all of them were recruits from outside the local labor market, advertising (newspaper and radio) and government agencies were much more important as means of finding jobs than in other situations.

The implication that the public employment service plays a minor role in bringing workers into contact with jobs perhaps requires qualification. Levine [19] observes that the influence of the public employment office varies according to industry, occupation, and size of establishment, and consequently is considerably more important in some situations than these studies indicate. He cites a U. S. Employment Service study of establishments in essential activities in 18 important labor market areas which found that the ratio of employment office placements to all "new hires" ranged from about 5 percent to 60 percent in the various localities. Nevertheless, for most workers and under usual circumstances the public employment service seems to play a relatively minor role in the finding of jobs.[20]

The patterns followed by workers in seeking jobs are apparently rather firmly ingrained. When Reynolds asked a sample of employed manual workers how they would go about finding a job if they were out of work, the responses followed rather closely the pattern of their past behavior (Table 6). A third reported that they would canvass their acquaintances and relatives, a fifth said they would try gate applications, and one in seven indicated he would apply to a previous employer. The remaining third were equally divided among those who would register with the public employment office, those who would consult advertisements, and those who would rely on union or other contacts.

[19] Louis Levine, discussion on "Dynamics of the Labor Market," *Industrial Relations Research Association Proceedings of Fourth Annual Meeting . . . 1951,* pp. 134–135.

[20] Haber suggests that the situation in England is probably not much different from that in the United States, despite the much longer existence of the National Employment Service there. He reports that a relatively small proportion of the total placements—"perhaps no more than 20 to 25 percent"—are made through the employment exchange. (William Haber, discussion on "Dynamics of the Labor Market," *ibid.,* p. 131.)

TABLE 6. PERCENTAGE DISTRIBUTION OF JOBS BY METHODS USED BY WORKERS IN FINDING JOBS, SELECTED STUDIES

Method of finding job	New Haven manual workers			New Haven male mfg. workers, changing status 1946–47		Nashua textile workers laid off		
	Present job	First job	"How would you find a job?"	Present job	First job	First job	Mill job	Present job
Friends or relatives	28	55	34	27	53	62	56	36
Application at gate	20	29	18	42	29	23	37	14
Returning to ex-employer	13	9	15	8	7	0	0	6
Public employment office	13	–	11	13	–	2	3	4
Private employment agency	–	–	–	–	–	4	0	0
Advertisement	13	–	11	5	–	2	2	0
Union	5	–	7	1	–	0	0	4
Other	8	7	4	4	11	7	2	36*
Total	100	100	100	100	100	100	100	100

Source: Data for New Haven, Minneapolis, and Fitchburg are from sources given for Table 3; for Nashua, from Myers and Shultz, *The Dynamics of a Labor Market*; for Philadelphia, from Dorothea de Schweinitz, *How Workers Find Jobs;* for Seattle, from Clark Kerr, "Migration to the Seattle Labor Market Area, 1940–1942."

* Employer solicitation accounts for most of the cases in this class.

This pattern of job seeking appears to be of relatively long standing. As early as 1930 de Schweinitz found that among Philadelphia hosiery workers contacts with friends and relatives and direct application at the mill were by far the most common methods of finding jobs.[21] In a questionnaire survey almost three fifths of about 4,000 workers said they had found their jobs through friends or relatives, while between a fifth and a fourth had applied directly at the mill. Advertisements and private employment agencies combined were responsible for only about 5 percent of the placements. (The present system of public employment offices had not yet been established.) No pronounced differences were found between the methods used by men

[21] Dorothea de Schweinitz, *How Workers Find Jobs,* p. 89.

TABLE 6. *(Continued)*

Method of finding job	Nashua workers, quit before shutdown, found jobs — Present job	Minneapolis mobile workers — All jobs, 1947–48	All jobs, 1943–48	Migrants to Seattle area, 1940–42 — Aircraft jobs	Shipyard jobs — Private	Govt.	Phila-delphia hosiery workers — Present job	Fitchburg workers moving between mfg. & utilities, 1937–39 — Jobs taken, 1937–40
Friends or relatives	41	30	28	36	52	34	58	39
Application at gate	21	32	35	–	–	–	23	33
Returning to ex-employer	9	–	–	–	–	–	–	22
Public employment office	2	6	8	–	–	–	–	0
Private employ-ment agency	0	5	3	–	–	–	2	0
Advertisement	11	14	15	28	37	19	3	2
Union	0	7	5	–	–	–	–	–
Other	16†	6	6	36‡	11§	47¶	14	4
Total	100	100	100	100	100	100	100	100

† Consists entirely of employer solicitation.
‡ Includes 31 percent who heard of jobs through government agencies.
§ Includes 9 percent who heard of jobs through government agencies.
¶ Includes 36 percent who heard of jobs through government agencies.

and by women, but younger workers relied on friends and relatives more often than did older workers.[22]

Extent of Workers' Knowledge of Job Opportunities. Closely related to the question of how workers find jobs is the extent of their information about jobs before taking them and their knowledge of alternative opportunities. The assumption that workers make job choices in terms of differences in the "net advantages" of available alternatives is realistic only to the extent that workers are aware of both the existence and the nature of such alternatives.

[22] *Ibid.,* p. 93. Findings similar to those reported in this section were also obtained by the Princeton University Industrial Relations Section in an unpublished study of the Trenton, New Jersey labor market. See Richard A. Lester, *Labor and Industrial Relations* (New York: Macmillan Company, 1951), p. 42.

Direct evidence on this question is rather fragmentary. Reynolds, in his study of New Haven manual workers, asked a series of questions designed to test their familiarity with wages and working conditions in other plants in the area. The responses led him to conclude that workers generally "are poorly informed about job opportunities," although there are exceptions, particularly among skilled workers in craft unions.[23] When asked where they would go to seek work if they were out of a job, three fourths of the respondents did not even mention a specific plant. Of the quarter who named what they considered to be desirable places to work, about half named plants where they had previously worked, while the remainder mentioned firms in their home neighborhoods, in the same industry as their current employers, or large plants whose names were well known in the community. Nor were the workers any better informed about "undesirable" places to work. When asked whether there were any plants in which they would not want to work, only 40 percent mentioned specific firms. Moreover, the information that workers had about the firms they mentioned as either "good" or "bad" places to work was quite meager. Most frequently they had only vague impressions, and seldom had any specific knowledge of wages or working conditions.

Another indication of employees' meager knowledge of labor market conditions in general, and of comparative wage rates in particular, is the lack of correspondence found by Reynolds between workers' attitudes toward the wages paid by their firms and the actual ranking of the firms according to wage levels. Although 95 percent of the employees of firms in the top half of the wage distribution felt that their wage level compared favorably with others in the area, 80 percent of the workers employed by firms in the lower half of the wage distribution had the same attitude. Indeed, almost 100 percent of the employees of the plant that had the lowest level of wages in the community believed their wages were fair in relation to those paid by other plants, while the firm at the median of the wage distribution

[23] Reynolds, *op. cit.*, pp. 84, 214. There is additional evidence that skilled union members may be relatively well informed about labor market conditions and job opportunities. Bezanson's study of the interfirm movement of Philadelphia upholstery weavers led her to conclude that "there is indicated a considerable amount of knowledge on the part of workmen of conditions and working opportunity in the trade. How far this is due to the specialized skill, . . . the organization of the craft, or the moderate size of the industry is uncertain." (Anne Bezanson, "The Advantages of Labor Turnover: An Illustrative Case," *Quarterly Journal of Economics*, 42:464.)

had the largest percentage of employees who felt their wages were unfair.[24] These results suggest that employed workers generally have little or no knowledge of comparative wage rates in the local labor market, and that a worker's attitude toward the relative "fairness" of his wage is perhaps more a product of his general feeling of satisfaction or dissatisfaction with his job than of any objective knowledge of the wage pattern in the community.

Somewhat different conclusions concerning the extent of workers' knowledge of jobs were drawn by Myers and Shultz from their study of the labor market behavior of textile workers displaced by a mill shutdown in a New England city of medium size. Their findings "suggest that in a small compact labor market, at least, displaced workers are likely to have a pretty good knowledge of job characteristics of other available jobs in the community."[25] For example, only about a tenth of the displaced workers who obtained other jobs knew absolutely nothing about the job or the company before being hired. On the other hand, over a third of those who had voluntarily quit their jobs at the textile mill in anticipation of the shutdown, and more than two fifths of those laid off, knew something specific about their subsequent jobs before taking them. An additional 12 percent of those who quit and 27 percent of those laid off had previously been employed in the plants in which they found work, and therefore presumably had some firsthand knowledge of their new jobs. Thus, over half of the workers "had fairly specific job information about their new jobs *prior* to being hired."[26]

These results may appear to contradict those in Reynolds' study, but there were differences between the workers covered by the two studies, the questions asked, and the methods of analysis. Also, the difference in the size of the two labor markets has been considered an explanation of the difference in results.[27] Reynolds studied a community of about 350,000 persons, while the study by Myers and Shultz was made in a city only about one tenth as large. Workers in a small town may well have greater knowledge of the nature of al-

[24] Reynolds, *op. cit.*, pp. 213–214.

[25] Myers and Shultz, *The Dynamics of a Labor Market,* p. 60.

[26] *Ibid.,* p. 58.

[27] See George P. Shultz, "Recent Research on Labor Mobility," *Industrial Relations Research Association Proceedings . . . 1951,* pp. 114–115; Richard A. Lester, book review, *American Economic Review,* 41:1005 (December 1951). As has been seen, Myers and Shultz seem to accept the same interpretation when they emphasize that they are dealing with a "small compact labor market."

ternative job opportunities than workers in a large city, but other factors are probably of greater importance in explaining the different results in these two studies.

Most fundamental is the fact that the investigators were really asking two completely different questions. Reynolds asked *employed* workers how much they knew about *other* jobs in the community. Myers and Shultz asked workers who had lost one job how much they knew about another specific job *before they took it*. Even if all the other elements in the two studies had been the same, the results could be expected to differ because of this basic difference alone. It is of course not impossible for workers to find out about jobs in a local labor market, and it is not surprising that workers *who are without jobs* have managed to learn *something* about *one specific job* before they "sign up" for it. Indeed, the difference in the results goes far toward substantiating Reynolds' major point: that satisfactorily employed workers are in no real sense "in the labor market" —that the chief reason for their lack of information about other jobs is their lack of interest in employment conditions in other companies.[28]

There is reason to believe that even the labor market information generally available to unemployed workers may be overstated in the data presented by Myers and Shultz. The questions relating to job knowledge were asked only of those displaced workers who had found other jobs by the time they were interviewed. But only 35 percent of the workers who had been laid off by the textile mill, and 86 percent of those who had voluntarily quit, were working when interviewed.[29] The remainder were either unemployed or had dropped out of the labor force. To the extent that job knowledge is an aid in finding work, it can be assumed that the workers who had found jobs possessed better information on available employment opportunities than those who had not. Consequently, the percentages of the employed workers with specific job knowledge are probably higher than those that would have been obtained had all the workers been similarly questioned.

Finally, Myers and Shultz apparently used somewhat more liberal standards than Reynolds in deciding whether a worker had any specific knowledge of other jobs in the community. It is, of course,

28 Reynolds, *op. cit.*, p. 85. See also Clark Kerr, "Labor Markets: Their Character and Consequences," *American Economic Review*, 40(suppl.):281 (May 1950), especially note 9.

29 Myers and Shultz, *The Dynamics of a Labor Market*, p. 28.

difficult to be certain on this point, but a careful reading of the excerpts from interviews presented in the two reports gives the impression that Myers and Shultz classified as "specific job information" responses that Reynolds would have regarded as quite "meager" and "vague." [30] For example, among workers classified as having knowledge of the chance for advancement in the job taken, Myers and Shultz include the individual who said "this company is supposed to be a wonderful place to work, everyone knows they give you every chance to get ahead." In contrast, Reynolds says, "The answers to this question were quite meager. It usually turned out that the worker had only a vague impression that 'they treat you right at the A—— company,' or 'a friend told me that B—— is really a good shop.' "

On the basis of the evidence reviewed, it may be concluded that most production workers who are employed and satisfied with their jobs are not accustomed to comparing their present jobs with available alternatives. It is unusual for them to be aware of other job opportunities in the locality, and even less usual for them to know about the specific characteristics of these opportunities. Once a worker leaves a job, however, whether as a result of a layoff or by his own choice, he is on the lookout for another and, in the process of seeking a job, he necessarily learns something about what is available. The methods that he uses for finding jobs are not systematic. Generally he canvasses his friends or relatives, who frequently can give him leads on jobs either in the plants where they work or in others. Frequently, also, he makes the rounds of the plants in the area, in a more or less random fashion. To what extent does the worker in these circumstances make comparisons among jobs and weigh "advantages" against "disadvantages"?

Do Job Seekers "Compare" Alternative Job Opportunities? Myers and Shultz found that a sizable majority (60 percent) of the displaced textile workers who were successful in finding other work had taken the first job applied for.[31] This in itself, of course, does not mean that these workers made no comparisons among jobs. It is conceivable that each of them weighed the known alternatives and then successfully applied for the job of his choice. The workers' comments on the point, however, seem to refute this hypothesis. The five excerpts from interviews presented in the report indicate without exception

---

[30] Compare *ibid.*, pp. 58–61 with Reynolds, *op. cit.*, p. 84.
[31] Myers and Shultz, *The Dynamics of a Labor Market,* pp. 62–66.

that the respondents had neither looked for nor even considered the possibility of any other job. Furthermore, there is a strong implication in each case that the worker considered himself particularly fortunate to have landed the job he took. Myers and Shultz justifiably conclude, "These people did not weigh alternatives; 'a job was a job' and they took it." [32]

What of the workers who did not take the first job they applied for, but did take another? This does not mean that they were all "weighing alternatives." Indeed, most of the workers who applied at more than one place did so because their earlier applications did not produce jobs. But there were some workers who did turn down one or more job offers as being unsatisfactory. The frequency of such refusals and the reasons for them are illuminating. A fourth of the employed workers who had voluntarily quit their jobs at the mill in anticipation of the shutdown, and a sixth of those who had been laid off, had turned down the first jobs they learned about. The absolute number of workers involved, however, was less than 20 for both groups combined. Undesirable physical characteristics of the jobs and inadequate wages were the reasons most frequently given for refusing jobs. Also, some workers turned down jobs because they were not "steady" or because they were too far from home. Of the 13 cases that are described in detail by quotations from interviews, only one was a worker who refused a job as the result of a comparison between it and another one which he took. In other words, in the overwhelming majority of cases the worker refused a job even though at the time he did not know of the availability of another. This suggests that workers generally evaluate prospective jobs according to certain absolute minimum standards, rather than by comparison with alternatives.

It should be pointed out that the study by Myers and Shultz was conducted in a relatively depressed labor market in which employment opportunities were scarce. Consequently, the pattern of behavior that was found would not necessarily persist when employment levels were higher. But Reynolds' study of the behavior of workers in a labor market characterized by "more than full" employment showed basically the same pattern.[33] Of all the workers in his sample who had changed jobs recently (and the majority of these represented voluntary separations), about two thirds had taken the first job they

[32] Ibid., p. 62.
[33] Reynolds, op. cit., p. 11.

found. The remainder had one or more offers in addition to the one they accepted. Reynolds claims that there is no basic difference between these two groups. The workers who took the first job offered were clearly not willing, he reports, to have taken *any* job, nor is there any evidence that many of those who turned down jobs had passed up *satisfactory* opportunities in the quest for still more desirable ones. In other words, the workers appeared to accept the first *suitable* job that came their way. Reynolds found only a very few exceptions to this general rule: "These were workers of unusual ambition and drive who, because of specialized trade skills and the high level of labor demand, were in a strong bargaining position and able to make prospective employers wait while they made up their mind." [34]

Conclusions from Long-Term Work Histories. The foregoing evidence on the extent of workers' knowledge of jobs and the nature of their job decisions has been derived principally from examinations of their behavior in, and attitudes toward, individual labor market transactions. The question can also be approached through examination of work histories covering extended periods of time—ideally, the entire working lives of individuals—to see whether there is evidence of the rational and purposeful behavior assumed by economic theory. Palmer has attempted this kind of analysis of work history data collected during the 1930's for several groups of Philadelphia workers.[35] More recently, the work history data collected in the six-city survey have been subjected to somewhat similar but more refined analysis by Palmer and Miller.[36]

From the lifetime work histories of almost 2,500 Philadelphia radio workers, weavers and loom fixers, machinists, and hosiery workers, Palmer "gains the impression . . . that the workers . . . had considerable knowledge of labor market conditions and pursued their occupational careers in a purposeful fashion, even though seemingly 'accidental' factors affected the decision to accept jobs or the choice of occupations, in the first instance." [37] She reports that skilled workers, and union members particularly, have substantial knowledge of con-

---

[34] *Ibid.,* p. 108, note 22.

[35] Gladys L. Palmer, "Interpreting Patterns of Labor Mobility," in Bakke and others, *Labor Mobility and Economic Opportunity.* For a list of the original studies which provided the data analyzed in this essay, see p. 25 supra.

[36] Gladys L. Palmer and Ann R. Miller, "Work-Attachment Patterns in Six Cities," unpublished manuscript, University of Pennsylvania Industrial Research Department (June 1953).

[37] Palmer, "Interpreting Patterns of Labor Mobility," *op. cit.,* p. 62.

ditions in their industry. Admittedly, if a worker is laid off he may have to accept any job he can get, but the subsequent history generally reveals either an attempt to get back to the kind of work preferred or, less frequently, a permanent shift to a new type of work. When the latter occurs, the worker usually gives reasons that are logical in terms of "economic realities." According to this view, most workers do have career orientations, and their behavior is purposeful with reference to their life-long records of labor market activity: "Economic considerations loom large in this context. Workers quit jobs to get 'steadier work,' 'more money,' . . . 'more experience.' " [38]

An outside observer can appraise this "impression" only with great difficulty, for the evidence that created it is necessarily highly intangible. Certainly, it is quite different from the conclusion that seems to be supported by the data presented by Reynolds and by Myers and Shultz. Palmer is of course cognizant of the difference and suggests that it may result from differences in methodology: she analyzed work records over time, while the other studies were "cross-sectional" analyses of specific job transactions. Indeed, Palmer's hypothesis is that individual job changes, although ostensibly random when viewed in isolation, form a meaningful and purposeful pattern if examined in the context of a person's total work history. This hypothesis is clearly untestable by the techniques used by Reynolds and by Myers and Shultz, and perhaps no comparison between it and the conclusions derived from their studies is warranted.[39]

Another possible explanation of the difference between the "accidental" factors stressed by Reynolds and the "purposefulness" indicated by the Philadelphia work histories lies in the differences between the two labor markets studied. As Palmer suggests, Philadelphia's greater size and diversification creates a greater potential for mobility. Another possibility, noted by Palmer, is that the experiences of workers during the depression of the 1930's and during World War II may have changed their attitudes and behavior patterns.

Additional evidence that most workers have "careers," or tend to follow specific "fields of work," was found by Palmer and Miller in their analysis of the work histories collected in the six-city survey. They conclude that the "work experience of men in the Survey runs counter to the thesis that American workers [as distinguished from

[38] *Ibid.*, p. 66.
[39] Cf. pp. 40–41 supra.

European workers] have 'jobs' rather than 'trades' or 'professions.' " [40] They classified almost two thirds of the men in the sample as "career" workers,[41] and this proportion was virtually identical for each of the six cities covered by the survey. Women had a considerably lower proportion of "career" workers, the weighted average for the six cities combined being 45 percent. This difference in the work-attachment patterns of men and women appears to be attributable to the difference in their labor force exposure. When comparison is made between men and women who had been in the labor force in 1940 as well as in 1950, the proportions of "career" workers are about equal.

Strong attachments to particular types of work were found to be not inconsistent with movement among jobs. Although male "career" workers had less than average mobility, about half of them had worked for two or more employers between 1940 and 1950. Moreover, almost a fourth had made at least one change between major occupational groups, a higher proportion had changed industry, and 13 percent had made one or more geographic shifts.[42]

While the findings of Palmer and Miller have significant implications for mobilization planning, it is doubtful that they throw much light on the "rationality" or "irrationality" of workers' labor market behavior or on the extent of workers' knowledge of job opportunities and labor market conditions. The authors point out that "career" workers, as defined for their purpose, "have not necessarily exercised any choice or do not necessarily indicate a preference for the type of work in which they have spent most or all of their working lives."[43] Thus, to impute purposefulness to all the workers who have been

[40] Palmer and Miller, *op. cit.*, p. 35.

[41] In this study, "career" was used "as a shorthand expression to identify the experience of those workers whose attachment to an occupation or type of work is readily discernible" (*ibid.*, p. 16). In most cases the work record had to show a minimum of 11 years in a given occupation or field of work in order to classify the respondent as a career worker. However, a minimum of 5 years of experience in a given field of work was sufficient for certain workers who had specific training or whose work records were interrupted by military service or illness, but who returned to the same type of work. Professional workers who had spent most of the decade (1940–50) preparing for their present occupation were classified as "career" regardless of the time they had actually practiced their profession. Finally, a very few respondents were classified as career workers solely on the basis of an exceptionally strong statement of their intention to stay in the occupation.

[42] *Ibid.*, pp. 43–45.

[43] *Ibid.*, p. 16.

classified as having strong work-attachments is not warranted. They may have been "trapped" in a "career," rather than having "pursued" it. But even if this were not so, "career" patterns measured by homogeneity of job experience do not necessarily connote "rational" behavior based on a knowledge of job opportunities and labor market conditions. A worker can pursue a "career" either "intelligently" or "unintelligently" in terms of market conditions. Thus, conclusions about the strength of work-attachment among various occupational groups may be quite significant for evaluating the prospective stability or flexibility of the labor force without indicating whether workers make "rational" job decisions in terms of relatively complete labor market information.

VOLUNTARY MOBILITY AND WAGE IMPROVEMENT

Another indication of whether the movement of workers among jobs in a local labor market is "functional" is the extent to which such movement results in improvement of wages. If mobility performs the functions generally attributed to it, one would expect substantial numbers of workers who make voluntary job changes to advance their own welfare thereby. Such advancement may occur in other than monetary terms, but wages are an important measure of workers' relative well-being. From the viewpoint of society, the larger the proportion of job changes that result in wage improvement, the more confident one can be that the responsiveness of workers to wage differentials produces desirable flexibility in their distribution among the various users of labor.

A word of caution is necessary before considering the evidence on this point. The extent to which voluntary job changes result in higher earnings for the workers involved is an indirect and inconclusive measure of the effectiveness of wage differentials in producing movement. Even if it is found that all workers who make job shifts gain higher pay, the most that can be concluded is that those workers who *do* move apparently move in the direction of higher paying firms. Such an analysis does not indicate whether the movement is commensurate with the prevalence and the size of wage differentials, or whether the movement is sufficient to perform its theoretical function of reducing or eliminating those differentials. To answer the latter questions, attention must be directed not at the experience of workers who move, but at the recruitment experience of firms in the labor market in relation to their position in the area's wage structure. This relationship will be examined in the next section.

The findings of studies of the extent to which the voluntary movement of workers results in wage increases are presented in Table 7. Again, the data are not directly comparable because of differences in the groups of workers studied, the time periods, and the measures used in making wage comparisons. In some studies, for example, comparisons were made in terms of average hourly earnings, while in others weekly earnings were used. For the present purpose weekly earnings seem to be the more appropriate measure, because they include the effect of the number of hours worked as well as the wage rate itself.

There is less variation among the quantitative findings of the several studies than might be expected in view of the differences among them, and the variations can be attributed largely to these differences. The proportion of workers who improved their financial situation as a result of voluntary job changes ranges from 40 percent to 73 percent. The latter figure is doubtless unrepresentatively high. It relates to the 1940–51 experience of skilled workers covered in the six-city survey,[44] and is based on only the job shifts that workers reported making for the reason either of "better wages" or a "chance for advancement." One would expect a higher percentage of these shifts than of all voluntary job changes to show wage improvement. Moreover, such a result would also be probable for a group consisting entirely of skilled workers, who generally have superior knowledge of job opportunities and labor market conditions.

Kerr's figure of 70 percent is also probably too high to be regarded as representing the normal situation in a local labor market. The workers included in his study were migrants into the high-wage Seattle labor market area during the war who took jobs in either the aircraft or the shipbuilding industries. Furthermore, the comparison was between weekly earnings on the last job held by the migrant at his place of origin and his weekly earnings in the Seattle war industry at the time of hire. It was possible for two years to have elapsed between these two jobs—two years in which the general wage level was rising.

Evaluation of Bezanson's findings is more difficult, because of factors that might be expected to have counteracting influences.

---

[44] Myers and Shultz, "Patterns of Mobility of Skilled Workers and Factors Affecting Their Occupational Choice, Six Cities, 1940–51."

TABLE 7. PERCENTAGE DISTRIBUTION OF JOB SHIFTS BY CHANGE IN WAGES,
SELECTED STUDIES

	Wages in new job			
	Higher	No change	Lower	Total
New Haven manual workers' gross weekly take home pay in jobs prior to and immediately after separation				
Workers quitting jobs, 1945–48	40	8	52	100
Workers laid off, 1945–48	18	7	75	100
Nashua textile workers' average hourly earnings in mill job and that immediately after				
Workers quitting before shut-down*	25	15	60	100
Workers laid off†	15	40	45	100
Fitchburg workers voluntarily shifting between mfg. and utilities, 1937–39‡				
Hourly earnings	57	13	30	100
Weekly earnings	54	17	29	100
6-city survey weekly earnings of skilled workers 25 and over, working 1 mo. or more in 1950				
Voluntary shifts for better wages or advancement, 1940–50 §	73	8	19	100
Shifts from layoffs, 1940–50 ¶	35	24	41	100
Minneapolis mobile workers' hourly wage rate				
Voluntary shifts, 1947–48	51	17	32	100
Voluntary shifts, 1943–48	53	36	11	100
Philadelphia upholstery weavers' weekly earnings in shifts among tapestry mills, 1926	61	–	39	100
Seattle migrants' weekly earnings in job taken in aircraft or shipyards, and in last job before migration	70	5	25	100

Source: Data for New Haven, Fitchburg, Minneapolis, and six cities are from sources given for Table 3; for Nashua and Seattle, Table 6; for Philadelphia, Anne Bezanson, "The Advantages of Labor Turnover: An Illustrative Case," *Quarterly Journal of Economics*, 42:450–464.

* No wage information in 9 percent of cases, not included in total.
† No wage information in 8 percent of cases, not included in total.
‡ No wage information in 12 percent of cases, not included in total.
§ No wage information in 9 percent of cases, not included in total.
¶ No wage information in 22 percent of cases, not included in total.

Her investigation of the relationship between mobility and wage experience involved 344 upholstery weavers who changed jobs among the 25 tapestry manufacturing firms in Philadelphia in 1926. Since they were all highly skilled workers in a highly specialized and concentrated industry, and since they were all union members, their record of wage improvement resulting from voluntary job shifts might be expected to be higher than that of workers in general. On the other hand, voluntary job changes and involuntary shifts necessitated by seasonal layoffs are not differentiated by the data, and the inclusion of the latter might be expected to decrease the proportion of shifts resulting in higher wages.

The percentages of voluntary job shifts involving wage increases that are reported for the samples of workers in New Haven, Fitchburg, and Minneapolis are quite close, ranging between about 40 and 55 percent.[45] In the Nashua study, a considerably smaller proportion of the workers made a gain in wages by changing jobs, but this would be expected since the workers concerned did not voluntarily quit in the usual sense, but left their jobs in anticipation of a layoff which they knew was inevitable.

Although it is neither necessary nor possible to state precisely the proportion of voluntary separations that involve wage increases, the data reviewed indicate that approximately 50 or 60 percent of workers who voluntarily change jobs achieve an immediate financial gain as a result. The differences in the effects on wages, depending on the circumstances in which job changes occur, are perhaps even more significant. The most striking of these is the difference in wage experience of workers who lose their jobs involuntarily and those who voluntarily quit. Every study that has differentiated between these two groups has shown a markedly higher percentage of the latter enjoying an increase in earnings. Reynolds, for example, found that only 18 percent of the New Haven workers who were laid off or discharged found other jobs paying higher wages, as compared with

---

[45] This conclusion differs from that of Heneman, Fox, and Yoder, who say: "These [New Haven] results differ markedly from the Minneapolis findings. Thus, for all employees in the New Haven study, 26 percent changed to jobs with higher pay, whereas in Minneapolis, slightly more than 50 percent shifted to higher paying jobs." (*Op. cit.*, p. 23.) This comparison, however, overlooks the fact that the 26 percent for New Haven is based on all job shifts, involuntary as well as voluntary. On the basis of the data, 40 percent of those who made voluntary job shifts experienced a wage gain. This is considerably closer to the 50 percent reported for Minneapolis.

40 percent of those who quit voluntarily. In their study of skilled workers in six cities Myers and Shultz report wage gains for 35 percent of the shifts resulting from layoffs, as compared with 73 percent for the voluntary shifts to improve wages or chances of advancement. As has been seen, all the workers in the Nashua study were in one sense or another the victims of a layoff, yet even there those who "beat the gun" by quitting were almost twice as successful in finding higher paying jobs as those who waited to be laid off.

It is also evident from these studies that workers who voluntarily leave their jobs are not a homogeneous group with respect to factors that influence their subsequent wage records. Reynolds found a considerable difference between those workers who quit jobs with others lined up and those who quit to look for other jobs. Of the former, 60 percent moved into jobs with higher gross weekly earnings, while only 25 percent of the latter were successful in finding higher paying jobs.[46] Supporting this conclusion is Myers and Maclaurin's finding that 66 percent of those workers who gave up a job in order "to take a better one" improved their hourly earnings and 60 percent improved their weekly earnings, while only 47 percent of those who voluntarily quit because of "personal or family reasons" eventually improved their hourly and weekly earnings when they took new jobs.[47] It is noteworthy that Reynolds' study shows considerably less difference in wage improvement between workers who were laid off and those who quit to find better jobs than between the latter group and the workers who quit with other jobs lined up. The percentages of each of these groups who moved into higher paying jobs were 17, 25, and 60, respectively.

A more detailed analysis of Bezanson's findings is appropriate, for her study was directed specifically and exclusively at the relationship between mobility and wage improvement. She obtained weekly records relating to earnings and working time for each of the 344 upholstery weavers from the local of the Upholstery Weavers Union. For purposes of analysis, the 25 tapestry mills among which the weavers shifted were classified into three groups according to wage level: [48] Class A,

---

[46] Reynolds, *The Structure of Labor Markets*, p. 215.

[47] Myers and Maclaurin, *op. cit.*, p. 65.

[48] Actually, piece rates were the same in all the union plants. Variations in earnings, however, resulted from differences among the firms in quality of equipment, type of fabric made, and volume of business. Thus, a worker making an interfirm shift could not expect to get a higher wage rate (unless he went to work on a dif-

consisting of 9 plants with the highest median earnings; Class B, consisting of 9 plants; and Class C, consisting of 7 plants with the lowest median earnings. As might be expected, the proportion of workers experiencing an increase in weekly earnings as a result of changing jobs was a function of the class of mill into which they moved and the class from which they came. Thus, more of the workers entering Class A firms raised their weekly earnings than of those entering Class B or C mills. Within each category of mills entered, workers coming from Class C mills were generally more likely to experience a wage increase than those from any other category. Significantly, however, three fifths of all the shifting workers increased their weekly pay, and even among those who moved from Class A to Class C mills, almost half (48 percent) received higher weekly earnings.

On the basis of this evidence Bezanson concludes that there is considerable advantage to workers in labor turnover. She observes that the financial gains made by the workers were apparently not offset to any substantial degree by time lost in changing jobs, for the workers frequently reported earnings in two mills during the same week. Also, the practice of work sharing in slack seasons insured the weaver of his job in one mill until he had obtained another. In addition to the monetary rewards which so frequently were involved in the turnover, Bezanson notes that the workers also increased their abilities by gaining experience with a variety of fabrics, a result that benefited both the workers and their employers as well.[49]

MOBILITY OF WORKERS AND WAGE DIFFERENTIALS

If it is true that little more than half of all voluntary job shifts result in wage improvement for the worker, no overwhelming tendency to gravitate toward the higher paying firms in a local labor market exists among employed workers. If the movement of workers among firms with various wage levels were completely random, one would expect that as many workers would improve their earnings in the process as would suffer a decrease. On the other hand, if voluntary movement were always in the direction of the higher paying firms, the records of all shifting workers would indicate wage gains. The

ferent fabric), but his earnings might increase if he worked longer hours or if his productivity was greater in the new firm.

[49] Bezanson, "The Advantages of Labor Turnover: An Illustrative Case," *op. cit.*, pp. 463–464.

evidence reviewed thus far suggests that the actual situation lies somewhere between these two theoretical extremes, perhaps closer to the former. But as has been observed, the wage records of workers provide only an indirect clue to the effect of wage differentials on the movement of workers and the influence of that movement on the size of the differentials. More pertinent is the recruitment experience of firms in a local labor market relative to their wage levels, and the effects of their recruitment problems on their wage policies.

In the Fitchburg study Myers and Maclaurin give considerable attention to the interrelationship of wages and the movement of factory workers in the late 1930's and early 1940's. The study was concerned primarily with determining the extent to which the shifting of workers among the major manufacturing and utility firms of a small New England community fulfilled the functions that such movement is "supposed" to perform—the equalization of wages and working conditions for similar jobs, the distribution of workers where the need for them is greatest, and the creation of opportunities for workers to utilize their abilities most effectively.[50] But the investigators find it difficult to relate the amount and the nature of the movement that actually occurred in the community to these functions. Job shifting did not serve either to equalize wages and working conditions or to distribute labor as effectively as possible. Although low paying firms increased their wage levels between 1937 and 1942, this is attributed more to the federal minimum wage law and to union pressure than to the voluntary movement of workers away from such firms. Moreover, the high paying firms also increased wages during this period, with the result that the relative ranking of the firms in the community wage structure was largely undisturbed, although wage differentials were somewhat narrowed. Despite this general conclusion, Myers and Maclaurin note a "slight tendency for movement to be in the direction of higher-wage firms in the period from 1937 to 1939, and a considerably stronger tendency in 1942." [51] Much more pronounced was the tendency of workers to move within "neighborhood clusters" of firms, particularly among the seasonal industries of a neighborhood.

The evidence on which these conclusions are based, however, is not entirely unambiguous. For example, in order to analyze the relationship between the movement of workers and wage differentials, the firms in the sample were classified in five categories according to

[50] Myers and Maclaurin, *The Movement of Factory Workers*, p. 1.
[51] *Ibid.*, p. 23.

wage rates. The investigators observe that only 4 percent of all the interplant shifts were from the firms in the three low-wage groups to firms in the two high-wage groups.[52] The implication is that very little of the movement represented a response to wage differentials. It is not clear, however, why the analysis should be made in this way. Elsewhere [53] the data show that somewhat over a fourth of all the job shifts were from lower-wage to higher-wage firms, less than a fourth were in the opposite direction, and about half were among firms in the same wage category. This presents a different picture from that emphasized by Myers and Maclaurin, for it can be said that more of the shifts were in the direction of higher-wage firms than in the opposite direction.

An even more fundamental question is whether it is reasonable to include all job shifts in such an analysis. If the purpose is to determine the extent to which movement of workers is toward higher paying firms, it would be more appropriate to consider only *voluntary* shifts, for those resulting from layoff or discharge are clearly not produced by a propensity to seek higher paying jobs. When this differentiation is made, the data show clearly that there is a relationship between the wage level of a firm and its ability to attract workers. In 1937, seven of the 10 firms in the two highest wage categories attracted workers through voluntary movement, while only three lost workers.[54] In the next two wage categories nine of the 16 firms gained workers, while seven lost. In the lowest wage category only two of the nine firms added more workers than they lost through voluntary job changes. In the wartime year 1942, the relationship between the firm's wage level and its success in attracting workers through voluntary movement was even more pronounced. Three of the four firms in the highest wage category gained workers, the 21 firms in the two intermediate categories were about equally divided between those that gained and those that lost workers, and all 10 firms in the lowest wage category lost workers through voluntary movement.[55]

The evidence does not suggest a perfect responsiveness of workers to differentials in wage rates, or perhaps even the degree of responsiveness that is assumed by traditional allocation theory. Yet it is difficult

[52] *Ibid.*, p. 31.
[53] *Ibid.*, p. 32, Table 4.
[54] A firm "attracting" workers is one that experienced more voluntary inward than outward shifts during the period.
[55] *Ibid.*, p. 57, Chart III.

to avoid the impression that the conclusions of Myers and Maclaurin understate the strength of the relationship between wage rates and labor mobility which their data show.

As to the obverse aspect of the relationship between wages and mobility, that is, the effect of the movement or potential movement of workers on wage differentials, Myers and Maclaurin conclude that mobility in the labor market they studied did not perform its supposed function of reducing differentials. Here again, however, the conclusion probably requires qualification. It is reported, for example, that "Movement of workers to better-paying companies caused some firms to raise their wages in 1937–39." [56] Also a few companies anticipated that wage increases would have to be made in order to combat the threat of movement. By 1942, additional firms in the low-wage category had found it necessary to make wage increases in order "to hold key workers, to reduce turnover generally, and to attract (if possible) sufficient replacements." [57]

Myers and Maclaurin recognize that differentials in the "attractiveness" of jobs cannot be measured exclusively in terms of comparative wage rates. Both in determining the extent to which voluntary movement of workers is in the direction of "better" jobs, and the extent to which such movement tends to equalize the "net attractiveness" of jobs, the nonwage characteristics of employment must also be taken into consideration. Accordingly, the investigators inquire whether these nonwage conditions tend to offset wage differentials. They conclude that in Fitchburg wage differentials were not compensated by differences in other job conditions. Indeed, the high-wage firms were generally also those that had better than average working conditions and comprehensive welfare programs.[58] Of the four "very high-wage" firms, three had comprehensive welfare programs, and all had above average working conditions. On the other hand, none of the nine "very low-wage" firms had comprehensive welfare programs or above average working conditions.

From his study of the New Haven labor market in the postwar period Reynolds draws conclusions rather similar to those of Myers

[56] *Ibid.*, p. 55.

[57] *Ibid.*, p. 56.

[58] *Ibid.*, pp. 59–61. It is not clear what criteria were used to evaluate working conditions. The firms are classified in three categories: those with "above average," "average," and "below average" conditions. Of the total 37 firms, however, only three are classified as "below average," while 13 are "above average" (p. 60).

and Maclaurin, although perhaps more moderately stated.[59] According to Reynolds, "All things considered . . . the processes of wage determination and labor mobility seem to be much less intimately related than one might expect *a priori*." [60] Concerning the effectiveness of wage differentials in producing mobility, he concludes that they are not nearly so significant as differentials in job opportunities. In most metropolitan areas the existence of a perpetual pool of unemployed is the chief factor that makes the link between wage differentials and mobility at best a tenuous one. Most job shifts by workers do not involve a comparison between a present and an alternative job, but rather a comparison between a job and unemployment. Differentials in job opportunities can produce a redistribution of workers even in the absence of wage differentials. The converse, however, is not true. Wage differentials, in the absence of willingness to hire on the part of high-wage firms, obviously produce no movement.

For basically the same reasons, interplant movement does not ordinarily result in improvement of the worker's position. In most cases he takes another job merely to avoid unemployment. "Workers will move uphill in terms of wages if they can, but they will also move downhill if they must." [61] Finally, concerning the effectiveness of actual or potential movement in reducing or eliminating wage differentials, Reynolds concludes that it is "inadequate to prevent large and persistent differences in aggregate job attractiveness." [62] Again the reason is persistent underemployment. Expanding firms, occupations, or regions need not compete with others for their labor supply. They can draw workers from the unemployed pool at any wage above the "minimum supply price of the unemployed." Thus, the "pressure for equalization of wage differentials becomes much less than it would be in a full-employment situation." [63] In this connection it is pertinent that Reynolds' study was made in a local labor market during years when levels of employment were quite high. Only 3 percent of the labor force was unemployed, and part-time work was practically nonexistent. Many plants, indeed, were working overtime.[64]

[59] Reynolds, *op. cit.* See particularly Chapters 7, 8, and 9, from which the present discussion is drawn and all quotations are made.
[60] P. 248.
[61] *Ibid.*
[62] P. 246.
[63] P. 247.
[64] P. 10.

In support of his conclusions, Reynolds notes that the actual movement of New Haven workers in 1946 and 1947 was not predominantly in the direction of higher paying jobs. Only 40 percent of those who had voluntarily changed jobs between V-J Day and the time of the interview in 1946 or 1947 had increased their weekly earnings, although 60 percent of those who had quit with a new job lined up were successful in doing so.[65] Furthermore, there was no significant relationship between the relative wage position of the firm on the one hand and either its voluntary quit rate or the number of applicants for jobs on the other.[66] Since the smaller plants tended to have lower quit rates *and* lower wages than the larger firms, however, it is possible that if the sample had been large enough to permit classification of the firms by size, a significant relationship between wage levels and quit rates would have been revealed.

With respect to the influence of actual or potential mobility on wage differentials, Reynolds points to the persistence of pronounced wage dispersion during the entire period from 1940 to 1948. In the latter year the range of starting rates in 28 large manufacturing plants, accounting for half of the area's manufacturing employment, was from $.69 to $1.185 per hour.[67] This dispersion is especially significant because it existed among a relatively homogeneous group of large firms, three fourths of which were in metalworking industries, employing predominantly male labor. Moreover, despite considerable change in the relative ranking of the firms in the wage structure, interplant wage differences on a percentage basis remained virtually unchanged during the eight years of a tight labor market: "Yet the low-wage firms were still able to hire and retain enough labor to meet their production schedules." [68]

Concurring with Myers and Maclaurin, Reynolds finds that the nonwage terms of employment accentuate rather than compensate for wage differentials. He reports a slight positive relationship between the total amount of fringe benefits, as measured by their cost, and

[65] P. 215. Cf. p. 178 infra.
[66] Pp. 217–218.
[67] P. 186.
[68] P. 190. Dispersion (interquartile range divided by the median) was 20.3 percent in 1940, 20.0 percent in 1942, 16.7 percent in 1945, and 18.9 percent in 1948. Reynolds explains the slight reduction during the war in terms of the wartime wage controls and the "very high level of demand for labor."

the wage level of the plant.[69] Moreover, visits to the plants in the area "left a strong impression that the larger plants (which tend also to be the high-wage plants) have better physical conditions than most of the small plants." [70] The larger firms seem to have better personnel policies and better-qualified supervisors also, although these advantages may be somewhat counterbalanced by the closer personal relations that prevail in a small plant.[71]

Despite these findings there is evidence that wage rates are not entirely unaffected by labor supply (mobility) considerations. Thus, it is reported that "Much of the interplant competition for labor in this area during World War II seems to have been carried on, not by raising base rates, but by setting piece rates so high that workers could earn much more than their nominal wage." [72] In explaining the reduction in occupational wage differentials during the war, Reynolds emphasizes the practice of making uniform cents-per-hour wage increases but admits that the narrowing of differentials also resulted in part from "deliberate management policy in a tight labor market, in which workers tended to flee the less attractive occupations and had to be held in them by special inducements." [73] And in describing employers' emphasis on "keeping up with the area wage level," Reynolds claims that although they generally explained the policy "in terms of ethical and prestige considerations, one judges from various side remarks that it also has something to do with getting and keeping workers." [74] Finally, he offers the hypothesis that wage differentials are reflected in differences in the quality of workers, with the poorer workers gravitating into the plants at the lower extreme of the wage scale, and better workers into the highest paying firms. He suggests, however, that these qualitative differences in the work force are not commensurate with the differences in wages.[75]

Although Myers and Shultz in the Nashua study were principally

[69] P. 202.

[70] P. 221.

[71] For similar conclusions, see Richard A. Lester, "Results and Implications of Some Recent Wage Studies," in Richard A. Lester and Joseph Shister, eds., Insights into Labor Issues (New York: Macmillan Company, 1948), pp. 197–225, especially p. 210.

[72] Reynolds, op. cit., p. 198.

[73] P. 196.

[74] P. 217.

[75] P. 219.

concerned with the impact of a plant shutdown on the operation of a local labor market, some of their findings pertain to the relationship between mobility and wage differentials.[76] Like Reynolds, they found pronounced wage differentials among the 39 major manufacturing firms in the area studied. The highest minimum rate was twice as great as the lowest, and the same was true when the firms were ranked by average hourly earnings at straight time.[77] On the basis of their discussions with employers on the question of competition for manpower, however, the investigators were able to distinguish at least four "submarkets for labor," involving "noncompeting groups." When the firms were grouped in submarkets, the amount of wage dispersion within each was reduced although it was still substantial.[78]

Unlike the situation found by Reynolds, the relative ranking of the firms in the wage structure of the community remained about the same from 1940 to 1949. (There is no evidence as to what happened to the magnitude of the differentials during this period.) The major exception was the largest manufacturing firm in the area, which moved from near the bottom to near the top of the wage structure between the prewar and the postwar periods. This change affected the recruitment problems of other firms, as was indicated by the comment of one plant manager: "Before the war, no one who could get a job here would go over to the mill. . . . But after the war they were hiring away from us all the time." [79]

Interviews with employers concerning their wage policies throw some light on the extent to which the mobility of workers affects wage decisions by management. Myers and Shultz report that the attraction and retention of an adequate labor supply, although impor-tant, seems to be only a secondary objective of wage policy in most firms. Thus, while less than a fifth of the manufacturing firms mentioned the recruitment problem in explaining their wage policies, over half stressed either the necessity of meeting product competition, or "keeping in line with the industry." [80] Nonmanufacturing firms referred to the labor recruitment problem more frequently.

Only guarded conclusions can be drawn from the evidence that has been presented in this section. Definitive statements concerning

[76] Myers and Shultz, *The Dynamics of a Labor Market.* See particularly Part III.
[77] *Ibid.,* p. 161.
[78] *Ibid.,* pp. 154–155, 161.
[79] *Ibid.,* p. 161.
[80] *Ibid.,* p. 164.

the responsiveness of workers to wage differentials and the effects of actual or potential movement of workers on those differentials do not seem to be warranted. Certainly the interrelationship between wages and mobility is not nearly so direct or intimate as economic theory would suggest. On the other hand, it is equally clear that some relationship does exist and that it is probably stronger when employment levels are high and job opportunities are abundant. Under these conditions the assumptions of economic theory are more nearly met.

Further research on this question in diverse labor markets and under various economic conditions is needed before a confident judgment can be rendered. In this connection, studies of the relationship between the wage levels of firms and their recruitment experience should be more productive of meaningful results than studies of the employment histories of groups of workers.

SUMMARY AND CONCLUSIONS

In this chapter the findings of empirical studies of labor mobility have been reviewed with reference to some of the premises and conclusions of traditional wage and allocation theory. Evidence concerning four questions has been appraised: (1) the extent of workers' knowledge of job opportunities and the ways in which they go about finding and taking jobs; (2) the criteria by which workers make their job decisions; (3) the extent to which the voluntary movement of workers is in the direction of higher paying firms; (4) whether the mobility of workers appears to be effective in reducing differentials in wages and other terms of employment among comparable jobs. The first three of these questions relate to the assumptions of wage and allocation theory, and the fourth involves one of its conclusions.

The importance of the first question is clear. Unless workers have reasonably accurate and complete knowledge of the extent and nature of employment opportunities, there is no basis for assuming a purposeful movement of workers among jobs, and the foundation for the entire theoretical analysis is weakened. The evidence on this point is not reassuring. The average manual worker seems to have very limited knowledge of job opportunities in the labor market and even less information regarding the specific characteristics of jobs in establishments other than his own. There are of course exceptions to this generalization, principally among skilled craftsmen and to a lesser extent among union members whether skilled or not; and there are undoubtedly variations among labor markets, depending on their size and homogeneity.

The way in which workers go about getting jobs confirms and rounds out this view. In the first place, unless the worker is dissatisfied with his present job, he generally does not look for other work at all. If he is dissatisfied, he may canvass his friends and relatives or, much less commonly, visit the public employment office in an attempt to line up another job. But more often he simply quits his present job and begins a search for another one. This "search" generally involves finding out from acquaintances where job openings exist, or even being "spoken for" by friends currently employed in companies that are hiring. Alternatively, or perhaps concurrently, it may involve applying more or less randomly at plants that the worker happens to know about. The more formal methods of finding work, such as through the public employment office or responding to newspaper advertisements, are used in only a minority of cases.

The unemployed worker does not necessarily take the first job that comes along, but neither does he locate a number of desirable jobs and draw up mental balance sheets of their relative merits in order to decide which one to take. There is strong evidence that if the worker does not take the first job that he finds, he will take the first one that appears to meet the standards he has subjectively established for a desirable job. These standards, of course, are subject to downward revision as the duration of the search for a job increases. Consequently, there is no assurance that the job ultimately taken will be better than the one just left.

Two important conclusions concerning the labor market behavior of workers emerge from these findings. First, only a very small minority of the labor force is at any one time realistically in the labor market in the sense of being interested in or available for jobs other than the ones currently held.

Second, workers are rarely in the position of comparing the desirability of two or more jobs, either of which they can have. This is true even when one is speaking only of workers who *voluntarily* quit jobs, for the evidence indicates that more voluntary job shifts occur through a process of leaving one job and then looking for another, than by lining up a new job before quitting the old one. Reasons for voluntary job terminations therefore cannot safely be interpreted as indicating the factors in terms of which job *comparisons* are made. In other words, to a considerable extent even workers who voluntarily change jobs are not really attracted by more desirable jobs elsewhere so much as they are "pushed out" of jobs that they find unsatisfactory, and there is no assurance that they subsequently will find jobs better than the ones they leave. Most analyses of reasons for voluntary job changes imply a degree of "calculation" that in fact does not exist.

What, then, do workers look for in jobs? What job elements appear to be significant in producing satisfaction or dissatisfaction? What factors make a worker decide to leave a job? Having quit, what are the criteria by which he decides whether another job offer is acceptable? And when a worker is in a position to choose between two or more available jobs, what criteria determine his choice?

On the basis of the job characteristics mentioned by workers in accounting for job decisions, several factors appear to be significant. Perhaps the most obvious is the inherent nature of the job itself— whether the work is interesting or uninteresting to the worker, whether it is clean or dirty, heavy or light. Related to this is the physical environment in which the work is done: the cleanliness of the plant and similar factors. Wages, from the standpoint both of their adequacy to meet living costs and of their fairness in relation to the worker's conception of the job's worth, are another important factor. The opportunities for advancement, the security of the job, and the steadiness of work are other elements of an economic nature which the worker generally considers. Finally, a host of "human relations factors," including fairness of treatment by management, freedom from too close supervision, opportunity to make suggestions as to how the job should be done, and satisfactory relations with fellow employees, are also important.

Workers quit and change their jobs for reasons associated with all those factors. Concerning the importance of the wage factor, at least three generalizations seem to be warranted. First, dissatisfaction with wages appears to account for well under half of all voluntary moves. Second, wage considerations play a more prominent role when the worker is in a position to compare two jobs, either of which he may have, than under other circumstances. Third, the wage factor explains more of the movement during periods of prosperity and high levels of employment than during less favorable periods. The reason is probably twofold. During prosperity there are ample employment opportunities so that the situation in which the worker is able to compare two job opportunities is more likely to prevail; and the upward price movement that frequently characterizes such a period is apt to focus the attention of workers on the inadequacy of their wages for meeting the cost of living.

Available evidence on the extent to which workers are successful in improving their earnings as a result of voluntary movement, although meager, is consistent with the findings on reported reasons for changing jobs. Only a few relevant studies have been made, and the diversity in the populations sampled as well as in the methods employed makes generalization difficult. The limited data suggest that manual workers increase their earnings as a result of voluntary movement only slightly more often than they do not. In interpreting this it must be kept in mind that even if job changes were random with respect to wages, one would expect the number of moves resulting in wage increases to equal the number resulting in wage decreases. As might be expected, wage improvement more often accompanies voluntary job shifting in a "tight" than in a "loose" labor market. Also, the worker who moves from one job to another that he has already found is more likely to increase his earnings than the worker who quits a job in the hope of finding a better one.

The earnings of mobile workers are at best only an indirect clue to the effectiveness of wage differentials in allocating labor. In studying the latter question attention must be focused not on the mobile worker, but on the firm's wage policy and recruitment experience in relation to those of other firms in the labor market area. Conclusions on this question are perhaps more tentative than on any of the others treated in the present chapter. On the one hand, it is clear that there is some tendency for workers to move in the direction of higher paying firms, particularly when the level of employment is high. There is also evidence that employers are not unmindful of the effect of their wage policies on their ability to attract and to hold workers, a fact that might be expected to reduce differentials in the "net advantages" of employment. On the other hand, it is equally clear that the persistence of significant wage differentials, even within a single local labor market area, is the rule rather than the exception; and that these differentials, far from being offset, are often reinforced by differentials in the nonwage attractiveness of jobs.

6 SOME SUGGESTIONS

FOR FURTHER RESEARCH

As the previous chapters have pointed out, research on labor mobility has contributed significantly to knowledge concerning the flexibility of the labor supply and the operation of labor markets. The extent to which workers move among jobs and into and out of the labor force is fairly well established, at least for periods such as the past decade or two. The general characteristics of this movement can also be described with some confidence; there are data concerning the relative frequency of occupational, industrial, and geographic job changes, and of voluntary and involuntary job separations. The mobility characteristics of broad occupational groups of workers can also be differentiated.

Less is known about the factors that determine the amount and the incidence of mobility, but several generalizations do rest on a firm empirical basis. That voluntary job changes are both absolutely and relatively more numerous under prosperous than under depressed economic conditions is well established. That mobility tends to decline with advancing age, at least between the ages of 20 and 65, and that manual workers make more frequent job changes than white collar workers, can also be concluded with assurance. Sex, race, and marital status are among the many other factors whose relationship to mobility has been studied, but additional research is needed before conclusions as to their effects can be reached with confidence.

With respect to the labor market behavior of workers, it can safely be asserted that at any given time the vast majority of employed workers are not "in the labor market" in the sense of being interested in or available for other employment. It is likewise clear that even when unemployed workers are looking for jobs they do not generally compare alternatives in an attempt to choose the best job available. They are more likely to take the first job that meets the minimum standards they have established subjectively. Their procedures in seeking jobs, however realistic they may be from a pragmatic point of view, seem casual when contrasted with the degree of "rationality" assumed by economic theory.

Although there is no basis for firm conclusions about the motivating factors in labor market behavior, there is evidence that the emphasis on wages implicit in the prevailing theory of labor allocation needs qualification. It is doubtful whether most voluntary job changes can be explained principally by a desire for better wages. Moreover, it may be that persistent wage differentials, far from compensating for differences in the nonwage attractiveness of jobs, actually reinforce them. Finally, the empirical evidence supports the a priori view that however important wage differentials may be in inducing movement during full or nearly full employment, they are not the most influential factor when employment opportunities are less favorable.

There remain highly significant questions on which the existing evidence is inconclusive, as noted in previous chapters. These questions will not be summarized here, but emphasis will be placed on certain of the more serious gaps in present knowledge, and types of research that seem most likely to yield valuable results will be suggested.

Parallel studies in diverse labor market areas, among specific occupational groups, and under varying economic conditions are needed to test the universality of some of the conclusions that have been reached in research on mobility. More attention should be given particularly to various groups of nonmanual workers, to agricultural workers, and to workers in areas of diverse economic structure. Also, periodic surveys in a single labor market would throw light on the effect of changing economic conditions on labor mobility. These studies of course should be so designed that their findings will be comparable with one another and with those from past research.

While study of local labor markets should continue, there is need for additional national statistics on labor mobility. The cost of interviewing a national sample of the labor force would probably be prohibitive for university research agencies, but valuable data could be obtained in the Current Population Surveys made by the Bureau of the Census. It has made studies of internal migration, of the work experience of the population, and of gross changes in the labor force, all of which have contributed to an understanding of labor market processes on an aggregative basis. If members of the households in the Census sample were asked each month about their employment and job status "a month ago," the data would not only permit measurement and analysis of mobility on a national basis, but would also show how mobility varies over time.

Much work remains to be done in identifying and measuring the relative independence and importance of the factors that determine the volume, pattern, and incidence of labor mobility. Improved research planning and more refined methods of analysis are needed if investigations of these factors are to yield conclusive findings. It is no longer profitable simply to classify measures of mobility successively by such characteristics as age, sex, race, marital status, and occupation for the sake of determining the correlates of mobility. There are frequently intercorrelations among these variables. Techniques for isolating the influence of one variable from the influence of others correlated with it have already been used in special analyses of the data collected in the survey of labor mobility in six cities. Further application of the same methods should indicate those characteristics of workers that have some independent effect on mobility. As an illustration, evidence on the relative mobility of men and women is at present inconclusive, although there is reason to believe that the greater mobility of men shown by most studies results more from differences in the exposure of men and women to the labor force than from differences in their propensities to make job changes. It is also possible that the concentration of women in white collar occupations and their somewhat limited opportunities for upward occupational movement account in part for differences in the mobility of men and women. The suggested techniques should make it possible to carry out more rigorous tests of these hypotheses.

Another refinement in methodology is necessary. In analyzing work histories over a period of time, it is unsatisfactory to classify workers according to their characteristics at the time of questioning if these characteristics have changed during the period covered by the work histories. The influence of marital status on mobility cannot be ascertained by collecting 10-year work histories and classifying respondents by their marital status at the time of the interviews. Rather, mobility measures per man-year while unmarried must be compared with mobility measures per man-year while married. This procedure is much more difficult than that generally used, but it is the only one that will yield unambiguous results.

Past attempts to determine the characteristics of workers associated with mobility have focused on readily ascertainable factors such as age, sex, marital status, and occupation. These, however, appear to account for only a small proportion of the total variation in mobility among individuals. Thus, either other characteristics are more influential, or the incidence of mobility among workers must be largely fortuitous. The latter hypothesis is suspect, however, because most of the job changes in any year are accounted for by a small minority of workers, and because fragmentary evidence indicates that it is largely the same group of workers who move among jobs year after year. There is a strong suggestion, therefore, that much of the variation in mobility among workers is attributable to traits or external circumstances that are only partially (if at all) related to characteristics that can be ascertained from personnel records or from enumerative surveys. If the personal determinants of mobility are to be ascertained, employment histories of workers must be analyzed with reference to individual differences in personality traits, aptitudes, interests, values, intelligence, and occupational aspirations, and by use of controls that will hold nonpersonal factors constant.

The difficulties in this proposal are obvious. Respondents, in addition to furnishing the usual information on work experience, would have to submit to intensive interviewing and testing. It is doubtful that a random sample of the labor force could be persuaded to sacrifice the time that these procedures would require. However, psychological tests are administered for a number of purposes unrelated to mobility research, and it should be possible to acquire work history data from samples of individuals who take such tests for other reasons. This would be a limited approach, to be sure, but it might enable research teams of psychologists and economists to begin to examine some unexplored questions about the determinants of labor mobility and the motivations of individuals in making specific job changes.

Little has been done to test empirically numerous hypotheses relating to the institutional determinants of mobility. The deficiency is perhaps best illustrated by the typical assertions in the literature about the effect of trade unionism on labor mobility. Students almost universally conclude that unionism has the net effect of inhibiting the voluntary movement of workers. The retarding influences of contract provisions concerning seniority and pension plans would seem to be self-evident. It is not known, however, how strong these influences are compared with other considerations that tend to keep workers, particularly those with long service, rooted to their jobs even in the absence of unionization. Empirical studies of the union's impact on the willingness and ability of workers to make different kinds of job changes under varying economic circumstances, and of the specific aspects of unionism that bear most directly on mobility, are needed.

Successful pursuit of this line of inquiry will depend on the care with which the research is planned and designed. The significant questions cannot be answered merely by comparing the mobility of union and non-union workers. It has been suggested that different types of unionism may affect mobility in different ways, and relevant hypotheses need to be tested. Moreover, since workers move into and out of union membership as well as into and out of jobs, knowledge of a worker's union status as of a particular time is no assurance that he has been in that status during the entire period covered by his work history. Also, non-union workers in a bargaining unit covered by a contract are affected by many of the same factors that influence the mobility of union members. For these reasons, the relationship between unionism and mobility ought to be studied on the basis of a sample of establishments rather than of workers. Union and non-union firms might be matched for such factors as size, industry, and wage rates. Within each firm, job attitudes, attitudes toward the union, and extent of active participation in the union's affairs are among the matters that must be investigated in addition to the employment histories of workers, in order to evaluate the aspects of trade unionism that affect labor mobility.

Private pension plans are another example of an institutional factor whose influence on mobility should be studied empirically. Most students of the labor market assume that private pension systems necessarily make workers less mobile. At the same time it is generally recognized that labor turnover is so great, despite the existence of pensions, that substantial majorities of workers currently covered by pension plans will probably be ineligible for full benefits upon retirement. There has been almost no systematic research on the extent to which pension arrangements modify a worker's labor market behavior or his attitude toward changing jobs. Moreover, existing pension plans vary in important characteristics, and whether different types of plans affect mobility in different ways should be ascertained. For example, do plans with vested rights encourage greater mobility than those without them? Do plans covering more than one employer restrict mobility less than those for a single employer? How are various eligibility requirements related to the mobility of the covered workers? If private pension plans do in fact impose undue restraint on the mobility of workers, answers to questions of this kind will at least suggest the types of program that exert minimal influence. Experimental studies, similar to those suggested for testing the effects of unionism on mobility, would be appropriate.

Additional research on factors that motivate labor market behavior is needed, but such studies require substantially improved methods. Techniques that have been used successfully in studying motivational influences in consumer behavior might be adapted for investigation of the factors that shape workers' job decisions. It is doubtful that reports by workers on their reasons for voluntary job changes can in themselves provide valid information on motives. Hypotheses concerning the motivation of workers must be tested in the light of their actual labor market behavior. This calls for intensive study of the circumstances surrounding workers' decisions to change jobs, and for careful and detailed comparisons of the jobs they leave with those they take. Entrance of a new plant into an area provides a useful laboratory for a study of this kind. However, attention must not be directed exclusively at the experience of mobile workers. The considerations that cause workers to *remain* in jobs despite the availability of other and possibly better ones are fully as important for explaining labor market behavior as the considerations that induce them to *leave* jobs.

The motivational factors underlying the movement of workers into and out of the labor force also need further study. Valuable work has been done in quantifying the extent of such movement and in identifying the groups responsible for most of it, but the factors that induce them to enter and leave the labor force remain to be determined. Why did large numbers of women enter the labor force during World War II and leave afterward? Was it primarily the higher wages during that period, the patriotic incentives, the absence of their husbands in the armed services, the increased cost of living, or simply the almost unlimited availability of jobs? Answers to such questions would be particularly useful in estimating the total labor supply under various economic conditions.

The extent to which the movement of workers fulfills its theoretical functions of insuring an optimum allocation of labor and of equalizing the net attractiveness of jobs in the labor market also requires additional examination. Studies of this question should be made in labor market areas with diverse characteristics, and in the same labor market at different phases of the business cycle. It is particularly important to study the interrelationship between wages and voluntary mobility during high levels of employment, for the evidence is already clear that unemployment rather than wage differentials is the principal cause of movement during depressions. It is unlikely that the relationship can be determined by concentrating exclusively on the employment histories of workers, for they do not permit adequate testing of the strength of wage differentials in producing movement or provide evidence on the effect of actual or potential movement on wage differentials. Research on this subject must be focused on the relation between the recruitment experience and the relative wage levels of employing establishments. Also, greater emphasis will have to be placed on qualitative comparisons of the work forces in the firms being studied, in order to determine whether and to what extent interfirm wage differentials are attributable to differences in the skill and efficiency of workers in ostensibly similar jobs.

A final suggestion may be made concerning methodology. It is clear from the illustrations in this chapter that progress in research on mobility will depend on the careful adaptation of research designs and methods of analysis to specific problems. There is no reason to expect, for example, that the research design best for studying motivational factors in labor market behavior will be equally appropriate for studying the effect of unionism on mobility. On the contrary, there is good reason to fear that an attempt to pursue both these objectives in a single study would necessarily limit the success of each. Studies with limited objectives are more likely than investigations having many purposes to yield conclusive results on questions on which past research has been inconclusive. This does not mean that the broader labor market studies are without value. On the contrary, they provide a framework of data and suggest specific hypotheses for more intensive investigation. But the explanation of individual motivation and of the institutional forces that condition labor market behavior will only be achieved through sharply focused studies.

INDEX OF NAMES

INDEX OF SUBJECTS

204

Philadelphia, 25n, 28–29, 32n, 35n, 36, 40, 43, 54, 57, 66, 75, 102, 104, 110, 113, 119, 121–122, 136, 138–139, 164–165, 166n, 171–172, 176–177
Prestige, 108, 148n, 185
Princeton University, Industrial Relations Section, 165n
Productivity, of labor, 17
Professional workers, 82–85, 89–90, 98, 112
Promotion policies, 7, 80, 126, 131, 142
Propensity, to move, 8, 11, 13–20, 21–22, 60n, 82, 96, 106–107, 109, 111, 113, 115, 124, 135–136, 181, 193
Psychoanalytic concepts, 148n
Public employment service, 14, 46–47, 130–131, 134–135, 163–165, 188

Questionnaires, as source of data, 42–43
Quits, see Voluntary job separations

Race differentials, 54, 103, 116–118, 124, 141
Rational behavior, in job choices, 105–106, 144–146, 158n, 173–174, 191
Reasons, for job changes, 41–42, 43n, 144, 147–160, 188–189, 196
Recruitment, by firms, 7, 197; and wages, 174–175, 180–187, 190
Relief programs, 135
Residence, change of, 33, 53n, 97, see also Intercounty movement, Interstate movement
Roles, social, 101

St. Paul, 28n, 37, 40, 67, 70, 72, 111n, 113, 119, 121n, 123, 151, 154–155, 157–159
Sales workers, 83, 85, 90
Sampling, bias in, 45, 46, 54, 64, 70
San Francisco, 28n, 74n, 76, 83n, 86n, 89–92, 95n, 113, 114, 119, 136
San Joaquin Valley, 84–85
Scientists, mobility of, 36–37, 43, 84, 88
Seattle, 44, 78–79, 106n, 120–121, 130, 162–165, 175–176
"Secondary" workers, 118–121
Self-employment, 24n, 134n, 152
Semiskilled workers, 30, 83, 91–93
Seniority, as factor in mobility, 10, 80, 106–108, 121–122, 125–126, 129, 142–143, 194
Service industries, interchange of labor with, 94

Service workers, 30, 82–83
Sex differentials, 8, 55–56, 59, 82, 85, 109–116, 141, 193
Six-city survey, 28, 32n, 33, 35n, 37, 38–39, 40, 43, 53, 56, 57n, 59, 66, 68–69, 72, 73–76, 82–83, 85–88, 89, 91–92, 102n, 104, 109, 111–113, 115–116, 117n, 118–120, 139, 151, 158, 171–173, 175, 193
Skill: acquisition of, see Apprenticeship, Training; transferability of, 13–15
Skilled workers, 29–30, 34–35, 70, 81, 83, 85, 87–88, 90–93, 101, 102, 112, 155, 166, 177, 187
Social change, 2
Social class, 2, 76n
Social Science Research Council, Committee on Labor Market Research, 28n
Social Security Act, 48
Standard Industrial Classification, 32, 75

Time, coverage of, 39–42, 171–174
Tool and die makers, 61, 66, 87–88, 92, 103, 123
Trade industries, interchange of labor with, 94
Trade unions: and labor market information, 126; as means of finding jobs, 163–165; and mobility, 7, 64, 82n, 121–122, 124, 125–130, 141, 194–195, 197
Training, of workers, 13–14, 81, 84–85, 92–93, 145
Trenton, New Jersey, 165n
Turnover, 136, 195; differentiated from mobility, 22–24; employer view of, 24n, 132, 142; limitations of data on, 63–64; and wages, 178–179; see also Interfirm mobility, Involuntary job separations, Voluntary job separations

Unemployed workers, labor market information among, 168–169
Unemployment, 12, 24, 35, 71n; as factor in mobility, 18–19, 60n; and job choice, 156–157, 160n; and theory of labor allocation, 142–143, 183
Unemployment compensation, 46, 47n, 133–135
Unions, see Trade unions
U. S. Agricultural Marketing Service, 38n
U. S. Bureau of Agricultural Economics, 38
U. S. Bureau of the Budget, 32n